Careers Tomorrow
The Outlook for Work in a Changing World

Selections from THE FUTURIST

Edited by Edward Cornish

**World Future Society
4916 St. Elmo Avenue
Bethesda, MD 20814
U.S.A.**

The Futurist's Library

The purpose of the Futurist's Library is to make available in a convenient form a selection of articles from THE FUTURIST magazine bearing on a single theme. Volumes that have appeared to date include:

1999: The World of Tomorrow. Edited by Edward Cornish (1978).

Communications Tomorrow: The Coming of the Information Society. Edited by Edward Cornish (1982).

The Great Transformation: Alternative Futures for Global Society. Edited by Edward Cornish (1983).

Global Solutions: Innovative Approaches to World Problems. Edited by Edward Cornish (1984).

Habitats Tomorrow: Homes and Communities in an Exciting New Era. Edited by Edward Cornish (1984).

The Computerized Society: Living and Working in an Electronic Age. Edited by Edward Cornish (1985).

(These volumes are available from the World Future Society at $6.95 each.)

Editorial Coordination: Daniel Fields
Production Manager: Jefferson Cornish
Front Cover: Painting by John Porter

Articles in this volume were originally edited for THE FUTURIST by Cynthia G. Wagner and Timothy Willard.

Copyright © 1988 by World Future Society.
All rights reserved. No part of this book may be reproduced by any means, nor transmitted, nor translated into machine language without the written consent of the publisher.

Published by:
 World Future Society
 4916 Saint Elmo Avenue
 Bethesda, Maryland 20814
 U.S.A.

International Standard Book Number: 0-930242-33-5

Printed in the United States of America

Note: The World Future Society published a book with the title *Careers Tomorrow* in 1983, but the present volume is a completely new work aside from the title and cover. All of the articles are new, as is the introduction.

Contents

Introduction 5

Tomorrow's Work Force: New Values in the Workplace 8
by R. Eden Deutsch

The Actualized Worker 12
by Marsha Sinetar

Emerging Careers: Occupations for Post-Industrial Society 17
by S. Norman Feingold

New Choices: Career Planning in a Changing World 25
by David C. Borchard

Rethinking How We Work: The Office of the Future 34
by Samuel E. Bleecker

Work in the Information Age 41
by Arthur J. Cordell

Work in the New Information Age 44
by Alan Porter

Technology and the Changing World of Work 50
by Fred Best

Working at Home: The Growth of Cottage Industry 55
by Tammara H. Wolfgram

Artificial Intelligence: A New Reality 59
by Joseph J. Kroger

Pixel Power: The Graphic Revolution in Computers 62
by Alexander Petofi

The Robot Revolution 67
by F.D. Barrett

Supercops: The Police Force of Tomorrow 71
by James R. Metts

Private Disobedience: The New Militancy 77
by Randall L. Scheel

The Menace of High-Tech Employment 80
by J.H. Foegen

Beyond "Trendy" Forecasts: The Next 10 Years for Work 83
by Sar A. Levitan

Overcoming Unemployment: Some Radical Proposals 88
by David Macarov

Labor Unions Look Ahead 94
by Lane Kirkland

Collective Bargaining for the Future 96
by Cynthia Burton and Edward Cohen-Rosenthal

Creating a 21st Century Corporation 100
by Roger B. Smith

Management in the Third Wave 104
by H. Alan Raymond

Business and Creativity: Making Ideas Connect 107
by Robert Rosenfeld and Jenny C. Servo

How to Think Like an Innovator 113
by Denis E. Waitley and Robert B. Tucker

Economic Conditions Ahead: Understanding the Kondratieff Wave . . 120
by Jay W. Forrester

Destructive Foreign Trade: Sowing the Seeds for Our Own Downfall . . . 125
by John M. Culbertson

Learning Our Lesson: Why School Is Out 132
by Lewis J. Perelman

Home Computers & Families: The Empowerment Revolution 136
by Rowan A. Wakefield

New Challenges for the Information Age 141
by John Diebold

Prosumers: A New Type of Consumer 142
by Philip Kotler

Reconsidering Retirement: Understanding Emerging Trends 147
by Bernard I. Forman

From Retirement to Re-Engagement: Young Elders Forge New Futures . . 152
by Mary K. Kouri

Introduction

Out in Montana, a man named Rich McIntyre has learned how to build trout streams. The fish are fussy. They won't breed in any sort of stream. But McIntyre knows how to make a stream they will like. Now he's building trout streams all over North America, so trout enthusiasts can have a stream close to home. The trout lovers are happy, and McIntyre has found a profitable career.

Trout stream building is among thousands of new occupations that are springing up in our fast-changing economy. Far more will appear in the years ahead. They offer opportunity to the millions of workers who are experiencing "career shock" because their present jobs have been phased out or are changing radically.

An unemployed steelworker goes into computers or nursing. A dentist wakes up one morning, decides he never wants to look into another mouth, and enrolls in a seminary. An actress finds that the theater no longer turns her on and joins a real estate firm. A plumber uses an inheritance to start a restaurant.

Jobs are springing up all over our society, partly because of technological advances that enable people to do all kinds of things that were impossible before. For one thing, these advances create new needs and greater wealth with which to indulge them. Producing more luxuries and specialized services creates all kinds of new businesses and jobs.

Take dogs and cats. As recently as the 1940s, most people scoffed at food prepared specially for cats and dogs. Today pet food provides jobs for thousands of people. There are also "beauty parlors" for dogs and cats as well as pet psychiatrists and ophthalmologists. All told, the pet industry has become gigantic.

The increasing scale and complexity of modern society creates many jobs. The economy is so complicated that computers have to be used to try to figure out what's happening and what should be done next. That means jobs for hundreds of econometricians who feed data into computers and study the results as intently as ancient augurs looking over the entrails of sacrificed animals.

The complexity of the law has created millions of jobs for lawyers, judges, tax accountants, secretaries, computer analysts, and others. For every lawmaker in Congress there are 100 lobbyists trying to influence his vote.

The world of finance has become incredibly complex due to the invention of hundreds of new financial instruments, changing tax codes, and the globalization of financial markets. Today a commodities broker may specialize in anything from heating oil to cocoa; a stockbroker may find himself selling not stocks but options, a new field that has been growing like crazy.

Telling right from wrong in our increasingly complex society is now so difficult that corporations and government agencies are hiring ethics officers to counsel employees who may face dilemmas unknown at the time the Ten Commandments were brought down by Moses. Many public figures now squirming in the spotlight of national publicity might have avoided a lot of grief if they had consulted an ethicist at the proper time. A few simple commandments like "Thou shalt not steal" might have been enough in simpler times, but not in today's environment where executives haven't got time to read the multi-page contracts they are required to sign and must make hundreds of yea-or-nay policy decisions on the basis of an aide's recommendation.

The income tax is a modern invention; today it is a global obsession — and provides employment not only for tax collectors but tax accountants, lawyers, judges, lobbyists, and numerous others.

Only a few years ago, an ordinary person could read and understand a telephone bill. Now the proliferation of new telephonic equipment, services, companies, and price structures has led to a new career opportunity — telephone management.

The complexity of our lifestyles is also producing new careers. The increase in divorce has led not only to a demand for more lawyers and judges, but for a new sort of professional called "divorce mediator." A mediator seeks to avoid the adversarial atmosphere of the law and helps a couple sort out the various issues in their divorce in a reasonably friendly way.

People now travel so much and so far that travel medicine, emporiatrics, has appeared as a new medical specialty. Illnesses to be treated range from frequent ailments like jet lag and traveler's diarrhea ("Montezuma's revenge") to more-obscure ailments like Lassa fever (an African disease) and tapeworms picked up from eating raw fish in Asia.

Government regulations can have strange effects on the job market. A requirement that land be restored to its original conditions by those who damage it has meant that there now are jobs for swamp builders — or, more politely, wetland restorers.

All of these proliferating career choices make it more

difficult than ever for people to decide what they want to do. And choices promise to be even more numerous in the future. People must be prepared to change not just their jobs but their careers four, six, maybe ten times during the course of their lives.

The authors presented in this volume suggest not only many more careers but ways in which we can prepare ourselves for them and how the workplace and attitudes toward work are changing. I think you will be very interested in what they have to say. Each has a different perspective and offers some exciting new insights.

Since these articles were originally published in *The Futurist* magazine over a period of several years, you will find that some statistics and references are dated. I hope that you, the reader, will accept these blemishes as being unavoidable and focus instead on the illuminating insights of these distinguished authors.

— **Edward Cornish**

R. Eden Deutsch

Tomorrow's Work Force

New Values in the Workplace

A new generation of workers is entering the labor force. Fiercely independent, the "Computer Babies" will demand more autonomy on the job and will brush aside many values of the older baby-boom generation.

The workplace of the future will be shaped by the values and consciousness of a new work force. Between now and the year 2000, the workplace will be seriously shaken by the struggles for survival and influence between the pre-World-War-II work force, the post-war generation, and the new generation now emerging.

Just as the "baby-boom generation" pulsed through society in the 1960s and 1970s and rocked the institutions established by the prewar generations, the new generation is beginning to sweep through the workplace, bringing its own set of values, and the workplace will once again have to adjust. The baby-boomers, now gaining influence in the workplace, will increasingly have their authority questioned and will be faced with the challenge of recognizing the needs of this new work force—just as they once demanded that their needs be recognized and met.

The post-war generation grew up in a booming economy and a *Leave It To Beaver* community. They are the "TV Babies," who grew up along with the new medium. The small black-and-white television screen turned large with living color during this generation's development. Everyone got essentially the same slice of news, sports, and entertainment from broadcast television.

The next generation grew up in a declining economy with the family structure changing toward single-parent households, stepfamilies, and fewer siblings. These may be called the "Computer Babies," since their growth and development paralleled that of the computer. Inaccessible, mysterious mainframes became personal, desk-top computers under the complete control of the user, and the slow, complicated programs became fast and friendly. New technologies allowed the members of this generation to be more selective in their information intake; the Computer Babies did not receive a unified cultural message, as the TV Babies before them did. They developed as society became segmented into a single-issues orientation.

When the Computer Babies looked around, they also noticed a less-peopled world than did the TV Babies. The TV Babies were sometimes constricted, sometimes comforted, but always in the presence of many siblings and peers. The Computer Babies have more room as they move into a workplace that has been expanded to accommodate the vast numbers of the baby boom. They are in a marketplace that is in the beginning of a labor shortage.

The Work Force of Today

In today's work force, the two waves of the post-war generation occupy the bottom and middle rungs, with the new generation of Computer Babies just beginning to enter the work force. The pre-war Transition generation fills the senior ranks, one step above the TV Babies. The Elders, born prior to the Depression, are at the very top.

The post-war generation of TV Babies is divided into two distinct waves. Although they share the same consciousness and values, they have been affected by different economic forces. The first wave of the post-war generation, the "Advanceds," were born in the beginning of the boom. They grew up in the flux after the war as new patterns of life were developing. They entered the work force in the early to mid-1960s while the economy was still on the rise.

The second wave of the post-war generation found themselves in a squeeze. They were born in the peak years of the baby boom and outnumbered the first wave. The "Squeezeds" entered the work force in about 1974, expecting the continued material advantages to which they were accustomed but rejecting the established values. The workplace that had expanded to fit their older siblings, however, could not expand any further. The economy, rocked by the oil crisis, took a downturn.

The TV Babies' involvement in social and political issues has led toward democratization in the workplace: Minority rights are recognized, issues such as quality of work life are explored, and people are perceived as valuable resources.

The workers of the post-war generation, now about 20 to 40 years old, fill the bottom half of the workplace. Their paradox is that their large numbers have had a tremendous impact on changing the values and structure of the workplace but also have created so much competition that it is difficult for most of them to get ahead.

THE FUTURIST, December 1985

Today's managers—primarily of the pre-war generations—find a work force made up of baby-boomers who believe that work is a means to gaining personal fulfillment. These workers want a say in the decision-making process, including the designing of their jobs and the running of the organization.

The role of the manager today is matching people with jobs. The capable manager must provide workers with opportunities to further their own personal growth and development while accomplishing corporate objectives. This psychological understanding is a necessary part of the manager's work of creating congruent work environments. The successful manager is now someone who can psychologically size up workers' needs and goals.

Participation, equalization of status through teamwork (and team pay), horizontal organization, and relationships are the tools of today's manager. Sensitivity, respect for individual development, and the understanding of the patterns of people, organizations, and world systems are the personal qualities that tie it all together.

The Work Force of Tomorrow

From 1985 to 1990, the workplace will become turbulent once again. Just when it seemed that the challenges of the post-war work force were being successfully met, the leading edge of the Computer Babies will be entering the work force, bringing values that differ sharply from those of the TV Babies who preceded them. Managers, including baby-boomers, will be forced to sharpen their interpersonal skills and take a closer look at the values of the new workers.

The Entrants, making their transition to early adulthood, will challenge the structures of the established order, just as the post-war generation did in the 1960s and 1970s. The Entrants will challenge recently established ideas of worker involvement, participatory management, and team building in ways that only young, fledgling workers can invent.

The new workers will dispute the now-accepted meaning of work

PRE-WORLD WAR II

ELDERS
Year Born pre-1926
Size 57.4 million
Entered Work Force pre-1944
Age (1985) 60+
    (1990) 65+
    (2000) 75+

TRANSITION
Year Born 1926-1945
Size 52.5 million
Entered Work Force 1944-1965
Age (1985) 40-59
    (1990) 45-64
    (2000) 55-74

TV BABIES

ADVANCED
Year Born 1946-1955
Size 38.1 million
Entered Work Force 1964-1973
Age (1985) 30-39
    (1990) 35-44
    (2000) 45-54

SQUEEZED
Year Born 1956-1965
Size 41.6 million
Entered Work Force 1974-198
Age (1985) 20-29
    (1990) 25-34
    (2000) 35-44

COMPUTER BABIES

ENTRANTS
Year Born 1966-1975
Size 34.2 million
Entered Work Force 1984-1993
Age (1985) 10-19
    (1990) 15-24
    (2000) 25-34

The manager's ability to recognize individual lifestyle and preference will become even more crucial as the next new wave of workers, weaned on choice, sweeps into the workplace.

and the value of the way work is being done. They will offer radical alternatives to existing ways of working as they explore new possibilities. The benefits won by the previous generation will most likely not be seen as benefits—or will be accepted only grudgingly.

The turbulence created by the Entrants will be complicated by the Advanceds, the first wave of the TV Babies. The older ones will be moving into the senior ranks of the workplace, having developed a sense of their own power and gained their own voice. As part of their maturation, they will be ending their mentor relationships with the pre-war Transition generation. They no longer want to be seen as the junior members of the organization but as leaders in their own right.

The evolution of the Advanceds, especially with the termination of their mentor-protege relationships, will leave a strained atmosphere between them and their mentors from the Transition generation. The smooth working relationship that apparently had been developed will be jarred. The authority of the Transition generation, which had previously been accepted, will now be resented. The Advanceds will want to try out their own ideas rather than follow the ideas of others.

The second wave of TV Babies, the Squeezeds, will add their own restlessness to the situation, though the manifestations will be more inner directed. They will be emerging from their initial phase in the workplace, struggling with making their own internal adjustments; they will look at the changes they wrought and wonder which ones are for the best. They will try to figure out how to live in this world that they are now beginning to understand.

The Manager of Tomorrow

The manager of the next 10-15 years will have two main tasks at hand: dealing with the entry problems of a new group into the work force and organizing work procedures and policies that mesh with the emerging values of the new workers.

The manager's ability to recognize individual lifestyle and preference will become even more crucial as the next new wave of workers, weaned on choice, sweeps into the workplace. They have been treated as and trained to be consumers from birth, and they bring that orientation to the job. Managers will thus need to offer a combination of benefits, work schedules,

The Work Force: Key Characteristics

Pre-WWII	"TV Babies"	"Computer Babies"
Preferred Work Environment		
Power hierarchy: work your way up the ladder of success.	Quality circles and teams; participatory management.	Autonomy; individual works alone, least amount of supervision.
Goal		
Get the job done because it is good for the company, good for the nation.	Get meaningful experience from doing the job; personal growth.	Get job done so individual can use his own leisure time more satisfactorily.
Work Medium		
Assembly line; human labor.	Mainframe computers.	Personal (desk-top) computers.
Time Values		
9-to-5; overtime.	9-to-5; flexitime begins.	Flexitime, flexiplace.
Information and Enculturation Media		
Radio in the living room; newsreels at movie theater.	Television news; rock-n-roll; transistor radios.	Walkman; VCRs; music videos.
Consumption		
Brand-name buying; few choices available, few demanded.	More choices available.	More choices demanded.

T he image of the Computer Baby work force is that of young workers wearing sunglasses and having their ears plugged in to their own private music.

working conditions, tasks, and job sites suitable to each individual's needs and situation.

The trend toward the importance of personal experience and personal choice—started by the TV Babies—will continue and be emphasized by the youth entering the work force. But the type of personal experience the Computer Babies value will be different. Rather than demanding more say in a team effort, as the TV Babies did, the Computer Babies will demand more autonomy—which their personal computers will facilitate. Managers will need to "fine tune" their ability to delegate by giving workers the discretion on the job that they already seek and that technology furnishes by assigning the nondiscretionary tasks to robots and computers.

Toward the U.S. Work Force 2000: A Scenario

The flurry created by the Computer Babies' move into the work force continues. Personal freedom and self-expression on the job are a central issue of the new workers, approached in their own unique way.

The image of the Computer Baby work force is that of young workers wearing sunglasses and having their ears plugged in to their own private music. The personal freedom they choose is having their inner consciousness free to roam. Some are glad to donate their bodies for programming, leaving their minds unfettered. Others want to provide the agreed-upon product only, with minimal direction from management.

Participation on teams or work groups is an imposition that violates the Computer Baby's inner freedom and self-expression. With materialism on the rise, the new Entrants see their new way as the most efficient means of making money without being hassled. Money is to be spent on their own self-expressive pursuits off the job.

In the long run, this attitude may be a convoluted step forward in the evolution of work. Workers wanting meaningful work originally sought involvement on the job through work groups and participation. With that end achieved, new workers seek the next level of influence, which gives them the autonomy and discretion to work in whatever way they want, even at whatever time and place they want, defining only the results or end product of their labors. In this way, the Entrants' move toward "ultra" freedom changes the focus of work from the interpersonal process back to the end product.

But tension in the workplace increases as the Squeezeds accept the values of the workplace they entered years ago and settle in to work hard and climb the ladder of success. In low-level positions of authority, committed to group process, and relatively inexperienced and immature, they may be the least able to cope with the Entrants and their new demands, despite their closeness in age.

The Squeezeds' new commitment to the system, still vulnerable, is one of the fragile structures of the new workplace that is most threatened by the demands of the Entrants. In order to protect their new position of control, some become unusually rigid. Others are frustrated and immobilized from over-competition and from not learning information-age skills.

The first wave of TV Babies, the Advanceds, are now in the senior ranks and serve as mentors for the Squeezeds who are reaching for the next step. This is a time of consolidation of the values that the post-war generation brought into the workplace. This consolidation further dichotomizes the workplace, providing a clearer, unified target for the Entrants' attacks.

The managers who anticipated the new values of the Entrants and who could identify the repercussions are better able to set up norms to deal with conflict. In this way, they apply their experience and expertise rather than defensive emergency measures to handle the situation.

The Transition generation, which now heads the work force, carries the torch that the Elders have passed to them, using the best of hierarchy and power. They also understand the generations below them and the changes that have been implemented. As has been their nature, they serve as an effective bridge from the old to the new, bringing the best of the past to the work of shaping the future.

Beyond the "Big Generation"

The macro forces that came together during and following World War II drastically changed the patterns of existence for America and set the stage for the development of the post-war generation—the boom babies. The unique factors under which the baby boom grew and developed created a generation who changed everything they touched.

The influence of this "big generation" will continue into the twenty-first century, but we must not ignore the generations following it, who will also influence society and the workplace in ways we are only beginning to see and understand.

About the Author

R. Eden Deutsch is president of Metaconcepts, a human relations and communications consulting firm. His address is 420 N.E. Ravenna Boulevard, Seattle, Washington 98115.

Marsha Sinetar

The Actualized Worker

More and more workers are saying that money isn't everything. Business will have to find innovative ways to attract the new "actualized" workers, whose values of personal development make them desirable — but hard to hold on to.

Yoga is therapy for high-stress professional. The actualized worker of tomorrow will increasingly explore inner-growth potential both inside and outside the context of work, says author Marsha Sinetar.

SAMATA INTERNATIONAL YOGA AND WHOLISTIC INSTITUTE

In the early 1980s, when I started my private practice as an organizational psychologist in large, Fortune 500 corporations, I saw that employees questioned management more freely than in the past. They spoke up when they felt unfairly treated. They turned down promotions or relocation opportunities when these were thought to interfere with the quality of their personal lives. One fast-track financial director told me he didn't want to move to the Midwest, even though the move meant a sizable promotion for him, because he felt the move would make it difficult to continue participating in marathons.

Today, he is not alone: Executives and mail-room clerks alike question the way in which they spend their time at work. Apparently it is not enough simply to have a well-paying job. As one client put it, "I have realized that the way I spend my working day turns out, in time, to be the way I spend my life."

A key management issue of the year 2000 will be these workers' increasing need for self-actualization. By actualization I mean a healthy personality, wholeness, a full-functioning being, and psychological "completion." The self-actualized person is creative, independent, and self-sufficient. These individuals will increasingly have as their primary focus personal goals, inner values, and the creation of distinct lifestyles.

More persons than we might imagine are becoming interested in their own psychological, physical, and emotional well-being. Once having "found" themselves, such individuals are hard to manage. They demonstrate more loyalty to personal goals and inner rewards than to corporate objectives. Usually, such individuals work diligently toward deeply meaningful private-life objectives.

Their emotional maturity makes them valuable employees to any organization, as does their intellec-

> "Business is only gradually becoming aware that those workers they covet most are the first ones to leave the workplace when things don't suit them."

Author Sinetar savors the serenity of a pasture with her bovine companions. The actualized worker enjoys autonomy and may appear to be a dropout while developing his or her inner self.

tual integrity, since their developmental path positively affects their thinking skills, their judgment, and their ability to take on more responsibility. Yet these very traits also prompt them to risk leaving secure jobs and handsome salaries for personal-growth goals. Business is only gradually becoming aware that those workers they covet most are the first ones to leave the workplace when things don't suit them.

New Values and Lifestyles

Two years ago, I began to explore the values and lifestyle patterns of self-actualizing adults. But that study quickly blossomed into a surprising preview of tomorrow's "psychological man." The study participants expressed the same things as my corporate clients: that they needed to heed their inner values, however illogical; that they felt themselves guided from within to pursue a private — if hard-to-define — dream; and that they would "sell all," if need be, to follow this inner prompting.

All those I interviewed were adults, over the age of 35 (except one who was 27), and represented many walks of life and lifestyles: professionals, entrepreneurs, retired persons, housewives (and a househusband or two), artists, peace activists, environmentalists, carpenters. Their comments about values provided me with clear and definite links to the workplace issues I observed in my client corporations. These are typically multinational corporations who were trying to find, and hold on to, entrepreneurial workers. Here I heard top-level executives who were torn between the investment they'd made in their careers and the desire to have more freedom in their work and be more autonomous, creative, and innovative.

Two central values of actualization have enormous economic and cultural ramifications in the workplace of the future, and clearly these can be seen to have escalated in importance to individual workers in the past two decades. These values are social transcendence and self-transcendence.

By *social transcendence* I mean an individual's achievement of emotional independence from societal influences, including those of authority figures, family, co-workers, and other previously significant persons. The person who has detached emotionally from a known, familiar, and comfortable way of life in order to embark upon an uncharted journey is "socially transcendent" and usually is also on the road to actualization.

By *self-transcendence* I mean the individual who has had a mystical experience wherein the "small self" (separate self or ego) disappears or dissolves. The value of self-transcendence is harder to spot than most values in the workplace. Perhaps the clearest symptom that it is present is when an individual begins to honor some inner directive, even when outer activities, rewards, or expectations of others appear to be significant motivators.

Millions of Americans have had such mystical experiences, and their lives have been changed forever because of them. In the late 1970s, a survey conducted by Yankelovich, Skelly, and White found that 80% of the respondents said they had a strong interest in an inner search for meaning. In another survey, over 50% said they were involved with such inner-growth processes as biofeedback, yoga, or other disciplines.

Spirituality is not usually evident in organized activities. Essentially, it is a completely private matter and thus is difficult to see in others. When persons are sensitive to the stirrings of the inner self, they are sometimes organizational dropouts in terms of church attendance, for example. Often, what *looks* like selfishness, or dropping out, is the individual's need for quiet, simplicity, and solitude so as to grow inwardly into a more competent, mature, whole person. At a later stage of development, the person drops back in at a deeper, more responsible level of participation with the world. Thus, in the long run, dropping out is actually a selfless act that serves the greater good.

The Actualized Worker

If we consider the similarity between the new work ethic and the values of self-actualization, we eas-

The New Careerists

Workers are changing their minds about what it means to succeed at work, but managers still treat all workers as though the only goal is to climb the corporate ladder.

In fact, only a small group of the new career-oriented individuals, or "careerists," hold the traditional value of "getting ahead," according to C. Brooklyn Derr, associate professor of management at the University of Utah.

In his new book, *Managing the New Careerists*, Derr identifies five distinct career orientations among workers: getting ahead, getting secure, getting free, getting high, and getting balanced. Managers must recognize the differing values of the new careerists in order to improve job–worker matching, increase productivity, minimize political game playing, and reduce turnover, says Derr.

- **Getting ahead.** New careerists who value getting ahead are most likely to seek rapid advancement within an organization, making it to the top of the hierarchy. Managers may feel threatened by workers who seem too eager to climb to the top, or wary of the "flash-in-the-pan." But getting-ahead careerists are very hard working and reliable, says Derr.

"In some ways, managing these careerists is easy, because they tend to manage themselves, especially in the early phases," he says. "What may be difficult, especially for larger companies, is managing their high-potential future executives during mid-career."

One solution, says Derr, is to make sure the getting-ahead careerist is fully informed at the start about potential promotion in the organization. The manager might also try helping this careerist expand the definition of "success," since "for some getting-ahead people, even being 'number two' is seen as failure," Derr points out. Alternatives to promotion that still symbolize success could include bonuses, increased authority, or being asked to entertain important visitors.

- **Getting secure.** Many new careerists value security in their positions more than advancement or challenge. They tend to be loyal and competent, but they fear radical change and are most vulnerable to external changes such as dips in the market or changes in top management.

"Pay and raises are important signs of appreciation and job security, not as primary motivations in themselves, and a getting-secure employee will pay much more attention to benefits than a getting-ahead person will," says Derr. Tokens of appreciation such as a reserved parking place or new office furniture will also show getting-secure careerists that their steady performance and loyalty are valued. "In exchange, they

(continued on page 15)

"New careerists" all have different values that must be acknowledged and dealt with by managers. These values include getting secure, getting ahead, getting free, getting high, and getting balanced, says C. Brooklyn Derr.

(continued from page 14)

are willing to work incredibly long hours and put the company's needs first," he says.

• **Getting free.** "Getting-free" careerists desire independence and the option to solve problems their own way. "They are hard to work with, impossible to work for, slippery as eels to supervise and manage, and infinitely resourceful at getting their own way," Derr says. Many of these new careerists are self-employed entrepreneurs who value autonomy — which "may be the most important emerging value among workers in the 1980s," he says.

Managers and getting-free workers have a natural antagonism for each other. But, Derr points out, creative managers can get the work they need by offering such options as contract work, which does not entail a long-term commitment from an individual who values freedom. Another strategy is to give the worker the project, deadline, and budget, and let him or her alone to get the job done.

• **Getting high.** A fourth group of new careerists value excitement and challenges in their work. They frequently need freedom to take on exciting work, but, unlike getting-free careerists, they will sacrifice freedom for an exciting project in a bureaucratic environment, such as the military. A potential problem is that the getting-high worker may be less concerned with making a problem come out just right than with the thrill of the challenge, Derr points out.

Like the getting-free careerists, getting-high workers are difficult to manage. They continually need new and interesting opportunities to test themselves. These workers may best be used as consultants or intrapreneurs.

"Not every organization can afford getting-high people," Derr says. "But those that depend on cutting-edge technology or innovative marketing to keep the jump on their competitors cannot afford to be without them."

• **Getting balanced.** A final group of new careerists give equal priority to non-work aspects of life, such as family, leisure, friends, and self-development. "Getting balanced is a relatively new phenomenon in the work force, especially in conspicuous numbers," Derr says. Though they are decisively career-oriented, getting-balanced workers insist that work remain in balance with relationships and self-development.

To the getting-balanced worker, organizations may seem like obstacles to overcome. The manager's task is to recognize the time and energy limitations that the getting-balanced worker has for work itself and to create a flexible environment within which that worker can provide high-quality work. Traditional awards are relatively ineffective, since the getting-balanced worker needs more than money to feel fulfilled. Programs and benefits that do work, says Derr, include job sharing, flextime, home work stations, on-site day care, and negotiable use of sick leave.

The key point that managers must remember is that all of these new careerists *are* career-oriented and are potentially of great value to an organization, even if they do not fit the traditional model of fast-track, high-potential workers. If mismanaged, these workers will be unproductive and may even engage in destructive organizational politics, warns Derr. "Well managed and rewarded for their unique strengths, they would become equally valuable, though in a different way, as the most promising young general managers," he concludes.

Source: *Managing the New Careerists* by C. Brooklyn Derr. Jossey-Bass. 1986. 288 pages. Available from the Futurist Bookstore for $32.45 ($28.45 for Society members), including postage and handling.

ily see a connection. People are simply acting out their wholeness, their psychological completeness in the workplace. Specifically, three major work-force trends illustrate this point: the rise of an increased entrepreneurial spirit in today's best business environments; the employee's desire for individual autonomy, freedom, and involvement in his or her work; and the global move toward more responsible corporate and governmental behavior.

• **Entrepreneurial skills and actualization.** Entrepreneurial skills are now felt to be critical to American business success. Both "entrepreneurs" and "intrapreneurs" are currently best-seller buzz words. American business wants to recapture the quick-response style of its earliest days through company restructurings, through searching for entrepreneurial-type leaders, and through "skunk works" projects, in which small groups of intrapreneurs go off to smaller, sometimes hidden, facilities to create new products in more flexible offshoot venture groups.

Psychologists have found that entrepreneurs desire and enjoy problem-solving tasks, are highly resourceful, and have the ability to deal with ambiguous circumstances, delays, and uncertainty. My interviews with actualizing adults show their amazing similarity to entrepreneurs in both working habits and personal characteristics.

For example, entrepreneurs and actualizers both are gifted, creative people who desire autonomy in their work and the chance to achieve visible results, with "success" defined in more than merely monetary terms. Personal fulfillment, the opportunity to make a meaningful contribution to self and

> "Individual autonomy, both as reward and incentive, is central as a work and life value for the actualizing adult."

to others, the desire for time to spend with family and friends and in leisure pursuits — all these are part of the word "success" for today's most talented workers.

- **Autonomy and actualization.** Individual autonomy, both as reward and incentive, is central as a work and life value for the actualizing adult. In the workplace, we have seen that employees want — and are getting — flexible schedules, benefits, and organizational structures.

Studies of recent college graduates confirm the notion that the new work force wants more autonomy. In the early 1980s, the research division of the College Placement Council concluded in a study that graduating seniors have high career expectations and goals and expect to work hard. They are unwilling to sacrifice personal happiness, family, health, or ethical standards to meet job demands. They perceive job satisfaction and success to be more dependent on the nature of the work than on relationships to others. And they expect to be both independent *and* interdependent.

In my research, people expressed a tremendous desire to pursue individually meaningful goals even when it meant personal sacrifice of comfort, approval, and security. They were unwilling to live up to what others in authority held up as standards of excellence.

Actualized individuals do not pursue a career or do work because of the so-called work ethic or because it is profitable or because their parents or teachers or managers approve, but because it is work that will make them happy and fulfilled. The steps and choices of life stem from inner rather than outer drives. It is as if countless numbers of individuals have recovered (or uncovered) the ability to perceive their own delights and values, have rediscovered their own selves, and now wish to merge that self with vocational and life activities.

- **Social responsibility and actualization.** I found stewardship to be a primary value in the actualizing personality. The individual takes care of others and the greater good along with his own interests.

For example, a city manager described his work as helping him fulfill his destiny: "Whether I'm helping local public schools design curriculum for environmental education, participating in a civic organization, or out in the field supervising one of the clean-up projects, it makes no difference to me. It's all a way to do what I do best within the context of contributing to others — within the context of what others call 'work.' To me, work is just one of the ways I express myself, my innermost self."

A woman working as a computer programmer turned down a promotion because it would take her away from what she felt was her "ministry." She also expressed the more cohesive self/world view that grows gradually in the actualizing person.

This, then, is the top-of-the-line worker of tomorrow: a man or woman who is confident, independent, creative. He or she seeks to merge inner truths and values with outer realities, hoping to embody — in daily life and through a life's work — the light, ideals, and unique talent found within. These workers will not structure their lives around just any "job," but will strive to incorporate whatever work they do into a meaningful and fulfilling life context — one that is both inwardly rewarding and outwardly creative.

Meeting the Challenges

In tomorrow's worker-short marketplace, employees will quite willingly and easily shift from one workplace to another, or create their own workplaces — as many electronic-cottage owners have already done. The challenge facing management, then, is to keep pace with rapidly evolving workers.

Some companies have made efforts at meeting this challenge. Progressive companies now freely experiment with creative compensation packages designed to draw in, retain, and motivate the actualized workers. Tandem Computer, Inc., for example, provides its employees a sabbatical every four years as a way to help them with self-renewal needs.

Twenty-nine percent of U.S. businesses now have some form of flextime, and 42% of U.S. managers polled believe that their uses of such individual work strategies will increase in the future. Organizations now actively encourage such things as Quality of Working Life groups, communication sessions, wellness or fitness centers, cafeteria-style or individualized benefits, and multileveled decision-making groups.

Creative, innovative workplaces are now a must for American businesses. Japanese and Western European encroachment upon product markets previously dominated by U.S. businesses now forces American management to change. Quality circles, consumer-driven product development activities, the host of novel incentive and morale-building programs that now characterize the "best" business environments are signs that American business recognizes it can only compete by enlisting the support, creativity, and energy of its people.

About the Author

Marsha Sinetar heads Sinetar and Associates, Inc., a human-resource development firm based in Santa Rosa, California. She is an educator, organizational psychologist, and mediator and is author of *Ordinary People As Monks and Mystics: Lifestyles for Self-discovery* (Paulist Press, 1986) and *Do What You Love, The Money Will Follow* (Paulist Press, 1987). Her address is P.O. Box 1, Stewarts Point, California 95480.

S. Norman Feingold

Emerging Careers
Occupations for Post-Industrial Society

Once upon a time Ben Franklin could take his son for a walk through the streets of Philadelphia and point out all the jobs that were available. Today there are more than 30,000 different job titles.

Careers have changed from time immemorial. First, food gathering was done by women, while men did the hunting. Then came a period when most people were subsistence farmers, growing plants and animals to meet their needs for food, clothing, and shelter.

In the Middle Ages, the emerging careers were those of craftsmen and artisans. These workers made a living in the villages by serving the needs of the upper classes. The serfs continued to grow food for themselves and the overlords and to provide military service.

During the Renaissance, a whole class of artists and craftsmen, assistants and guilds developed. Business, trade, and manufacturing expanded. People worked in jobs that never existed in the preceding agricultural age.

Next, the Industrial Revolution expanded the number and types of jobs and careers. Boosted by science and technology, the expansion of jobs has intensified.

We are now entering the post-industrial period. In 1980, just 28% of the work force was in manufacturing, and it will probably be only 11% in the year 2000 and 3% in the year 2030. More people now work at McDonald's than at U.S. Steel. Businesses are adapting by diversifying their operations. Today, for example, sewing machines make up only 1% of Singer's business; the rest is in electronics.

New occupations and careers emerge all the time while others become obsolete. In comparing a past *Dictionary of Occupational Titles*, published by the U.S. Department of Labor, with the most recent one, many changes are readily observed.

The future holds in store a multitude of exciting new occupations, from treasure hunting to moon mining, says a careers expert.

Numerous job titles have been added, and many hundreds of others have been deleted.

One career, for example, of short duration in the nineteenth century was that of the pony express rider, though vestiges reappear in today's courier and messenger services. The elevator operator, the bowling pin setter, the milkman, and hundreds of other jobs and careers have virtually disappeared, and others will follow them into oblivion. The meter-reader will soon be extinct; instead of somebody reading the gas meter at your home, gas meters can be tied in to a computer and monitored more cost effectively.

All of us are in occupations and careers that are in transition. For some, the job titles will remain the same while the work tasks and concepts change. For some, there will be new titles and new tasks.

An emerging career has all of the following characteristics; it is one that:

• Has become increasingly visible as a separate career area in recent years.

• Has developed from pre-existing career areas, such as medical care and personal or business services.

• Has become possible because of advances in technology or actual physical changes in our environment. For example, home computers, solar industries, satellite television, and water pollution equipment are a few of the many areas that have engendered new, emerging careers.

• Shows growth in numbers of people employed or attending emerging education and training programs.

• Requires skills and training.

• Does not appear and then disappear in a very short period of time.

Careers in the Information Industry

One of the biggest areas of emerging careers is the information industry. Today, 55% of the workers in the United States are in information industries. More people are involved in information and communication than in mining, agriculture, manufacturing, and personal services combined. Some experts are calling the changes an "information revolution." By the year 2000, 80% of the work force will be information workers.

Here are some of the emerging career areas in the information industry:

Operation of information systems. Abstractor-indexers process the intellectual content of documents for convenient retrieval. Bibliographic searchers use modern computerized information systems and data bases to identify or retrieve pertinent publications. Information brokers perform specialized information retrieval services for a fee.

Management of information systems. Information center managers supervise facilities that organize knowledge of a specific subject area.

Design of information systems. Application or systems programmers write large-scale computer programs or modify existing programs in order to solve information problems in business, science, education, and other fields.

Research and teaching. Computational linguists analyze word and language structure to determine how the computer can manipulate text for indexing, classification, abstracting, search, and retrieval. Information scientists conduct basic research on the phenomenon

> "More people are involved in information and communication than in mining, agriculture, manufacturing, and personal services combined."

of information. Teachers of information science educate others in the planning, design, management, evaluation, and use of the total information process.

Consulting (or the selling of information). There has been an explosive growth of consultants of all kinds. For example, image consultants work with clients on a variety of problems such as dress, speech, and color. One of the earliest types of image consultant was the public relations consultant, who handles information and communications problems for a variety of organizations.

Information is a limitless resource. Unlike finite industrial resources such as oil, ore, and iron, there is an inexhaustible supply of knowledge, concepts, and ideas as people gain further education.

Robotics Careers

Robots are to manufacturing and mining jobs as calculators are to white-collar jobs. Each takes the monotony of repetition out of the job. Additionally, robots can do the hazardous tasks—with bottom-line effectiveness, no retirement pay, no vacations, no coffee breaks, and no strikes.

Robotics means that people will have to be trained for new skills or remain unemployed—and this includes thousands of people who

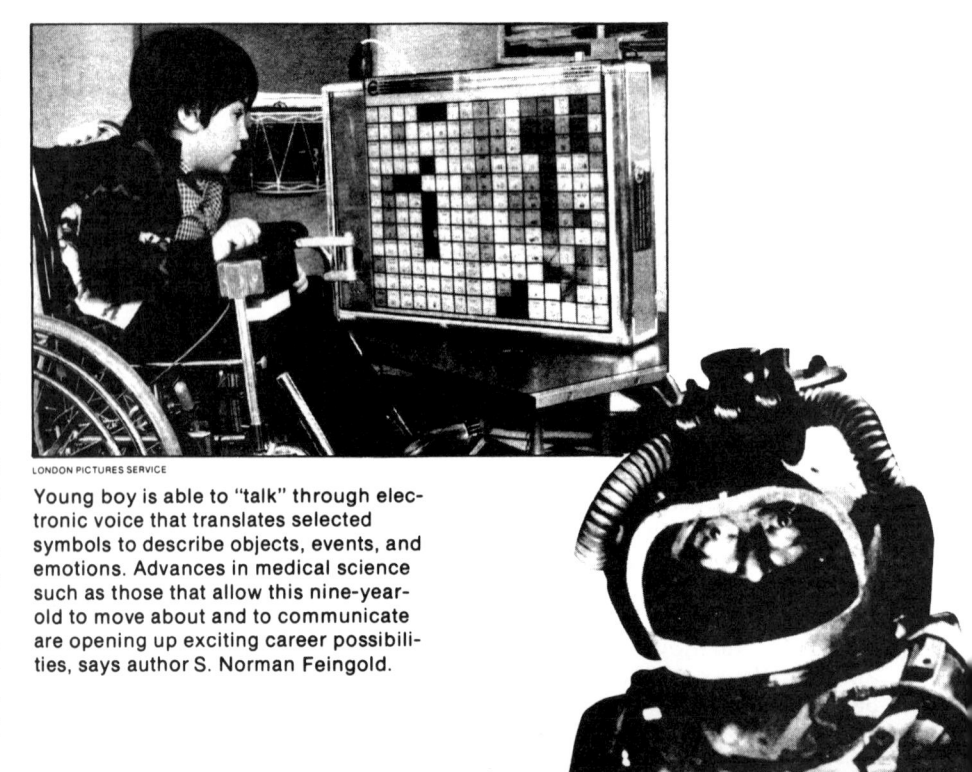

LONDON PICTURES SERVICE

Young boy is able to "talk" through electronic voice that translates selected symbols to describe objects, events, and emotions. Advances in medical science such as those that allow this nine-year-old to move about and to communicate are opening up exciting career possibilities, says author S. Norman Feingold.

formerly worked in the automobile and steel industries.

In addition to the new jobs for scientists, mechanics, and technicians that the development of robotics has created, there will be an increasing need for such workers as robots' supervisors in new, largely automated factories. But whether the development of robotics will create more jobs than robots displace is unknown at this point.

Robots are taking away thousands of blue-collar jobs. The jobs they are creating are not in these fields. The changes are of a magnitude comparable to those the Industrial Revolution created.

Overall employment in robotics is small but will grow with the increasing demand for robots. The three general types of jobs now available in the robot industry are:

> "Unlike finite industrial resources such as oil, ore, and iron, there is an inexhaustible supply of knowledge, concepts, and ideas as people gain further education."

Planning. Robotic engineers select jobs a robot could perform based on a thorough knowledge of the robot's capacities and of the tasks to be performed and the environment in which they are done.

Installation. Technicians install the robots and adjust them to the specific tasks involved. These people could be technical-school graduates with a special interest in robotics.

Monitoring. Supervisors check the operation of the robot on the line and keep it supplied with any needed raw materials, such as wire for a welding gun.

Ocean Industry Careers

The ocean industry is growing, with new careers ranging from catching new kinds of fish to finding ships that have sunk at sea carrying gold and other precious items. We are now cultivating the ocean the way we do the land. And researchers have discovered new kinds of sea-grown food that could

Engineer controls robot connected with vision system designed by Westinghouse. As the robotics industry grows, there will be increasing demand for robot scientists, engineers, technicians, supervisors, and salespeople, says author Feingold.

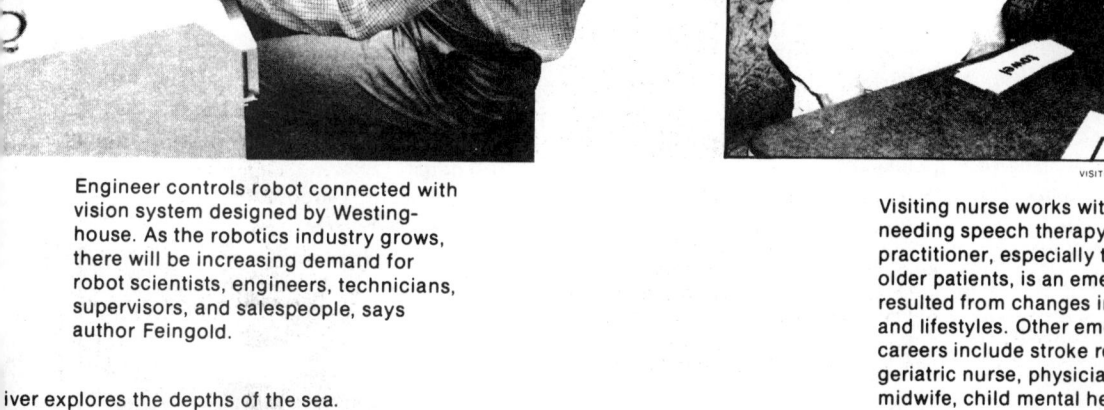

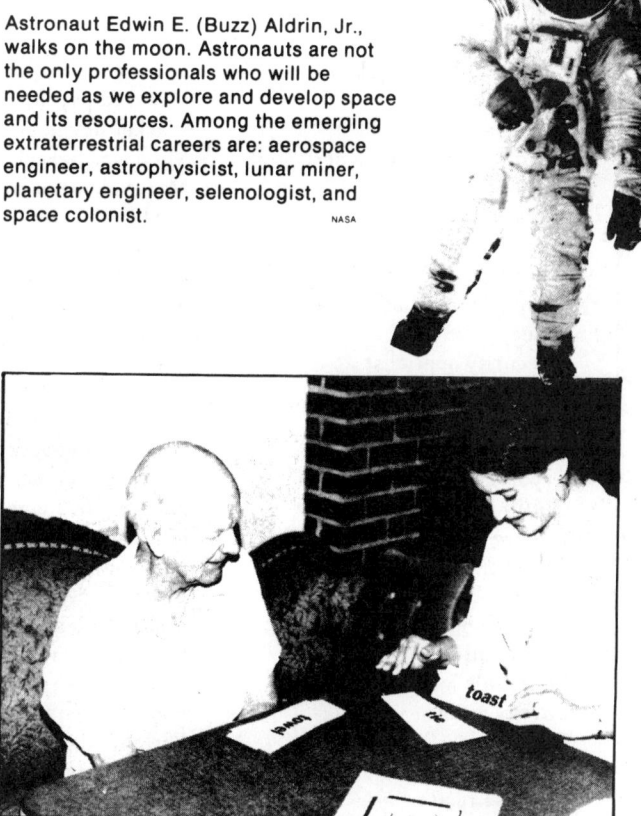

Astronaut Edwin E. (Buzz) Aldrin, Jr., walks on the moon. Astronauts are not the only professionals who will be needed as we explore and develop space and its resources. Among the emerging extraterrestrial careers are: aerospace engineer, astrophysicist, lunar miner, planetary engineer, selenologist, and space colonist.

Visiting nurse works with home-bound patient needing speech therapy. The home health-care practitioner, especially those working with older patients, is an emerging career that has resulted from changes in society, population, and lifestyles. Other emerging health-care careers include stroke rehabilitation nurse, geriatric nurse, physician's assistant, nurse-midwife, child mental health specialist, alcoholism counselor, and music therapist.

iver explores the depths of the sea. merging careers in ocean industries nge from treasure hunting to fish rming.

Occupational Titles of the Future

Here is a list of job titles that might appear in a *Dictionary of Occupational Titles* of the future:

Aquaculturist
Armed courier
Artificial intelligence technician
Arts Manager
Asteroid/lunar miner
Astronaut
Battery technician
Benefits analyst
Biomedical technician
Bionic medical technician
Cable television auditor
Cable television salesperson
CAD/CAM technician
Career consultant
CAT scan technician
Certified alcoholism counselor
Certified financial planner
Child advocate
Color consultant
Communications engineer
Community ecologist
Community psychologist
Computer:
  analyst
  camp counselor/owner
  designer
  graphics specialist
  lawyer
  microprocessor technologist
  programmer (software writer)
  sales trainee
  security specialist
  service technician
Contract administrator
Cosmetic surgeon
Cryologist technician
Cultural historian
Cyborg technician
Dance therapist
Dialysis technologist
Divorce mediator
EDP auditor
Electronic mail technician
Energy auditor
Ethicist
Executive rehabilitative counselor
Exercise technician
Exotic welder
Family mediator/therapist
Fiber-optics technician
Financial analyst
Financial consultant
Forecaster
Forensic scientist
Fusion engineer
Genetic biochemist

Genetic counselor
Genetic engineer technician
Geriatric nurse
Graphoanalyst
Hazardous waste technician
Health physicist
Hearing physiologist
Hibernation specialist
Home health aide
Horticulture therapy assistant
Hotline counselor
House- and pet-sitter
Housing rehabilitation technician
Image consultant
Indoor air quality specialist
Information broker
Information research scientist
Issues manager
Job developer
Laser medicine practitioner
Laser technician
Leisure counselor
Licensed psychiatric technician
Market development specialist
Massage therapist
Materials utilization technician
Medical diagnostic imaging technician
Medical sonographer technician
Microbial geneticist
Microbiological mining technician
Mineral economist
Myotherapist
Naprapath
Neutrino astronomer
Nuclear fuel specialist
Nuclear fuel technician
Nuclear medicine technologist
Nuclear reactor technician
Nurse-midwife
Ocean hotel manager
Ombudsman
Oncology nutritionist
Orthotist
Paraprofessional
Peripheral equipment operator
PET scan technician
Physician's assistant
Planetary engineer
Plant therapist
Plastics engineer
Pollution botanist
Power plant inspector
Protein geometrician
Radiation ecologist
Recombinant DNA technologist
Relocation counselor

Retirement counselor
Robot:
  engineer
  salesperson
  scientist
  technician (industrial)
  trainer
Security engineer
Selenologist (lunar astronomer)
Shrimp-trout fish farmer
Shyness consultant
Software club director
Software talent agent
Soil conservationist
Solar energy consultant
Solar energy research scientist
Solar engineer
Space botanist
Space mechanic
Sports law specialist
Sports psychologist
Strategic planner
Systems analyst
Tape librarian
Telecommunications systems designer
Thanatologist
Transplant coordinator
Treasure hunter
Underwater archaeologist
Underwater culture technician
Volcanologist
Waste manager
Water quality specialist
Wellness consultant

Energy consultant reviews thermograms and photographs in a heat-loss survey to show homeowners where they can save money. Energy industries offer a broad variety of job opportunities requiring a range of skills. In addition to workers with traditional skills—such as welders, pipefitters, carpenters, materials handlers, and truck drivers—emerging energy careers will require more and more people with knowledge in a number of areas.

have tremendous value to feeding the world's people.

Fishing and other occupations exploiting the sea are almost as old as the human race, but marine technology is making possible many exciting emerging careers, such as ocean mining, fish farming, oil prospecting, treasure hunting, and underwater archaeology.

Now let's take a closer look at some of these emerging career areas.

Ocean mining. Scientists and engineers work to solve the problem of how to retrieve and process the millions of tons of undersea minerals. Marine ecologists study how ocean mining operations could affect the ocean's environment. International sea-mining claims and law-of-the-sea treaties are new specialties for maritime lawyers.

Other areas such as off-shore drilling and deep-sea exploration require people with knowledge in more than one area, including oceanography, geology, seismology, marine engineering, and meteorology.

Underwater archaeology and treasure hunting. Until recently, no technology was available to recover artifacts from sunken ships. Now, treasure hunting using the most modern underwater techniques can be profitable, although the chances of making a fortune are small. Among the positions relating most directly to underwater exploration are project directors, professional divers, crew members, equipment handlers, sonar operators, and television camera operators.

Aquaculture. As fish supplies diminish and world population increases, scientific farming of fish and other seafoods will expand. One technique used with increasing effectiveness is polyculture, or the raising of several species together, which maximizes utilization of food and water.

Fish farming requires workers skilled in land and water management and in the care, feeding, managing, harvesting, and marketing of fish.

Exploring New Frontiers

Space, "the final frontier," has already opened up undreamed of

> "Treasure hunting using the most modern underwater techniques can be profitable, although the chances of making a fortune are small."

occupations and will demand many new kinds of pioneers in the future.

Exploring space and developing its resources will require highly skilled technicians in addition to the astronauts and pilots now serving in U.S. and other space programs. Specialists in communications, computers and electronics, energy, and pharmaceuticals, for example, will work on the space shuttle or Skylab.

Eventually, as humans can remain in space for longer and longer periods of time, space programs will require miners, mechanics, ecologists, geologists, and other technicians to explore extraterrestrial materials and energy resources; to mine raw materials on lunar bases; to build and staff industrial facilities, factories, processing plants, and solar-power stations; to build space habitats and work in closed-ecology agricultural production; and to develop transportation systems connecting a growing number of space facilities.

Health Careers

Breakthroughs in genetics, bionics, cryology, laser surgery, and other medical sciences are creating exciting new career possibilities. The replacing of body organs with transplants or artificial parts represents a marriage of medical and engineering fields that has engendered such emerging careers as bionic-electronic technicians; orthotists or prosthetists, who develop surgical devices to activate or supplement weakened limbs or functions; spare-human-organs technicians; and many other previously unimagined occupations.

Electronic devices activated by voice, the blink of an eye, or a puff of breath have enabled mobility-impaired people to open doors and

Technology Tracking

Large companies are turning to "technology trackers" as a way to keep up with technological advances

The speed of technological change is giving birth to a new profession—the "technology tracker." "It is no longer feasible for large organizations to stay on top of what's happening without creating a senior position devoted solely to this end," says Herb Halbrecht, president of Halbrecht Associates, a firm that specializes in technology-related research.

Large companies are beginning to hire managers whose sole job is to track advances in technology and to introduce promising innovations into the organization.

Researchers cannot be expected to keep up with developments in areas ranging from telecommunications to bioengineering, says Halbrecht. The technology tracker, however, can spot those innovations that might be useful to a company. The technology then has to be "sold" within the company. Once this is accomplished, the tracker has to deal with outside suppliers.

Traditional managers and department heads often fail to push—or even look for—new applications of technology. This resistance to change "can be a persuasive reason why companies separate technology tracking from other duties," notes Halbrecht.

Merrill Lynch and American Express both have vice presidents for advanced technology, and Citibank has an office of technology assessment. The people involved in this field, says Halbrecht, "are broadly technology-literate and possess an intuitive sense of what's important. Most of all, they don't isolate themselves."

Source: Herb Halbrecht, Halbrecht Associates, Inc., 1200 Summer Street, Stamford, Connecticut 06905.

Fifty-Four Ways to Get a Job

All things being equal, the more job-seeking techniques used, the better your chances of locating a truly appropriate position. The following ways can be used. They are not listed in any order of priority.

1. Newspaper: Place or answer an ad in a newspaper.
2. Magazine: Place or answer an ad in a periodical.
3. Read the *Professional and Trade Association Job Finder* (available from the Garrett Park Press, Garrett Park, Maryland 20896).
4. Job banks: Use services that list candidates for jobs.
5. Job registries: This is another form of a job bank.
6. Clearinghouse of jobs: Use employment services that list candidates and vacancies.
7. Clearinghouse of jobs: Use employment services set up in conjunction with national or regional meetings of professional organizations.
8. Cold canvass in person: Call on employers in the hope of finding a vacancy appropriate for your skills, personality, and interests.
9. Cold canvass by telephone: Call employers to identify organizations with appropriate vacancies.
10. Union hiring hall: Use employment services set up by labor organizations.
11. Alumni office contacts: School or college alumni offices may suggest former students in a position to help you.
12. Public career and counseling services: Use state employment and other public career-oriented services.
13. Private career and counseling services: The fees charged by these organizations may be more than justified by the job search time saved.
14. Employment agencies: These may charge a fee or a percentage commission—but only if you take a job through them.
15. Executive search firms: These are "head hunter" organizations retained by employers to identify persons for specialized jobs.
16. Volunteer work: Millions have begun their careers by first gaining experience or a "foot in the door" through unpaid work.
17. Part-time work experience: A part-time job may be easier to obtain than full-time work and may lead to a permanent position.
18. Temporary or summer work: These provide experience and an introduction to the employer's organization.
19. Make your own job: Freelance work may lead to self-employment or a job with an employer.
20. Join a 40-plus group: Most cities have these job clubs that specialize in older workers.
21. Join a 65-plus group: These organizations provide jobs and other services for senior citizens.
22. Join a job search group: Sharing job hunting experiences can provide new ideas and psychological support.
23. Tell friends and acquaintances: Most studies show that friends and family are the best single source of job leads.
24. Federal job centers: These offices, located in major cities, are a good source of job leads. Look them up in the telephone book under "U.S. Government."
25. Computerized placement services: Many organizations inventory candidates and employers by computers to make job matches.
26. Social agency placement services: Along with social services, many of these groups now provide job counseling and placement assistance.
27. Membership services: Many professional and other organizations maintain employment assistance programs to aid their members.
28. Mail order job campaign: Send out dozens or hundreds of

---

windows, use the telephone, etc. Closed-captioned television and movies allow the deaf to "hear."

Other new health-related careers result from changes in society, population, and lifestyles. As the population ages, for example, there will be a greater need for geriatric nurses and social workers, home health aides, nursing home counselors, stroke rehabilitation nurses, and thanatologists.

Small Business: Going Out on Your Own

From the end of World War II until the mid-1970s, small business was not looked upon favorably by the mass of young entrants into the labor force. Ten years ago, one study showed that while 27% of the parents of high-school students owned their own small business, only 3% of the children were willing to enter the same business.

This has changed. In the past five to ten years, the number of self-employed rose significantly. Small business is the key to high employment today and in the year 2000.

Twelve hundred new businesses are formed each day in the United States. In an era of bigness, more and more people are now starting to see that small is beautiful and that they can turn their interests, potential, and abilities into salable products and services. The root of American economic success has been in entrepreneurship. Today, high schools and colleges all over the United States are offering courses in small business.

Women are more involved than ever before in starting their own small businesses. Many are entering small business for self-actualization, growth, and development. Though money is still important to them, more and more people want to be able to control their lives and to believe that they are making some sort of contribution to society.

Many new small businesses are at the cutting edge of new career developments, such as communications, aids for the handicapped, and the information industry. But there are all kinds of people needs. Creative people can translate them into a successful small business.

For example, one man who earned a high salary but just couldn't get along with his supervisors decided to start his own letters to potential employers, hoping to identify suitable openings.

29. School or college placement services: Both current students and alumni generally are eligible for help from these groups.

30. Association placement services: Many professional and other organizations include employment assistance as part of their service program.

31. Trade placement services: In many occupations, an organized placement program operates.

32. Professional placement services: Use professional career placement specialists, particularly if seeking a high-level job.

33. Hotlines: Use these answering services (many operate 24 hours a day) maintained by community organizations or libraries.

34. Federal civil service offices: Contact employment offices of federal agencies in your area of interest.

35. State merit service offices: Get in touch with appropriate state government agencies.

36. County or city personnel office: File for suitable openings with agencies of local government.

37. Internships: Use a paid or unpaid short-term internship to gain experience and make contact with potential employers.

38. Work-study program: Use a cooperative work-study program to gain experience and to make contacts in a field of prime interest.

39. Networking: Expand contacts that may help you by working with peers, supervisors, friends, and others.

40. Mentor: Cultivate an older, more experienced person to whom you turn for advice. Such a mentor may take a special interest in your proper placement.

41. Television job and career announcements: Don't overlook ads placed on television for employees.

42. Radio job and career announcements: Many employers, with numerous jobs, use radio to help solicit candidates for them.

43. Bulletin board posting: Check ads placed on career-related bulletin boards.

44. Check the *College Placement Annual*, published by the College Placement Council (P.O. Box 2263, Bethlehem, Pennsylvania 18001).

45. Check in-house job vacancies: Most progressive employers now post all vacancies for their current employees to examine and, if interested, apply for. This permits maximum use of upward mobility techniques.

46. DVR job placement services: All state divisions of rehabilitation services offer disabled persons extensive job counseling and placement services.

47. Former employers: Don't hesitate to ask former employers for help.

48. Fellow employees: Persons who work with you might know of suitable vacancies in other offices or organizations.

49. Personnel office counseling: Many times, the personnel office will counsel with you about career paths or alternative jobs in your organization.

50. Religious leaders: Often ministers, rabbis, and priests know of potential employers among their members.

51. Library resources: Check Moody's Industrials, the Fortune "500" list, and other library reference books for employment suggestions.

52. Overseas work: Major religious groups and other international agencies may hire for jobs in other countries.

53. Sponsored interviews: If possible, have persons you know set up employment contacts for you.

54. Military services: Enlistment in one of the armed forces may provide both an immediate salary and job training in fields of interest.

---

chauffeur business because he loved to drive a car; he now has a Rolls-Royce and drives it for anyone who wants to rent it for a special event. He is busy every day and is now on the way to buying another Rolls.

What kind of economic impact does small business have? Plenty. Of all nonfarm businesses in the United States, 97% are considered "small" according to the Small Business Administration's definition. Small business accounts for nearly $7 out of every $10 in sales made by retailers and wholesalers annually. Nearly 80% of all U.S. businesses (excluding farms) employ fewer than 10 people. The small business part of the economy creates more jobs than any other; it provides, directly or indirectly, the livelihood of more than 100 million Americans—that's almost half of the current U.S. population.

Small business has been growing at the rate of 2.4% annually for the past couple of years. With more sophisticated financial planning and action by entrepreneurs, the failure rate will undoubtedly drop during the next five years.

Computers and the Changing Workplace

Computers and the information revolution are changing the workplace in many ways, and these changes affect how people work, relax, travel, think, and feel.

Recently I visited a paperless office in Washington, D.C. Most of the staff worked at home with their computers and came together only once every three or four weeks. They got their instructions for the day or week via their computers.

Computers may markedly change human behavior by altering the ways people relate to each other. Over the phone, you hear the other person's tone of voice. Face to face, you see a person's smile or anger. You also see who takes the head seat at a meeting. When people use a computer to communicate, they lack nonverbal cues since they cannot see or hear the other person. There are no cues as there are when you meet someone in person or talk to someone on the phone.

Over the next 20 years, there will be more pressure to increase job satisfaction by changing the content of jobs; today, few people seem to deeply enjoy their work and to have real psychic satisfaction. At the same time, people are likely to spend less time at work, either through shortened workweeks or through absenteeism.

While there is likely to be greater employee participation in decision-making, loyalty to one's company will probably continue to decrease. More people will change jobs or even careers more often. Training policies will be reassessed to meet an increasing need to train and retrain people. The proportion of women in the work force is likely to increase, and more of them will be career-oriented.

More people will work at home. There will probably also be more work for people in neighborhood work centers. These centers will be similar to the firms that offer a business address, an answering service, and an office to rent on an hourly or daily basis. There also can be community communication centers for sharing particularly expensive facilities, including video telephone booths, rooms for electronic meetings, etc.

While sophisticated technical skills will be needed in the twenty-first century, I believe we need to add life- and love-enhancing skills or our technology will accelerate alienation.

The concept of Win-Lose must be replaced by a Win-Win ideal. Rather than "King of the Mountain," the game we must learn now is "People of the Mountain."

When people are made to feel that their self-image and worth depend on their being on top, complex problems are created. They experience high levels of anxiety, display destructive tendencies, and show increased insensitivity to the feelings of others. They lie, cheat, hurt, maim, and kill to make it to the top. In the process, some people destroy not only their colleagues but their families and themselves.

We need to develop a special kind of sensitive balance for cooperation and individualism that allows people to live and work in harmony. People can compete in a psychologically healthy way.

We can enhance individual initiative and creativity and, at the same time, stimulate the ability or potential to work well as a team.

"Special Interest" Colonies For Oceans and Space

The key to successful underwater colonies—and to outer space exploration—will be to make life there so interesting that able young workers will be lured to jobs there. This could lead to "special interest" colonies staffed entirely by chess players, compulsive gamblers (complete with their own casino), young single men and women, musicians, or others with like interests, according to a report from International Resource Development Inc. (IRD), a Connecticut-based consulting firm.

Long-term undersea habitation has moved from the realm of pipedreams to reality. For example, marine scientists increasingly use underwater habitats to study the biology and geology of the world's oceans. New undersea habitats will allow scientists to live beneath the ocean's surface for months at a time and in relative luxury. And, despite recent setbacks for the U.S. space program, plans still call for a permanent manned space station to be in operation before the year 2000.

Special interest colonies could help to alleviate the loneliness and isolation experienced by workers engaged in deep ocean research and commercial activities or on extended trips to outer space. "There's going to have to be a lot more attention paid to compatibility between the workers, and especially to commonality of interests," says IRD researcher Mark Pine.

Pine points to offshore oil drilling projects as an example of a current-day isolated working and living situation. "Wages at offshore oil rigs are among the highest anywhere, but the physical strength required in most of today's offshore colonies tends to limit job applicants to 'roughnecks' and artisans with special skills," he says. In deep ocean colonies or on space stations, however, a large proportion of the work will be done by computer-operated robotic manipulators and systems. Workers will thus need a high level of computer skills but much less muscle.

With this intelligence-oriented job market, a broad range of workers, from recent college graduates to retirees, will apply for high-paying "aquaspace" and outerspace jobs. This wide range of experience and interests, however, will make problems of compatibility on deep ocean or outer space projects even more difficult—and important.

Soon, there may be a new agency to come up with solutions to these problems. IRD believes that today's space agency NASA will evolve into NAASA—the National Aquaspace, Aeronautics, and Space Administration. The functions of this new agency will encompass the frontiers of the deep ocean as well as the frontiers of space.

"There is even a school of thought that says some of the pioneering leading-edge technology developed in these environments should be handled by a single trained group of Astronauts/Aquanauts; so many of the actual activities and skill requirements are the same in each case," says Pine.

Source: International Resource Development Inc., 6 Prowitt Street, Norwalk, Connecticut 06855.

About the Author

S. Norman Feingold, a licensed psychologist, is president of the National Career and Counseling Services (1522 K Street, N.W., Suite 336, Washington, D.C. 20005).

David C. Borchard

NEW CHOICES

Career Planning in a Changing World

Not so long ago, career/life planning would have served little purpose. People had few career choices available: most men were farmers or factory workers, and most women were homemakers or teachers. Those circumstances were perceived to be as stable as the dollar, and the future promised little change other than growing older. Those were the days when America's work and lifestyles were associated with agriculture and manufacturing.

There is little doubt that we have left the old world behind and are now in the post-industrial revolution—the transition to a new age. The realities that once restricted occupational and lifestyle choices are no longer the governing realities of today. The magnitude of today's possibilities is staggering. Now life seems as *un*stable as the dollar.

Career/life planning is the process of identifying your choices and then choosing goals suited to both your individual uniqueness and to the realities of the world of work. This is a time-consuming and on-

> As society enters the post-industrial age, career choosers and changers have more options than ever before. Yet traditional methods used by career counselors fail to take into account the rapid changes affecting the world of work.

going process. For people to have invested much effort in this process in the agrarian and industrial eras would have been essentially futile. Today, however, we live in an age of almost unlimited choice. This makes career/life planning an essential undertaking for anyone desiring a satisfying career and life.

A Career/Life Planning Model

John L. Holland, a vocational psychologist at Johns Hopkins University, created an occupational-choice model that has become a very popular career-planning tool over the past decade. Holland's model establishes a general classification system for personality styles and another for occupational environments. In this theoretical framework, personality styles are classified into six general categories based on patterns of interests (see Figure 1). The six styles are linked to a classification structure that organizes occupations according to similar traits (see Figure 2).

Therefore, the task in Holland's model for career planning is to identify your strongest interests and to see where these fit in the personality style hexagon. You then select your occupation from among those choices that are included within the corresponding category of the occupational environment hexagon.

For example, let's assume that you complete an interest-assessment evaluation, using assessment tools such as Holland's *The Self Directed Search* or Edward K. Strong,

THE FUTURIST, August 1984

Figure 1
The Six Personality Types

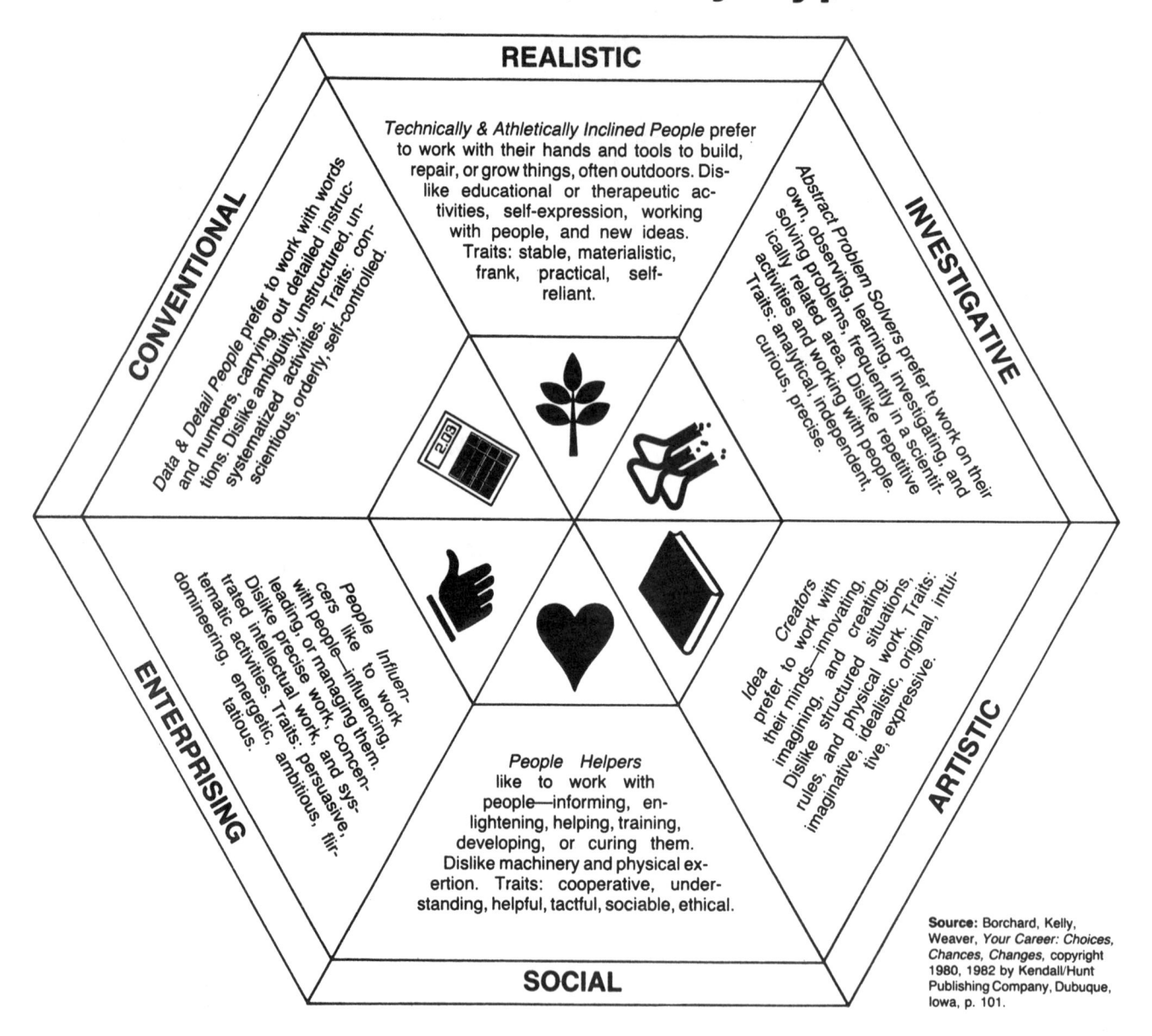

REALISTIC

Technically & Athletically Inclined People prefer to work with their hands and tools to build, repair, or grow things, often outdoors. Dislike educational or therapeutic activities, self-expression, working with people, and new ideas. Traits: stable, materialistic, frank, practical, self-reliant.

INVESTIGATIVE

Abstract Problem Solvers prefer to work on their own, observing, learning, investigating, and solving problems, frequently in a scientifically related area. Dislike repetitive activities and working with people. Traits: analytical, independent, curious, precise.

ARTISTIC

Idea Creators prefer to work with their minds—innovating, imagining, and creating. Dislike structured situations, rules, and physical work. Traits: imaginative, idealistic, original, intuitive, expressive.

SOCIAL

People Helpers like to work with people—informing, enlightening, helping, training, developing, or curing them. Dislike machinery and physical exertion. Traits: cooperative, understanding, helpful, tactful, sociable, ethical.

ENTERPRISING

People Influencers like to work with people—influencing, leading, or managing them. Dislike precise work, concentrated intellectual work, and systematic activities. Traits: persuasive, domineering, energetic, ambitious, flirtatious.

CONVENTIONAL

Data & Detail People prefer to work with words and numbers, carrying out detailed instructions. Dislike ambiguity, unstructured, unsystematized activities. Traits: conscientious, orderly, self-controlled.

Source: Borchard, Kelly, Weaver, *Your Career: Choices, Chances, Changes*, copyright 1980, 1982 by Kendall/Hunt Publishing Company, Dubuque, Iowa, p. 101.

Psychologist John L. Holland's identification of six personality types is based on unique patterns of interests and skills. Most people can be placed in one to three of these categories, which can then be used to help them to discover the occupations for which they are best suited (see Figures 2 and 3).

Jr., and David P. Campbell's *Strong-Campbell Interest Inventory*. You learn that your primary interest patterns fall within the Artistic (A), Investigative (I), and Social (S) categories. A career counselor might then assist you in identifying a list of occupations to consider from the A, I, and S groups, such as psychologist, psychiatrist, biology instructor, writer, architect, graphics designer, etc. While this is an overly simplified description of the process, it does serve to illustrate the general nature of Holland-oriented career planning.

Career Planning and Change

One of the major problems confronting the neophyte career/life-planning professional is the pace at which the occupational world is now changing. Many of the specific career-related programs that college freshmen and technical-school students enter into today may no longer offer good employment prospects or long-range career potential by the time they obtain their degrees.

Rapid change does not alter the effectiveness of the Holland model for assessment purposes, but it certainly could affect its utility as a vocational-selection methodology. The Holland model works well in a stable world where the occupational future remains consistent with the past. Vocational choice in stable conditions is a simple matter of selecting the occupation that

Figure 2
Occupational Environments

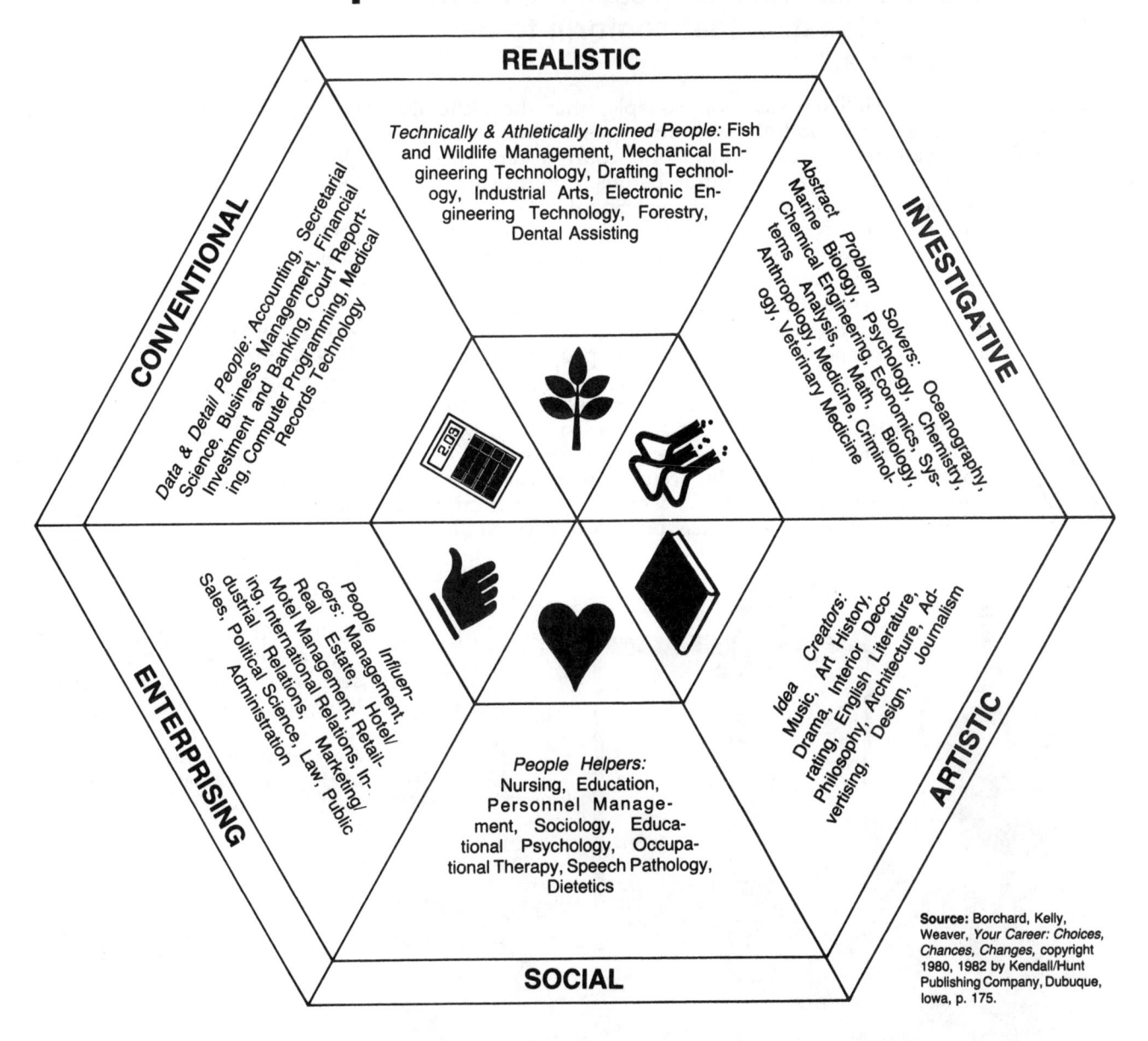

REALISTIC

Technically & Athletically Inclined People: Fish and Wildlife Management, Mechanical Engineering Technology, Drafting Technology, Industrial Arts, Electronic Engineering Technology, Forestry, Dental Assisting

INVESTIGATIVE

Abstract Problem Solvers: Oceanography, Marine Biology, Psychology, Chemistry, Chemical Engineering, Economics, Systems Analysis, Medicine, Math, Biology, Anthropology, Criminology, Veterinary Medicine

ARTISTIC

Idea Creators: Music, Art History, Drama, Interior Decorating, English Literature, Advertising, Philosophy, Architecture, Design, Journalism

SOCIAL

People Helpers: Nursing, Education, Personnel Management, Sociology, Educational Psychology, Occupational Therapy, Speech Pathology, Dietetics

ENTERPRISING

People Influencers: Management, Hotel/Motel Management, Retailing, International Relations, Industrial Relations, Marketing, Sales, Political Science, Law, Public Administration

CONVENTIONAL

Data & Detail People: Accounting, Secretarial Science, Business Management, Financial Investment and Banking, Court Reporting, Computer Programming, Medical Records Technology

Source: Borchard, Kelly, Weaver, *Your Career: Choices, Chances, Changes,* copyright 1980, 1982 by Kendall/Hunt Publishing Company, Dubuque, Iowa, p. 175.

This chart shows traditional occupations associated with the personality types identified by Holland (see Figure 1).

best fits your interests and skills. But how do you know what occupation your interests suggest when the future is so uncertain? In a time of rapid change, you can't even be sure what choices will be in existence in the future, let alone which has the best match for your particular attributes.

However, two features of the Holland model make it an excellent tool for futures prediction in the occupational arena. The first has to do with the assumption that an individual's dominant personality-based interest patterns have pretty much crystallized by the end of adolescence. These patterned interests then remain fairly stable throughout life. What this means is that when your personality style has been accurately classified in Holland's terms, your primary interest patterns have been revealed for life. Thus, if an assessment test found you to be an Artistic or an Investigative type at age 20, a similar test retaken at ages 40 and 60 would again detect the same prevailing interests.

The second feature of the Holland model that gives it credence as a tool for futures prediction lies in the relationship between human interest patterns and the structure of the occupational world. In essence, Holland found that occupational activities in the workplace are reflections of human interest patterns. It seems unlikely that the evolved structure of our occupational world is due to chance or ac-

> "While we can't be sure what specific names the occupations of the future will have, we can be rather sure that these unknown occupations will possess characteristics that conform to the Holland structure."

cident. The fact that Holland was able to classify the inner world of personality so neatly into six general styles seems to attest to a natural ordering. But why does this same pattern exist in the occupational world? The answer, no doubt, is that people gravitate to, or create, work that enables them to express their primary interests. In this regard, the Holland structure appears to be an occupational model for all time.

No matter what historical period we might select as a reference, we could fit all of the known occupations in existence at that time into Holland's six categories. We know, for example, that the alchemists were Investigative types, blacksmiths Realistics, court jesters Artistics, cattle barons Enterprisings, and midwives Socials.

There is every reason to believe that the Holland model will continue to serve as a convenient scheme for organizing the occupations of the future. We can also assume that people in the future will be happiest when they enter occupations best suited to their natural interests. Thus, while we can't be sure what specific names the occupations of the future will have, we can be rather sure that these unknown occupations will possess characteristics that conform to the Holland structure. The Holland model helps us to know a lot about what people's interests will be in the future, and a little about the nature of work in the future.

Designing Occupational Scenarios

Figure 3 illustrates how the Holland model can be used as a reference for facilitating occupational-scenario designing. Three scenarios have been developed around six factors that shape the nature of jobs and career patterns over the next 20 years. These six factors are: technology, economics, international politics, brain/mind capabilities, health and longevity, and values. Figure 4 depicts a continuum representing extremes for these variables. From this continuum it is possible to weigh the overall effect of possible trends and then to envision likely occupational scenarios using Holland's six categories as a base for prediction.

The three scenarios are:

1. Little change in the environment or in human qualities.

2. Rapid change in human creations, such as technology, economics, and politics, with little change in humans themselves.

3. Rapid change in humans, such as brain/mind capabilities, health, and values.

Scenario 1 lists a few sample occupations that we might expect in each of Holland's six code categories if there is little change over the next 20 years. In this scenario, the occupations would not be very different from those of today. However, there are some current trends that would probably continue modifying the occupational environment. For example, there will almost certainly be fewer physical-labor jobs of the kind associated with a heavy-manufacturing-based industry and more of the highly skilled jobs associated with high technology.

JOE DI DIO/NATIONAL EDUCATION ASSOCIATION

People who like to work with other people—teaching, healing, developing, informing, or training them—are attracted to occupations in such fields as education, sociology, and therapy. This teacher has the rapt attention of his young pupils.

Figure 3
Three Scenarios for Occupations in the Year 2000

PERSONALITY TYPE	1 • LITTLE CHANGE	2 • EXTERNAL TRANSFORMATION	3 • INTERNAL TRANSFORMATION
Realistic *Technically & Athletically Inclined People*	Electronic Technician, Robot Technician, Pre-Fab Construction Worker, Cable-TV Technician, Medical Technician	Laser Technician, Solar Technician, Space Station Technician, Satellite Communication, Bionic Limb Technician	Brain/Mind Lab Technician, Bioenergetic Technician, Actualization Abode Carpenter, Thought Transmission and Recording Technician, Health Food Farmer
Investigative *Abstract Problem Solvers*	Pollution Control Scientist, Systems Analyst, Nuclear Engineer, Computer Scientist, Intelligence Analyst	Space Medicine Scientist, Computer Scientist/Medical Analyst, Space Habitation Analyst, Extraterrestrial Geologist, Weapons Disposal Engineer	Genetic Engineer, Well-Being Medical Doctor, Mind Expansion Researcher, Human Communications Specialist, Peace Scientist
Artistic *Idea Creators*	Graphics Design/Commercial Artist, Cable-TV Writer, Conservation Architect, Military Musician, Curriculum Developer	Computer-Assisted Design and Computer Graphics Artist, International Satellite Communications Script Writer, Solar Energy Architect, Computer Musician, Right Brain Curriculum Developer	Thought Transmission Artist, Human Expansion Writer, Human Milieu Architect, Mind Expansion Musician, Whole Brain Curriculum Developer
Social *People Helpers*	Nurse, Stress Psychologist, Marriage/Divorce Counselor, Public Education Teacher, Geriatrics Nurse	Computerized Medicine Nurse, Space Psychologist, New Modes of Living Counselor, Private Computer Learning Facilitator, Retirement/Longevity Counselor	Psychic Healer, Actualization Psychologist, Mind/Body/Spirit Counselor, Personal Enlightenment Tutor, Age 70+ Career Counselor
Enterprising *People Influencers*	Industrial Robot Salesperson, Hospital Administrator, Military Officer, Electronics Office Manager, Criminal Lawyer	Solar Car Salesperson, Electronics Medical Diagnosis Center Manager, International Peace Project Officer, International Data Bank Manager, Euthanasia Lawyer	Rapid Learning Machine Salesperson, Actualization Center Manager, Quality of Life Projects Manager, Brain/Mind Data Bank Manager, Genetic Manipulation Lawyer
Conventional *Data & Detail People*	Data Entry Clerk, Word Processing Specialist, Medical Records Technician, Computer Programmer, Accountant	International Data Base Clerk, Paperless Office Administrative Aide, Electronics Medical Diagnostic Records Technician, Computer Security Inspector, Computer Accountant	Brain/Mind Data Bank Clerk, Thought Transmission Recorder, Actualization Center Administrative Assistant, Psychic Research Aide, Personal Efficiency Advisor

This chart shows what job titles might be found in Holland's Occupational Environment hexagon (see Figure 2) in three different scenarios of the year 2000.

Figure 4
Factors Shaping Careers of the Future

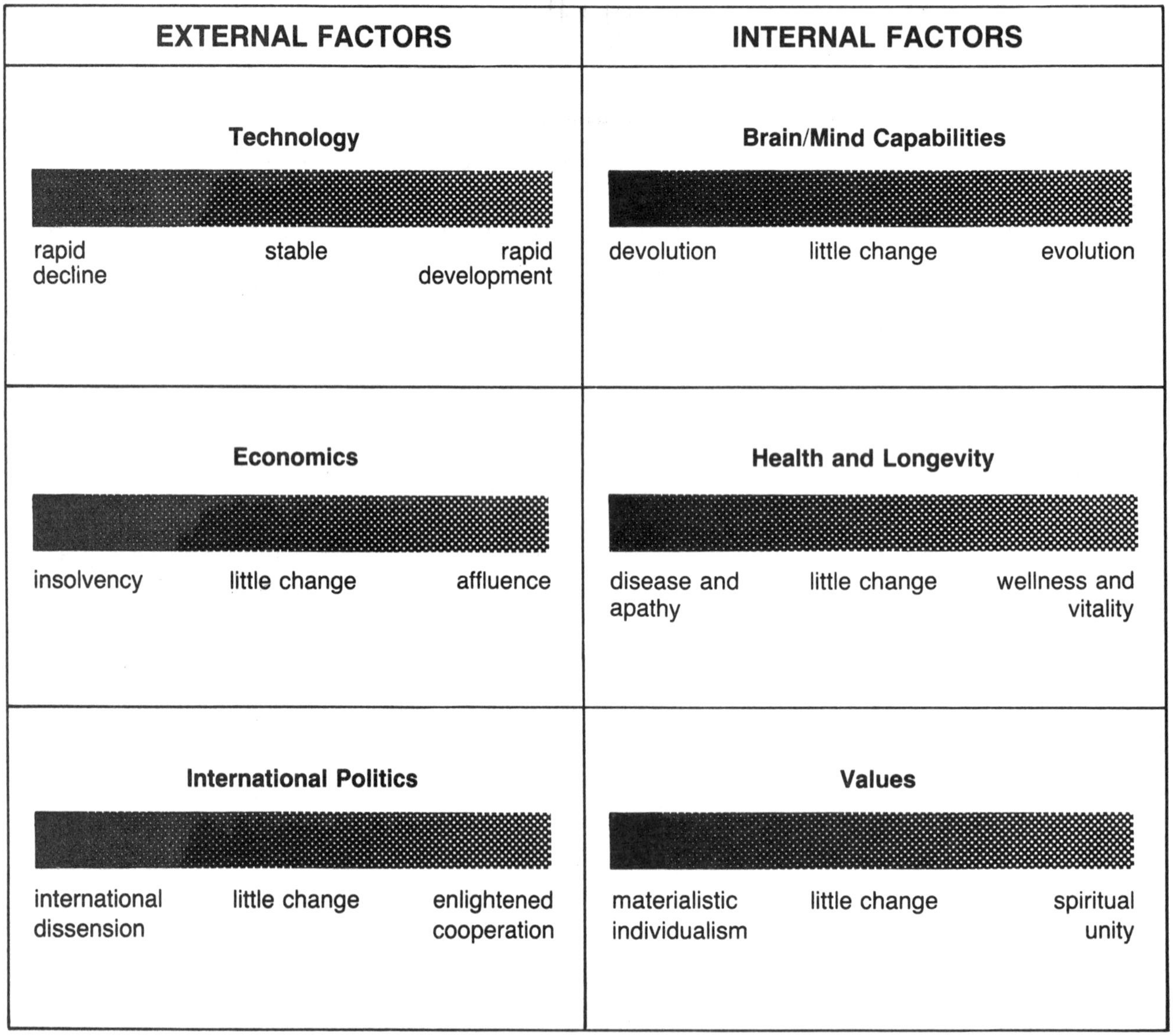

EXTERNAL FACTORS	INTERNAL FACTORS
Technology rapid decline — stable — rapid development	**Brain/Mind Capabilities** devolution — little change — evolution
Economics insolvency — little change — affluence	**Health and Longevity** disease and apathy — little change — wellness and vitality
International Politics international dissension — little change — enlightened cooperation	**Values** materialistic individualism — little change — spiritual unity

This chart summarizes a continuum of possible changes—from negative to positive—in six factors affecting the future of work. Author Borchard's occupational Scenario 1 assumes "little change" in either external or internal factors. Scenario 2 assumes rapid positive change in external factors, but little change in internal factors. Scenario 3 assumes little change in external factors, but rapid positive change in internal factors. Other scenarios can also be developed assuming rapid negative changes in either external or internal factors or both.

The current upheaval in the school and college system generated from the baby-boom years will have stabilized. The result should be a much rosier employment situation than is currently the case, and the education field may once again offer promising, prestigious, and stable careers.

In a population that is growing older, increased numbers of workers serving the over-60 age group are sure to be needed. With most of the U.S. population possessing home computers and cable television service, the early twenty-first century should be a boom time for the deliverers of life-long learning services, including educational-system designers and software developers.

Scenario 2 illustrates the kinds of occupations we can expect if rapid, positive transformation should occur in government, technology, and economic conditions over the next 20 years. Major breakthroughs in the technological areas that produce better living conditions (abundant and cheap energy, clean environment, food sufficiency, clean and efficient mass transportation, space capabilities, etc.), combined with rapidly developing world affluence and international cooperation, would create profound changes in the array of occupations available. This would be especially true in the defense, health, and education industries.

Under these circumstances we could expect to see a great reduction in military expenditures with significantly more capital resources available for health, education, and

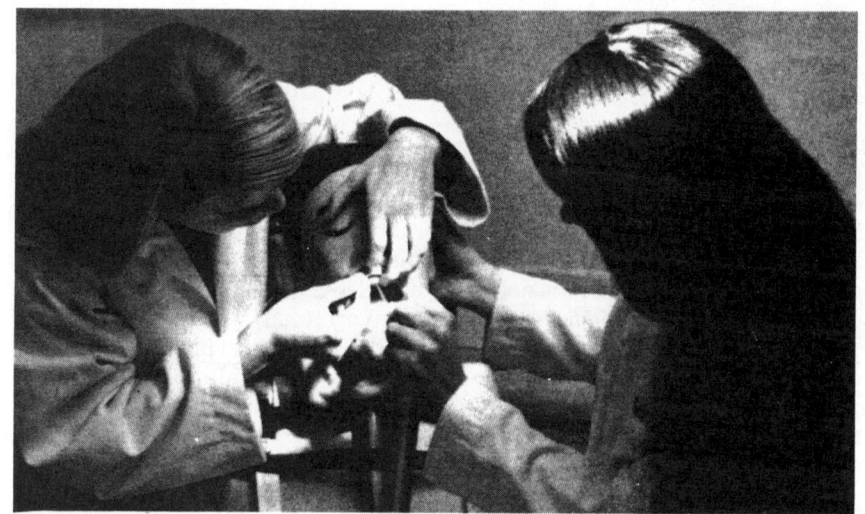

Dental-assistant students prepare for a career suited to "Realistic" type individuals—those who are technically or athletically skilled and like to work with their hands. Other Realistic careers of today include mechanical and electronic engineering, drafting, and forestry.

People who are analytical and precise and who prefer to work on their own frequently gravitate toward scientific and technical careers such as chemistry, biology, medicine, and mathematics, says author Borchard. Here, a technician measures chemicals during research at Goodyear lab.

nonmilitary research and development. The emphasis might shift from protecting national interest and security to global problem solving through science, technology, and education.

In this scenario, the year 2000 ushers in an age of international peace and cooperation. The world's military expenditures might be re-employed for international construction projects, peace-keeping missions, environmental restoration tasks, and space and ocean exploration. Multinational corporations would become aware of the business benefits created in an affluent, cooperative, and peaceful world, while industries with vested interests in promoting the arms race would transform their product lines into goods and services with market value in a peaceful world.

Scenario 3 envisions a revolutionary transformation in people, with a growing awareness of the amazing potential of the mind. Here we would see a value-system transformation from individual materialism to spiritual wholeness. People would live long, healthy lives through their ability to manage personal, mental, and emotional health and to move to higher levels of well-being. This high state of wellness would be achieved through inner transformation rather than through advances in medical technology. In this scenario, the major focus for career activity might center on "inner technology" and our ability to expand our creativity and intellect, promote mind/body/spiritual well-being, and conduct fully expressive and loving relationships.

Career Planning Example

Mark, a 30-year-old automobile-assembly-line worker, was laid off from his job in 1982. After several months of lying around the house waiting for the union to get his job back, he realized that the automobile industry wasn't rehiring very many laid-off workers. Mark also knew that the plant was using robots to do the tasks that he used to perform.

At first he felt bitter and angry; later, helpless and depressed. His job was gone, his self-concept was devastated, and he felt he had no skills to do anything else.

After much encouragement from a friend, Mark visited the career-development center at a nearby community college for assistance. There, a career counselor introduced him to the career-planning process, and he began to explore new possibilities. After completing several interest- and skills-assessment exercises, Mark learned that his top interests could be classified as R-I-C (Realistic-Investigative-Conventional) on the Holland model. He was pleased to learn that he had valuable skills that were transferable to other jobs and careers.

The counselor then showed Mark how to develop a list of occupational alternatives suited to an R-I-C personality style by using the traditional sources of occupational information, such as the *Dictionary of Occupational Titles* and the *Occupational Outlook Handbook,* as well as computerized searches and group brainstorming. From these sources, Mark was able to compile a lengthy list of options that offered both good employment prospects and future development potential.

With the assistance of his career counselor, he narrowed down his choices to these occupations: electronics technician, radiology technician, computer operator, solar technician, cable-TV technician, and laser technician. After researching these options in the college's career library and conducting information interviews with people working in these fields, Mark chose to pursue a new career as an electronics technician. This occupation both suited his interests and seemed to be viable in almost any future scenario that he and his counselor could envision.

Now, one year later, Mark is beginning his second year at the community college and soon expects to complete the electronics-technology program. He obtained financial aid to assist with family finances while pursuing his degree. After successfully completing a semester of work experience through the college's cooperative-education program, he obtained a part-time job at a nearby electronics firm. He has already had several job leads and is excited about beginning his career in either the robotics industry or computer production.

ROBERT A. ISAACS

The average secretary's skills and interests place her in Holland's "Conventional" category—people who are orderly and efficient and prefer to work with words and numbers. Other Conventional types include accountants, medical records technicians, and computer programmers.

"Career-planning practitioners need to become occupational-scenario designers as well as personal-assessment experts."

Students seek the advice of career counselor at a community college. To help career choosers make wise choices, the counselor must also be a futurist capable of constructing alternative occupational scenarios.

Life/Career Planner As Futurist

Career planners need to tune in to the future if they are to remain equipped to assist today's career choosers and changers. Many of the methods, tools, and resources currently in use are outdated. Even our current computerized career-search systems are not fully adequate sources of occupation information for people who wish to have careers that span into the future.

Career-planning practitioners need to become occupational-scenario designers as well as personal-assessment experts. By educating themselves about the future, counselors can develop new resources and rejuvenate existing tools. Most counseling tools are showing their age when it comes to assisting people with career planning toward the year 2000.

For example, the Holland model has features that make it particularly adaptable for occupational-scenario development and future-oriented career planning. With a bit of creativity, the counselor can use the model to predict the kinds of occupations likely to develop in the future, even when the times are changing as dramatically as they are now.

About the Author

David C. Borchard, president of the Middle Atlantic Career Counseling Association, is director of career development at Prince George's Community College, 301 Largo Road, Largo, Maryland 20772. He is co-author of *Your Career: Choices, Chances, Changes* (1980) and *Winning Your Career Game* (1983), both published by Kendall/Hunt Publishing Company, for whom he is career planning consultant.

Samuel E. Bleecker

RETHINKING HOW WE WORK
The Office of the Future

Until now, the office has been modeled after the factory. But the foremost product of the office — ideas — cannot be handled like factory output.

The office of today is organized like a factory where the product is paper. And, since paper is the perceived product of the office assembly line, the desire to exchange information on paper has directed the development of office design and technology.

If we are seeking the solutions to today's problems in factory-modeled offices, we're hunting in the wrong field. Before we throw more technology and billions of dollars more at the problems of work and the workplace, we must recognize that the product of the office isn't paper but ideas — that people and not machines are the source of economic power.

However, what hampers our move from the office of today to the office of tomorrow are the shackles of a machine age mentality — an inappropriate worship of technology and progress.

Computers *do* speed paper flow. The automated office cranks out two, three, four times the documents of the office before it was automated. The American Productivity Center reports that American businesses churn out 370 million new business documents totaling 190 billion pages every single day.

New technologies stand ready to quicken the pace further: The IBM 3800 printer knocks out 20,000 lines a minute — 576,000 pages daily, or enough output to lay down a daily paper trail 100 miles long.

But, as former Xerox Vice President Paul Strassmann notes in his book *Information Payoff: The Transformation of Work in the Electronic Age*, "if a secretary types 300 lines of mostly useless text per day, it does not follow that replacing the typewriter with a word processor capable of generating 3,000 mostly useless lines of text per day will be

TERRY GRAVES

THE FUTURIST, July-August 1987

"How can we impartially measure the productivity of the mind, the impact of an idea, or the value of a thought?"

an improvement enhancing profitability of the firm."

Increased speed and what we measure as "productivity" should not be the final goal. If computers and automated processes do nothing but spawn new ways to race paper around the office, America will certainly lose its competitive edge.

Throwing billions of dollars more into technology will do little to transform the office of today into the office of tomorrow. In fact, the exclusive emphasis on technology is an anchor that may well sink us all.

The roots of the problem of creating a profitable workplace stretch back perhaps more than 200 years to the start of the Industrial Age. The problem arises from applying mechanical-age principles to Information Age technologies: Office organization derives from principles that simply do not apply to society today.

The Rise of the New Office

In an office, not all that goes on is tangible. As Paul Strassmann notes, "The closer one examines the details of office work, the less one knows what is going on."

The paper work surely is tangible. But its content isn't. The accuracy of figures or the persuasiveness of a marketing piece or letter to a customer cannot be measured by the automated standards of the mechanical age. Quality must be judged, not measured.

The Industrial Age did just fine measuring the contributions of the body. It essentially pitted man against machine and drew its measure from the competition.

Today, it is the mind and not the body that sits at the core of the economy. Information is the currency. Ideas are products. Information is power. How well people understand is critical to the means of production. Knowledge workers are asked to inquire and to think, to gather information, to evaluate it, communicate it, and act upon it.

But how can we impartially measure the productivity of the mind, the impact of an idea, or the value of a thought? Clearly, an idea is not like a cord of wood that burns predictably at so many calories per minute. Not all ideas are alike. To offer two ideas an hour may not be better than offering two a day or one a month. Chester Carlson, the inventor of xerography, proved the point: One idea in his lifetime was enough to create one of the world's largest industries.

The difficulty in measuring the value of a single idea or the productivity of the office worker has baffled many. It has stifled automation in the workplace. How can the creative contributions, ideas, and insights of office workers be automated? The uniformity of the work force powered the factory; individuality drives the new office.

The New Office Structure

In an office driven by information, secretaries don't need to be near their bosses. Aides can be in the next room or in the next country. Workers can be home or in the office. We find new flexibility in office planning because ideas are not restricted by location. Two people don't need to be near one another to improve a product that can flash electronically around the globe in seconds.

If the office is organized around information flow, then the office work can be viewed as enriching data as it flows through the organization. In effect, each office worker works as a kind of value-added reseller of information, taking it in, massaging it, and passing it along.

Information flow in the office is decidedly different from the product flow in the factory. In the factory, every step of the production process is orchestrated like a massive symphony with each voice heard at just the right moment.

Nothing in the manufacturing process is left to chance or the serendipitous result of accident. The assembly line, like the machine age itself, minimizes chance. It works to overcome the individuality of craftsmen and the unpredictability of the seasons.

But not so for the office. The office feeds on spontaneity and flexibility. In the office, people share ideas and exchange information. People go off in different directions to contemplate particular — often individualized — problems.

Managers may prefer to operate their offices like factories because of the comfort implied in the predictability of the factory organization. In reality, though, people come up with creative thoughts as they have them, not as they are directed. These ideas can be encouraged, but they certainly cannot be orchestrated like a great symphony.

In addition, the products of today's office aren't run-of-the-mill or off-the-shelf solutions to clients' problems. Most companies pride themselves on customized approaches or on knowing how to get out of the tight spots with specialized expertise. General Motors isn't like the Chrysler Corporation — and they wouldn't want to be treated the same.

In the office, pieces of the puzzle are acted upon simultaneously. People don't operate like machines in tandem. They process information and assignments in parallel, interweaving bits of one problem with pieces of the solution to another.

A study by a group of psychologists, reported in the *New York Times*, shows that chief executive officers generally play several alternatives over in their minds simultaneously and often do not think in a serial, organized way.

A well-oiled office, therefore, is flexible where the factory was ordered, spontaneous where the fac-

Expert Systems in the Office

The slogan of American corporations today is "Work smarter, not harder." Helping office workers to work smarter will be the job of software, most particularly self-learning and modifiable expert systems.

Capturing the knowledge of industry experts on a computer is a way to work smarter. Expert systems are instruction sets representing the collective knowledge, inferences, and rules-of-thumb of experts. Relatively unsophisticated expert systems are already working their way into the factory and the office. Increasingly, these systems will invade the executive office, bringing basic changes in the way the office works.

Expert or knowledge systems will, in essence, do for the office what the stirrup and gun have done for battle: They will serve as the great equalizer for individuals of widely different skills and intelligence. Expert systems will make everyone smart.

But there's a catch. Someone must devise expert systems. Someone must write the programs. Someone must tailor the systems to the needs of the office. Who will that someone be? The office workers themselves!

Modifying expert systems to the needs of the corporation will occupy more office workers' time in the future. The task will be an extension of existing tasks. Currently, information is the product of the office. People gather, process, and transmit it. At the highest levels, processing includes analysis and repackaging of information. So, in fact, people invent expert systems all the time. However, they don't always record them.

To reduce costs and pump up efficiency, companies will employ programmed expert systems that, without human intervention, issue reports and recommend actions on data gathered electronically. Increasingly, data will be automatically captured and manipulated by computer systems such as the computerized trading programs that triggered the stock market's near-record 141 point sell-off of September 11 and 12, 1986.

The new office workers, in essence, will become programmers, tailoring off-the-shelf programs to the specific needs of the company. Fewer will be engaged in data collection and research or in routine work such as claims or form completion. Rather, workers will be trained to spot those factors that influence decisions.

The new worker must understand the basic information needs of the organization and tailor the electronic services and software to them. For example, an office worker concerned about VCR product development might instruct an expert system to capture all articles and production figures related to VCRs. The computer would scan all the electronic sources recovering data on numbers of VCRs sold, the manufacturers, suppliers, etc. From these data, the expert system would generate trend analyses and recommendations.

But the office worker might believe, as a result of experience, that other factors could influence the company's decision to manufacture VCRs in the United States rather than overseas. In order to make the program more effective, the office worker/programmer might rewrite the program to also capture financial data about Japan, a major VCR manufacturer, and the differential between interest rates of the two nations. Trade balance deficit data also play an important part in determining the direction of prices of overseas goods. And so these too would be added to the program's arsenal.

Installed expert systems tailored by office workers/programmers will be electronically fed data and will respond with solutions. Bolstered by self-learning artificial-intelligence techniques, these programs also would learn to accommodate user preferences. They would learn the individual's wants from the way that he or she uses the system. Increasingly, software developed for today's marketplace includes natural-language programs that allow the user to modify the program to taste.

— Samuel E. Bleecker

---

tory was pre-planned, and processes in parallel where the factory processed serially.

The Office of the Information Age

In the Information Age, the strategic resource is the mind — ideas that fuel the economy.

The very nature of the "products" of the Office of the Future — ideas and information — holds vast promise for the development of companies in the coming decades. Information is a nondepletable resource. Sharing it does not diminish it; in fact, for the first time in history, the basis of our economic strength actually increases with usage. As more people share ideas and information, the better off we all are.

The rise of the new currency — ideas — has prompted authors John Naisbitt and Patricia Aburdene to suggest in their book *Reinventing the Corporation* that the new labor force emerging in the workplace requires what I call "through-life" education. To stay on top of their jobs, workers continuously need new information to sharpen their skills. The consequence, note the authors, is a new alliance between business and education, with the corporation undertaking a larger share of lifetime learning.

Ideas, like the people who generate them, are by their very nature

> "The farther we move away from the factory model, the closer we move toward the empowerment of all employees and the diminution of central authority."

unique. If based on the work at hand, ideas are born custom-made, tailored to circumstance.

And since people, not machines, have ideas, it is people who should be valued as the economic resource in the new office society.

Companies often protect capital equipment with maintenance contracts, preventive maintenance programs, and even specially developed environments that protect valuable assets and assure their longevity. Does it make any less sense to protect our new economic resource — people?

Enlightened organizations pamper their people with effective work environments — from ergonomically designed chairs and work environments to gymnasiums and full health facilities. These enlightened organizations value their workers. As Harvard Business School professor Robert H. Hayes suggested in a *New York Times* editorial, "In such organizations everybody is assumed to be responsible for the organization's prosperity."

Responsiveness in the Information Age

The introduction into the workplace of new, faster technology has enabled workers to produce more in less time. And as time in the Information Age becomes "multiplexed" — as more and more things begin happening at once — response time to stimuli becomes critical.

Just as temperature sensors indicate a buildup of heat in a nuclear reactor, so marketing sensors indicate a buildup of heat in the competitive marketplace. And companies need to respond quickly. Cycling memoranda up and back through a dense corporate hierarchy no longer yields answers soon enough when critical deadlines are set in terms of days or minutes rather than months or years.

In response to the quickened pace of technology and decision making, companies have streamlined the corporate ladder and shifted authority to a larger portion of the work force.

In situations where the office is styled after the factory model, corporations tend to have steep, pyramidal hierarchies. In contrast, Information Age companies such as Intel Corporation, Apple Computer, and the new artificial intelligence concerns housed in Boston's "AI row" tend to have flat organizational structures.

The desire or the necessity in these new offices to process information in parallel determines to a large degree the steepness of the organizational chart. The farther we move away from the factory model, the closer we move toward the empowerment of all employees and the diminution of central authority.

According to Peter Drucker in a column for the *Wall Street Journal*, "Traditional organization basically rests on command authority. The flow is from the top down. Information-based organizations rest on responsibility. The flow is circular: from the bottom up and then down again."

When one large multinational company organized itself around information, it was able to delete 12 levels of unnecessary management.

Distinguishing Features of the Factory and the Office

Factory	Office
Serial processing	Parallel processing
Physical space	Conceptual space
Preplanned	Spontaneous
Ordered	Flexible
Linear time	Multiplexed
Depletable resources	Nondepletable resources
Speedy processes	Customized processes
Quantity	Quality
Automated machinery	Intelligent machinery
Durable goods	Disposable goods
Steep pyramid office hierarchy	Flat hierarchy
Workers indistinguishable	Individuality
Central control	Empowerment
Productivity	Effectivity
Processed energy	Mental energy
Accounting	Valuing
Specialization	Conceptualization

As the nature of work has changed, so have the distinguishing features of the workplace. This chart contrasts the distinguishing features of the factory — the predominant workplace of the Industrial Age — with the distinguishing features of the office.

Changes through the Ages

	Agricultural Age	**Industrial Age**	**Information Age**
Defining technology	Craftsman	Clock	Instruction-based systems
Strategic resource	Raw materials (seeds, water, soil)	Capital (money)	Ideas (minds)
Transforming resource	Natural energy (sun)	Processed energy (coal, electricity)	Synergy (minds working together)
Product	Food	Mass-produced items	Information
Organizing principle	Seasons	Product design	Inflow (information flow)
View of time	Cyclical	Steadily onward	Multiplexed
View of progress	Progress in history	Perfectibility of man and society	Merger of man and machine
Machine paradigm	Spindle	Heat engine	Organism (instruction-based machine)
Communication	Conversation (transfer ideas locally)	Face-to-face conference (transfer ideas by transporting people)	Teleconference (transfer ideas by transmitting images)

The transition from the Agricultural Age to the Industrial Age to the Information Age has changed the means, methods, and materials with which we work. This chart notes the changes that have taken place for a number of work-related items and activities.

Empowerment delegates to employees the responsibility, resources, and authority to act in particular circumstances. Thus, employees in the best position to know what is going on handle day-to-day decisions effectively and cost efficiently. Such delegation frees top management for more important chores and accords to jobs at all levels the characteristics cherished by contemporary workers: the ability, power, and resources to exercise control over their own job responsibilities.

Instruction-Directed Systems

It may seem that computers are the catalyst in the transformation from the Industrial Age to the Information Age. That is true — indirectly. But the real engines of change are the instruction-directed systems — the software that drives computers and other equipment.

For example, few people would consider the stereo system the economic heart of the music industry. Most would agree that the "software" — the record albums, cassettes, and so forth — accounts for the industry's large revenues.

Without software or programs to run, the fastest, state-of-the-art supercomputer serves as little more than a costly silicon or gallium arsenide boat anchor.

Ultimately, the future points to the merger of man and machine. At the simplest level, this means that machines may have some of the intellectual attributes of man. At the highest level, microchip circuitry may be biologically based.

Though the computer is the most recent installment of this marriage between man and machines, it is neither the last nor the most effective. The computer, however, *is* helping us to automate our work, reducing the time and tedium of doing repetitive tasks. Most importantly, the computer is capable of liberating us by helping us develop mechanical servants.

Six Levels of Understanding

Information flow organizes the office. An examination of office work demonstrates that people, to varying degrees depending upon job function, must be capable and efficient at one of six levels of Apprehension — apprehension not in the sense of fear or capture but as perception and understanding of ideas.

A secretary, for example, does not merely answer the phone and take dictation. A secretary screens information: Is this call important? Should the executive be interrupted? Does the boss need this memo to make a decision?

A product manager evaluates a large number of signals each day to make intelligent decisions. In announcing a new product, for example, a manager must, in addition to making decisions about the manufacture of the product, collect information about the competition. What are they offering now and at what price? Can we beat it? With what consequences? What do the shifts in personnel announced in the newspapers signify about the competition's internal problems?

As we advance to executive levels, the strain of collecting and evaluating information rises exponentially. How, for example, will the national debt affect interest rates within one week? two months? five years? How does this affect plans for expansion, here and overseas? Will the political unrest in the Middle East jeopardize low oil prices? How do we market our product in China or in Japan?

Work performed in an office — regardless of the individual's position or title — requires processing at one or more of these levels of apprehension:

1. Data — unconnected numbers, dates, names, and items that flood us daily. They can be seismic readings or even daily Dow Jones figures alone (unconnected to dates). "Albany," "macaw," and "1776" are data.

2. Facts — connected data. When we combine daily Dow Jones quotes with dates, we can obtain a picture. Examples of facts: Albany is the capital of New York, a macaw is a tropical bird, and the American Revolution began in 1776.

3. Knowledge — a particular assemblage of facts, providing firmer connective tissue among them. Knowledge can be taught; it can be acquired by being "schooled," where a student gains perspective on a range of issues related to a field of study. However, having knowledge of all parts of an engine does not, for example, guarantee that a mechanic can repair a car. Knowledge, too, can be compressed. The trials and errors of generations can be boiled down to a two-semester course in economics.

4. Experience — primarily from self-directed interactions with the "real world." Experience broadens knowledge and gives it a richness unavailable through study alone. Experience internalizes knowledge; it takes time to acquire.

5. Shared visions — philosophical and emotional collective understandings founded in our universality, not individuality. It is the stuff of leaders, people who are able to perceive the common denominator, the universal need. It is the motivating force that galvanizes organizations into actions and gives them purposes. Democracy is a shared vision, for example.

6. Epiphanies — a level of apprehension that reaches beyond logic and even beyond intuition. It is an understanding that comes to an individual rarely and in great flashes — a creative brilliance that sees beyond the immediate boundaries and strikes at the heart of the matter.

Each of these levels of apprehension is transformed into a higher level by application of an organizing principle. For instance, data become facts with order or association. Facts elevate to knowledge with synthesis. Knowledge transforms into experience with perspective. Shared vision transcends experience by application of a single unifying force or a view of underlying principles. Epiphanies demand a supralogic to bring new insights into focus, often without appeal to reason.

It is the application of the organizing principle that demonstrates our skill. And it is the level of apprehension exercised at our job that primarily determines the person's function and status within an organization.

— **Samuel E. Bleecker**

This is why the computer plays such a unique and pivotal role in the development of the office and why it has been embraced and heralded as the messenger of a new age. But, in a sense, it is a case of mistaken identity. It is not the computer that is responsible for the new age; rather, the computer allows us to break with an established and restrictive factory civilization.

We might have gone on praising the computer and its impact on the way we work if the new age had not stumbled. Wall Street politely says the industry is "experiencing a contraction."

But the office revolution is not simply slowing down. It seeks a new, firmer footing, one grounded in a new perception of what office work is.

Machines That Work As People Do

The computer has become an accessory to people rather than the Industrial Age model of people as accessories to the machine.

Modern office technology, such as this advanced word-processing system, have greatly increased the speed of office work but have not necessarily increased true productivity.

BRITISH INFORMATION SERVICES

Whether machines mimic man or vice versa is a long-standing conflict. With computers, we have some of the first instruments capable of working the way we do.

Currently, executives don't engage computers productively because computers won't bend to executives' ways of working. Instead, computers demand obedience to machine rules.

In the office, executives spend more than 90% of their time communicating face to face — over the phone or at meetings. People talk. With the development of digitalized voice-recognition and voice-synthesis systems, computers also will be spoken to and listened to. And when artificially intelligent computers become commonplace, computers will also understand and do our bidding — by listening, not by our typing in commands.

Ultimately, the organization of the office and office work are not driven by technology. New technologies will simply allow us to be more of who we are.

A New Language For a New Age

The office, like the farm and factory before it, is a microcosm — a laboratory for new ideas and new technologies. In the office, we can observe the world in transition.

Early indications of change often show up first in our language. For example, "user-friendly" indicates machines taking their first halting steps toward working the way people do.

The transition from factory to office is starting to reorganize the way we work. We need a new language to express our new perceptions of the forces at play.

Industrialists invented the language of the machine: rate, efficiency, productivity, specialization, delegation, accounting. Perhaps the new language should eschew concepts such as depreciation that compensate for how much less value our assets represent as time goes on. Instead, we might apply appreciation factors to our idea-assets — our people — based on years of experience and increased levels of understanding within the organization.

Futurist Wilford Lewis suggests alternatives that also reflect the new organization of the office. According to Lewis, we should speak not of productivity but of creative synthesis; not of specialization but of conceptualization; not of delegation of authority but of empowerment; not of accounting but of valuing; and not of processed energy but of mental energy.

In this new age teeming with information management, we must redefine our concepts to recognize that a strong mind, not a strong back, rests at the root of our economic power.

People form the core of our economic wealth; they are the means of production. In the Industrial Age, people aided machines; today, machines aid people. This shift is central to the most dramatic change in the history of production. This is the first time in history that our most valuable strategic and transforming resource is internal and nondepletable: the human mind.

About the Author

Samuel E. Bleecker is a technology consultant. His address is 712 Northeast 71st Street, Boca Raton, Florida 33431.

Arthur J. Cordell

Work in the Information Age

A smooth transition to the computerized society will require a realistic approach to the choices and trade-offs.

Will technology in the workplace be a "boom" or a "bust"? That is, will new technology increase or decrease the number of jobs available? In fact, the technology will lead to *both* a "boom" and a "bust." It depends on whether we are looking at the short term or the long term and on which job category is being examined.

Saying that we will experience *both* "boom" and "bust" is another way of saying that we will experience profound change in the labor markets. With change will come winners and losers.

To better appreciate where we are today, it is helpful to introduce a historical perspective on technology and employment. The first part of the industrial revolution was characterized by replacing machines for muscle power. Machines replaced human and animal labor in very many areas. This is probably why we still measure the output of many machines in terms of horsepower. Machines represent capital, and increased capital intensity means that the productivity of labor is increased.

A simple example is the use of a bulldozer, which can do the work of many people with shovels. The bulldozer is both technologically complex and capital intensive, and its use displaced labor and made the remaining labor more productive. Since the remaining labor was more productive, it received increased wages. In a growing economy, the displaced workers would be able to find new work.

We are in the midst of a profound transition that began within the past 15 years. Machine intelligence is being substituted for human intelligence throughout society. Computing power is being built into machines, both on the factory floor and in the office, with the result that labor is displaced. Fewer and fewer people will be needed in the actual production of both goods and services, and the remaining workers will be more productive. However, in a growing economy, the displaced workers will be able to find new work.

New skills will lead to new types of goods that will be sold in the markets of the future. The use of microelectronics and the related technologies of satellites, fiber optics, digital networks, and the coaxial cable system will profoundly transform the nature of Western society.

The Emergence of the Service Sector

As advanced society industrialized, the number of people in the agricultural sector declined and people moved off the land to work in factories. At about the mid-point of this century, productivity advances in the manufacturing sector led to another displacement of labor—and the service sector began to grow.

While the service sector is relatively labor intensive, new technologies are making the service sector (including the information sector) more productive. With increased capital based on computer technology of all types, we can increase the productivity—that is, the output of the remaining workers—of banks, insurance companies, department stores, and government departments. With computer-aided learning, we can even expect to see increased productivity in universities.

Increases in productivity will cause further job displacement. When we automate the service sector, where will people go? How do people find work in a society that is capable of developing machines with intelligence?

In actuality, the use of computing power not only displaces labor but also creates new services that can be performed by the remaining labor. This is what economic development is all about. Industrialization and the development of computerization have led to the emergence of whole new categories of employment. New industries and job descriptions, which only 20 years ago were either unheard of or were to be found in science fiction, are now part of our daily life.

We have all heard about places where jobs will be lost. The key question is: Where will jobs be created? In an information society, the new and important resource will be information itself. Economist Peter Drucker believes that information is the *new* capital resource in the new economy and will be the main capital input leading to growth and development. In an information economy, schools are as much primary producers as farmers—and the productivity of schools may turn out to be more important for national well-being.

The productivity of other information producing and manipulating institutions will become equally important. As Drucker notes, in an information-based economy, much of what we now consider "expenditure" or "social overhead" is actually "capital investment." He concludes that this investment must produce a return both to the institution and to the nation in general.

We are seeing the emergence of new hardware, new software, new content, new skills, new jobs, new industries. Just as the automobile age led to the creation of jobs in whole new industries—shopping centers, suburban development, petroleum sales and related services, highway construction and

THE FUTURIST, December 1985

maintenance—information technologies, too, have created jobs in the building of microcomputers, creating wealth for those who can provide interesting, educational, and entertaining *content*.

Content As Commodity

Content will more and more become an article of commerce. Content refers to the vast range of ideas, experiences, concepts, reports, directions, and recipes produced by a society. Until now, the most common vehicles for conveying content have been the written and the spoken word and the photograph. Now, advances in information technology enable content to be stored, retrieved, and delivered to anyone, anywhere in the world, at lower and lower cost. Information "packages" can be personalized according to a client's requirements.

The information economy places a value on all sorts of content. That content is turned into a commodity and sold. Whether it is a pornographic film on a cable channel, or a laser videodisc walking tour of Paris, or a satellite weather map, the information or content has value to someone. As such, it can be sold. Someone can make a profit. Someone will have a job. Taxes will be paid. The economy continues, but it has a different shape, configuration, and tempo.

Thus it would be a mistake to think that the information consumed is only an extra and that the real business of the economy is and will continue to be the provision of food, clothing, and shelter. It is also incorrect to think that services are somehow second-class elements of the economy whose existence and value depend on the exchange of "real" goods.

The information industries will contribute the major part of the future gross national products of developed countries. Goods will be sold as part of a total information package. In fact, it is altogether likely that more of the goods industry will depend on the information industry than vice versa. The use of televisions, telephones, computers, communications satellites, microwave networks, and typewriters, for example, already depends on the content provided by information activities. Unlike houses, shoes, and doughnuts, these products are useless in themselves.

Information is the raw material of the new economy. Information is central to manufacturing, services, and the operations of government. Inquiring, communicating, evaluating, and deciding have become predominant activities. In industry, the "need to know" fuels the search for information on which business decisions are based. The corporation is slowly evolving into a kind of information-rich, organic learning system that transforms data from various sources into the capital knowledge base on which the corporation ultimately rests. Information is consumed by business and, in a different form, is consumed at the level of the household.

Information derives its value in many ways. It has value to those industries that manipulate fashions and mold public opinion. Political parties also spend vast amounts of money for information of this type.

Fingertips on the world's foreign-exchange and money-market operations: Lloyds Bank in London. Machine intelligence is replacing human intelligence in many areas, but it is leading to new types of skills, says author Cordell.

Cumbersome and deteriorating documents such as these deed and mortgage records can be stored on microfilm and computers so that the information is accessible for more people.

Policy Issues for the Information Age

The issue is not the simple binary notion of "boom" or "bust." We will have to cope with profound change in labor markets and in economic, political, and social institutions. The changes associated with the transition to an information society will set national agendas for the next decade.

At the beginning of the widespread implementation of electricity (or of the automobile), it would have been very difficult to devise a policy or set of policies for an orderly transition to the electrical era or to an automobile culture. The transition itself led to the change in values, attitudes, and institutions, and then and only then could a set of policies be devised that was appropriate and operational.

The same is true for computers. Computer technology is blurring the boundaries between work, leisure, and education. Now is *not* the time to devise a comprehensive or integrated policy or set of policies on employment and computers. Rather, now is the time to prepare a policy for the transition to a computer culture.

Change will bring winners and losers. Some businesses will be in trouble; others will grow and prosper. And whole new industries—some of which we can now only dimly imagine—will spring up. By trying to rush in too quickly with policies designed to safeguard industries or culture or jobs or governments, we may develop policies that at best are neutral or useless and at worst cause more harm than good. The change or transition to a computer culture does, however, call for some policy development. Such policies should have the following characteristics:

- A policy for change will stress flexibility. There must be an ability to respond to new situations and unexpected events. Inherent in flexibility is the concept of resilience. Existing policy modes and institutions must adapt to new problems, knowing that in 5 or 10 years the change will be so profound that a whole new set of policies can be designed and made operational.

- A policy for change will have an image or a set of images of what changes are likely to occur. With an image of the future will come the ability to anticipate a new institutional landscape. "Crisis management" will be necessary regarding such probable events as a privacy scandal resulting from penetration of a data base or the closing of a one-industry town as the Western world turns from resource-based hardware to intelligence-created software. Such crises should be anticipated and planned for in advance of their occurrence.

- Most important, a policy for change will deal with the casualties of change in a benign, supportive, and constructive way. Thus, when people are displaced by new technology, we must develop humane policies for retraining and resettlement. If that doesn't work, we should develop humane policies for income distribution.

The computer era promises enormous gains in productivity and efficiency. It promises to lead to a society of abundance and widespread leisure. In fact, many systems are already in place that have led to remarkable reductions in the need for labor.

But no matter how we try to develop policies that will allow computer technology to evolve in an orderly way, the trade-off will have to be faced: The transition to an information society will bring about vast disruption and personal and social dislocation. The productivity and efficiency inherent in information technology that is labor saving, capital saving, and energy saving are the reasons advanced society is willing to go through change on such a vast scale.

About the Author

Arthur J. Cordell is a science advisor for the Science Council of Canada, 100, Metcalfe Street, Ottawa, Ontario K1P 5M1, Canada. He is the author of numerous studies and articles on economics and the implications of information technology for Canadian society.

WORK
In the New Information Age

Alan Porter

Just 25 years ago, John F. Kennedy was president of the United States, the space race was on, we were into the upbeat sixties, and we were discovering the computer. Twenty-five years from now, we will be living in the new Information Age. Many uncertainties cloud our images of this future. Yet we can sense what differences the new Information Age will make in our work lives.

There can be no doubt that the Information Age has arrived for the working world. We meet it driving to work as we use our cellular phones, at work in our electronic offices, and back home as we plug in our personal computers to do our "homework."

When we think of "work," the image of smokestack industry in the Ohio Valley has faded into the background. Silicon Valley is the model every governor wants to imitate in building home state industry. We live in a post-industrial society—but "we ain't seen nothin' yet."

In archaeology, the terms "Old" Stone Age and "New" Stone Age sound similar, but in fact represent vastly different periods. Similarly, we now find ourselves in the "old" Information Age, with the "new" Information Age yet to come. The new Information Age will bring with it an upheaval in the world of work.

Among the changes that the new Information Age brings may be a

> We are moving from the "old" Information Age into a "new" Information Age. And this new age promises dramatic upheavals in the world of work.

massive shortfall of jobs. Preparing for and adjusting to this shortfall could require a radical change in our attitudes toward employment and unemployment. We must consider the implications of such changes today if we aspire to manage a graceful transition to this new Age.

The Bureau of Labor Statistics projects employment by economic sectors only through 1995 (see Table). We can extend their projections to give orders of magnitude of population, labor forces, and jobs 25 years into the future—*not* taking into account the impact of large-scale adoption of information technologies. Note the shortfall of some 18 million jobs in 2010 due to demographics (the baby boomers remain in the labor force through this point).

Three sectors of the labor force taken together—mining, private households, and farming—will provide about 3 million jobs, or only 2% of the projected labor force in 2010. That leaves seven labor sectors for examination: construction; transportation and utilities; finance, insurance, and real estate; government; manufacturing; trade; and services.

New Information Age Scenarios

Here is a short look at some of the changes we'll find in each of these employment sectors as we enter the new Information Age.

The speculations presented here take into account available or nearly available technologies; they do not make provisions for future technological breakthroughs. In other words, these new Information Age scenarios will likely prove too conservative.

The scenarios to follow assume:

• No major war.

• An economy that alternates between growth and recession, without devastating depression, uncontrolled inflation, or collapse of the worldwide monetary system.

• Political stability in the United States and the world.

• No deliberate efforts to forestall the new Information Age (e.g., through legal restrictions on automation, trade blockages, or widespread labor revolt).

• No major countermeasures to lessen the impact of widespread adoption of advanced information technologies.

Construction

In the new Information Age, as before, growth fuels growth. Office/apartment complexes use modular structures, prefabricated in a semi-automated factory, then trucked to site. Labor costs are a fraction of traditional construction, which has ground almost to a halt nationwide. Demands for architecture, engineering, and planning have all been restricted by the use of modular units. Mass production wins every time.

Transportation

Telecommunications takes a big bite out of transportation. Individual calls and teleconferences, utilizing telephone, video, and holographic images, now substitute for much business and personal travel. The high cost of vehicles and energy, along with the consequent high cost of services, results in even lower transportation demand. Railroad employment continues to be halved every 25 years. Ship crews are skeletons with a computer brain. Automated material handling dominates freight movements.

The airlines are down to three major carriers. All-American Air flies half the flights once available on its component carriers prior to consolidation. Larger planes and reduced demand account for the drop. Safety has improved greatly, thanks to in-flight self-fault diagnosis and repair, overlaid on automated ground maintenance routines.

Crews today consist of the autopilot and one human co-pilot, who actually intervenes on less than one-tenth of one percent of all flights. Robo-servers and one human attendant take care of the passengers. (Customers accept self-service everywhere these days.) In air travel, people make their own arrangements at computer terminals. Airline and travel agents have been decimated; they only work on

Job Growth From 1982 to 2010
(In Millions)

Jobs (Millions)

Sector	1982 (BLS)	1995 (BLS)	2010 (Ext.)
Mining	1	1	1
Private Households	2	1	1
Farming	3	3	1
Construction	5	8	9
Transportation & Utilities	6	7	8
Finance, Insurance & Real Estate	6	8	9
Government	16	17	19
Manufacturing	19	23	26
Trade	23	29	31
Services	23	31	35
Total Jobs	102	128	139
Labor Force	112	130	157
Population	231	256	280

Note: BLS (Bureau of Labor Statistics) figures for 1982 and 1995 (moderate projection) are rounded to the nearest million. The sums of the sectors do not exactly match the total jobs because of rounding. The extension to 2010 is a rough extrapolation by the author. Population level is based on a small improvement in life span. Labor force participation rate uses Predicasts values of .74 for the 15-64 age group in 1982 and .79 in 1995 as a basis to extrapolate to .84 for 2010. Ten-year age group population figures are moved forward over time. A small decline of 1 hour per work week is assumed. Jobs are factored upward by population ratios as a demand factor. These are adjusted among sectors taking into account Predicasts allocations among work categories. Subjective adjustments are added to consider current technological trends on work and basic implications of surplus labor and pressure on wages. In contrast, an alternative forecast not presented here that considers automation effects explicitly by type of worker yields only 105 million jobs in 2010, a shortfall of more than 50 million jobs.

intricate international packages. In terms of employment, the skies are not friendly but lonely.

Finance, Insurance, And Real Estate

Integration in the airlines doesn't hold a candle to what has happened in this sector. It's now called Financial Services, integrated from head to toe. Investment (stocks, real estate, venture partnerships, and legalized betting), credit (debit cards to mortgages), daily transfers (payments sent and received), and insurance of all sorts have fused. The top ten national banks devoured the local banks when deregulation hit, ate up other financial services, and now fight each other over shares of the pie.

Government

Federal, state, and local governments, squeezed by budget pressures, have failed to maintain the role of employer of last resort. Most government work is white collar, information work. Those inertial bureaucracies chock full of professionals, managers, and clerks certainly feel the computer shaving away like an electronic razor. Computerized records, expert system query handlers, electronic funds transfer (EFT) systems (e.g., Social Security automation), and automatic reporting and accounting procedures clip away the bureaucratic behemoths. That officious clerk doling out tidbits of information has been swept away by your direct terminal access to an intelligent system.

The profit-conscious U.S. Postal Service is a showpiece of efficiency. Competition on both the electronic and hard copy fronts keeps the Postal Service lean and mean. EFT has eliminated billing and check writing, corporate and personal. The physical mail mainly consists of unusual correspondence and packages.

Reduced mail demand means increased price. Businesses retain daily delivery, but homes can't afford it. The surcharge for personal handling is up to $2 per piece (in 1986 dollars), so virtually all mail is prepared for optiscan, direct routing, and automated handling. No human touches it unless it's going to so rural a destination that we still use a "mailman" (most delivery is by automated guided robotic vehicles). Ninety percent of neighborhood branches are self-serve stations that weigh and sort your mail, calculate charges, and collect fees from your debit card.

Manufacturing

The image of the enormous, dark, unpopulated factory producing almost without human workers has become widespread reality. Indeed, all three major production systems—process industries, mass production, and small batch production—utilize full-scale automation.

The chemical plant presents an eerie scene: acres of gleaming steel machinery, hissing sinisterly, with pungent odors wafting to and fro. But no people. A few humans await emergencies as intelligent computers monitor and control other computers that operate the plant.

"One-man" publishing operations exemplify modern mass production. A manuscript arrives electronically. The expert system selects fonts and sizes and colors and so on. Then it publishes the volume, even doing most of the editing, formatting, and proofreading. Materials handling, printing, and assembly are fully automated. Of course, most publications are electronic, received via computer with automatic royalty fee transfers.

Gone are the days of the tool and die shop manned by a dozen expert machinists. Today, one person oversees on-demand automated

Boeing 747, which can carry over 350 passengers, takes off. Larger planes and reduced travel demand will characterize air transportation in the future.

UNITED AIRLINES

production. Orders are placed electronically. Flexible manufacturing cells are reprogrammed dozens of times daily. Inventories and distributors are creatures from the past. Production on demand headlines a truly integrated system—automated throughout order processing, design, materials handling, production, distribution, and funds transfer.

Trade

This sector was once divided into wholesale and retail. Wholesale is no more. Information technologies mean direct links. Direct links and automated production enable production on demand, minimal stockpiling, and direct sales. The traditional role of the wholesaler disappears. Retailing feels the change, too.

Take auto sales. The consumer has home access to action videos and full data on performance. Options can be selected at will with detailed video representation and price comparison. When Renault decided to drop its dealer network in favor of lower prices and more convenient direct home sales, the competition shortly followed suit. Service largely relies on self-fault detection and diagnosis with many easy to replace modules—either do-it-yourself or by the independent service center.

Now over 50% of retail sales are conducted electronically via home computers. CompuSears offers a good example. The electronic catalog with easy search capabilities saves consumers time and hassle. The consumer calls up videos and documents as desired to compare products, delivery dates, and price. Ordering and payment are handled electronically. Your item, even if produced to your personal specifications, will probably never involve direct human action.

Services

You might imagine that all the jobs reside in the services. But the information technologies driving factory and office automation integration are doing the same in many key service areas.

The "one man and a computer" operation takes over many professional services. Furthermore, many of the ordinary providers are driven out of business by the truly expert system. Nowhere are the gains in efficiency more pronounced than in programming. Software engineering, high-level languages, and artificial intelligence mean the really outstanding systems designer dominates, doing the work of a hundred humdrum programmers of 25 years ago.

Some of the most surprised victims of the Information Age have been the would-be salespersons. Take medical supplies. When pharmaceutical firms set up computerized distribution systems and provided hospitals and M.D.'s with free terminals with which to order drugs and supplies instantly, the old sales system collapsed under the weight of better information.

Repair opportunities evaporated as do-it-yourself fault detection became a hot selling point. Not just cars but household appliances, most electronics, and office equipment all offer either user-friendly repair or prices so low that repair is unwarranted.

Let's look at three essential service areas: food, health services, and education.

Food

Use your phone to place your order ahead at Autoburger, the "one man" fastest food dispensary. Fully automated order-taking, cooking, and packaging has it

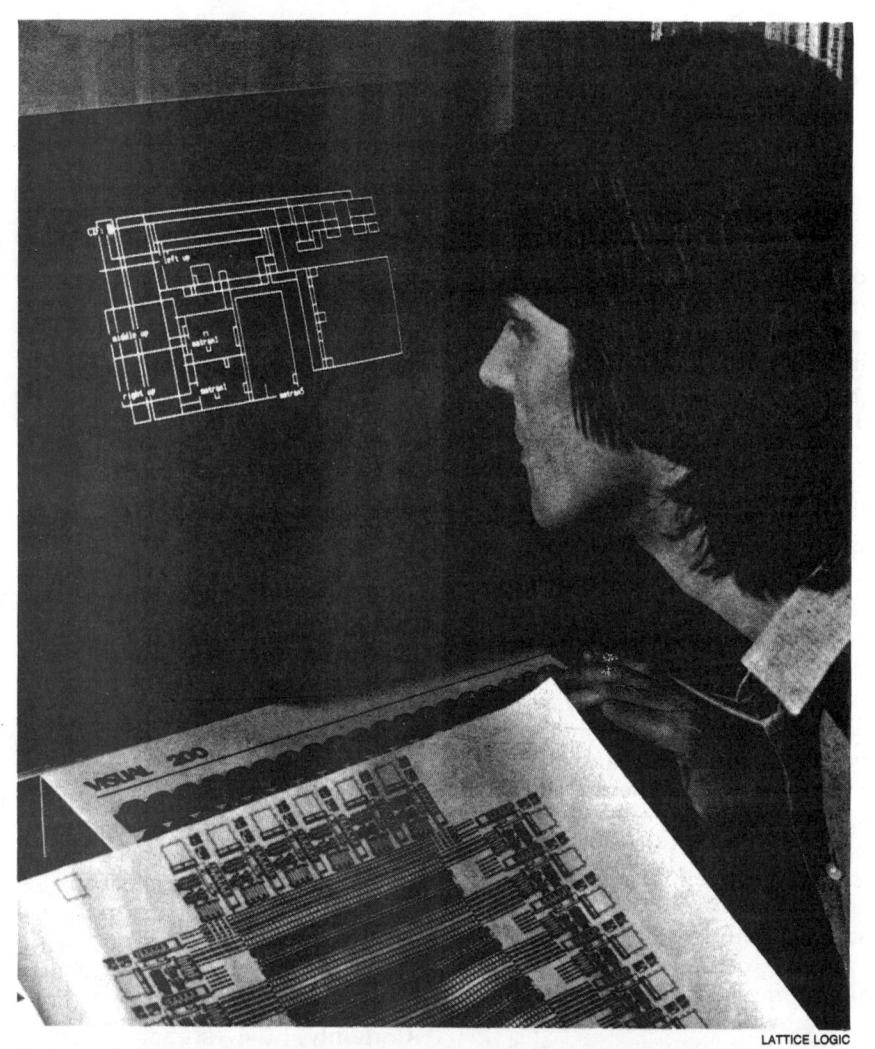

Systems designer, utilizing a high-level hierarchical design language, creates integrated circuit patterns. New, complex computer languages and artificial intelligence mean that one outstanding designer will do the work of a hundred ordinary programmers today.

"Expect the nature of work to change abruptly in the next 25 years."

ready for you to pick up. Or perhaps you'll gather groceries from the Autoshop. Walk the aisles remotely from home; pinpoint the fruits you like and watch the autopicker gather them, package them, and charge you. A cold and sterile environment—better for food, cheaper to maintain, and easier on the consumer. Come by for readi-pick-up or pay for home delivery.

Health Services

The primary care physician is "The Doctor"—a computerized generic expert health system. It counsels on your personal health needs (diet, exercise, and the like), diagnoses your ailments, and prescribes treatment, all for free. The government found that maintaining this service was the only viable alternative to prohibitively expensive government-funded programs such as Medicare. "The Doctor" also compiles results of its diagnoses, recommended tests, and prescriptions, building a data base to increase medical knowledge and continually refine its guidance.

The health-care system still employs medical researchers, surgeons, emergency care personnel, and frontier-of-knowledge specialists. However, M.D.'s, routine medical care, and even hospital operations have been squeezed hard by "The Doctor."

Education

In the new Information Age, teachers train and programs teach. That is, the role of the human in the education system is to facilitate use of computerized modules and to foster social relations. The federal government supports production of thousands of multi-media modules at all levels. So instead of thousands of teachers redundantly teaching algebra or physics, we have one (or two or three) Hollywood-scale efforts involving video action, computer feedback, etc. Teachers coordinate the use of these programs and assist special students. The educators who remain (down 30% from 1980) find the new system rewarding and challenging.

The New Information Age And Change

Once upon a time, these scenarios might have seemed unbelievable. No more. The notion that the Information Age will see such changes in a quarter-century is eminently believable.

Technically, everything postulated is within our grasp today. Socially, we have choices, but fullspeed development appears unstoppable. Anything else and our economy will simply become uncompetitive. From Japan to the Third World, adoption of information technologies is leading to higher productivity, better quality, faster delivery, enhanced reliability, and lower cost.

Certainly, the scenarios presented depend on step-changes from present-day work practices. The scenarios are built on particular steps, representing only one of many possible courses of development, so these specific scenarios may not occur. However, what is likely is a qualitative, system change of a corresponding magnitude.

The adoption of the telephone illustrates such a change. One telephone is useless; two telephones are a novelty. A hundred telephones in a community become slightly useful. Then, bang! The network reaches a critical mass; everyone has to have one; and life changes abruptly.

Expect similar degrees of change driven by new information hardware as well as by smart, friendly, and cheap software. New systems with new capabilities will exert positive pressure to induce further innovations. Expect professional workstations to be linked together, home computers to become as ubiquitous as the telephone, and the development of a full, national video-audio-data network. Expect the nature of work to change abruptly over the next 25 years.

The Changing Nature of Work

On the individual level, the form that jobs take will be radically different. This means that we need to rethink education and job training systems. More importantly, we must recognize the potential of an aggregate effect. Increases in productivity could be so sharp that we could no longer pretend to have full-time work for everyone who wanted it.

Imagine what the automation reflected in the scenarios does to the numbers extrapolated in the Table. It shatters those employment projections. Adjust the 2010 projections yourself to take into account the system changes we can anticipate:

- Construction—Move much of the actual material preparation and pre-assembly to the factory, substituting computer-integrated manufacturing for on-site labor.
- Transportation and utilities—Reduce transportation and energy demand per capita in the Information Economy; computerize everything from clerical details to piloting.
- Financial services—Consolidate and computerize all information work.
- Government—Bureaucracy constricts everywhere, with less need for middle management and clerical work in particular.
- Manufacturing—Integrated automation makes possible production-on-demand, boosting quality and reducing cost.
- Trade—Squeeze out middleman operations, superfluous with electronic sales and ordering; redo retailing around a national information network, cheaper and more convenient for the customer.
- Services—Set up new systems to take advantage of artificial intel-

"Drastic unemployment could instigate vicious riots, government overthrow, class war."

ligence/expert systems and basic computer/communication capabilities to transact business and to entertain, lowering costs and improving service.

Taken together, these system changes could mount to a shortfall of 50 million jobs in 2010.

The evidence mounts that the shortage of work will constitute the Number One political issue of the coming quarter-century. We attempt to legislate work. Since 1946, the U.S. Congress has committed, and periodically recommitted, the United States by law to the goal of full employment. We believe that we must offer a job to every able-bodied person and that, by God, they had better take it. We strain the economy to connive unneeded and often unfulfilling work.

What can we do about the shortage of work that looms ahead? Let's look at some of the typical responses. A quick scan finds:

- Unions resisting introduction of microelectronics as "job killers."
- Training programs with endless wrinkles, perhaps viable at the micro level in getting one worker prepared for a job but barely relevant in terms of the macro level of too many workers in the labor force for too few jobs.
- Government subsidizing industry to create work, whether through partial payment of wages to induce hiring of disadvantaged workers or a $300 billion defense program propped up by the press for jobs.
- Cries by management and labor to raise trade barriers to keep out cheap steel and quality cars, increasingly futile in a world economy.
- Welfare itself, the cursed last resort, roundly condemned as demotivating, wasteful, and sinful.
- And, most intriguing, plans to reduce work hours—resulting in capable people moonlighting while the less able starve, dropping international competitiveness, growing poverty for everyone, or all of the above, depending on how wages are adjusted.

In a closed economic system, these actions might succeed to some extent. In the face of hard-charging international competition, they fail. Automation means cheaper and better-quality products and services. Even the developing countries with dirt-cheap labor cannot compete with highly automated production processes. Labor-intensive today translates to loss of jobs tomorrow. Furthermore, we must question the value of using people to perform work that a machine can do.

Changing Attitudes Toward Unemployment

The potential to produce what we want without having to do very much work could bring about the biggest system change of all. The cost of many goods and services should drop significantly. Government will cost less by computerizing routine and expert functions. Likewise for goods, housing, education, health care, and so on. This means less income will be needed. All of this could help ease the transition toward a less-work society.

The peaks and valleys of unemployment together present a strong upward trend across recessions and boom times. Official unemployment hovers between 6.5% and 7% in the present "good" times; 25 years ago that would have been deemed awful for a recession!

At some point, society may well give up the act. We must stop trying to provide 40-hour jobs for all and start rethinking our socio-economic system. Fewer people will be employed, and those who are employed will work fewer hours.

We need to begin thinking about these issues now. Our track record is that technological change moves faster than social institutions adapt. The adaptation required to handle a surfeit of would-be workers is staggering.

The "job" is the cornerstone of our social structure. It provides for economic, social, and psychological needs. Take it away and society could collapse—unless we plan ahead. Drastic unemployment could instigate vicious riots, government overthrow, class war. The alternative is to begin to formulate productive policies now.

Our system of government is loathe to plan. It finds greater rewards in responding to crisis than in avoiding it. We cannot afford to wait on the issue of work. Industry and labor need to work with government to set a clear agenda to build effective policy.

The first step is to recognize the probability—not the certainty—of drastic long-term employment shortfalls. Forecasts in hand today make this case clear. Next, we must set aside the fruitless Industrial Era remedies for unemployment. Then, policy experiments on employment alternatives can test uncharted waters prudently. We must study the kibbutz, run guaranteed income programs for restricted populations (like the New Jersey Negative Income Tax studies), try out paid volunteer programs, back pioneers in flexible work careers, and vary co-op arrangements.

Working out the details will take decades. Should society pay for volunteers to work with the elderly, or for housework? How do we cope with the generation caught in transition to a new economic system? What work mechanisms will function well in a new system?

Effective work strategies depend on early answers to these questions. The future of society, in turn, depends on these strategies working.

About the Author

Alan Porter is associate professor of industrial engineering at Georgia Tech and is senior author of *A Guideline for Technology Assessment*. His address is School of Industrial and Systems Engineering, Georgia Tech, Atlanta, Georgia 30332.

Fred Best

Technology and the Changing World of Work

Computers and other technological innovations are changing the nature of work and the balance between our jobs and our personal lives. Here, an expert on the impacts of new technologies offers some long-term speculations on the future of work.

The United States and other industrial nations are now experiencing wave after wave of innovations that bring profound changes in our personal and occupational lives. At the core of these changes is the computer. If the cost of purchased or rented computer time continues to decline at its historical rate of 50% every two and one-half years, and if the complexity of utilization is reduced by "user-friendly" software, computers and allied technologies will soon be assimilated into every aspect of our lives.

The impacts of such technological change on the economy, the world of work, and our personal lives will be phenomenal. These innovations are likely to alter the nature of work activities within all economic sectors, dramatically affect the growth and location of employment opportunities, and shift the relationships between our jobs and personal lives.

Changing Skill Requirements

Up to 45% of existing U.S. jobs will be significantly altered by technological changes over the next 20 years, many through an upgrading of skills.

The historical trend toward mechanization is becoming increasingly sophisticated as robots and computer-coordinated operations take over routine and dangerous tasks now performed by workers. For example, the installation of robots in the United States has been growing by 30% per year, increasing from 200 in 1970 to 3,500 in 1980. Moderate estimates indicate that there will be 35,000 installed robots in America by 1990 and that applications will skyrocket during the last decade of the twentieth century.

Small computers, sophisticated sensors and servo-mechanisms, and design and control instruments that are easier to understand and use are moving us rapidly toward the "cybernetic promise" of highly integrated and flexible production systems. For example, the growing application of CAD/CAM systems (computer-assisted design/computer-assisted manufacturing) now allows industrial planners to design products on computer screens and then reformat machinery on the shop floor to produce products by centralized programming. The implications for increased productivity and product diversity are spellbinding.

Many workers will have to be reassigned to new tasks. While some of these new tasks might not require greater skill, many necessitate an understanding of new and more complex technologies. For example, General Motors Corporation predicts that 50% of its work force in the year 2000 will be categorized as skilled tradespersons (technicians, inspectors, monitors, etc.), compared with 16% in 1980. Thus, there will be a need for more highly trained personnel such as engineers, technicians, computer specialists, and managers with basic technical skills.

THE FUTURIST, April 1984

Applications analyst compares computer-generated drawing with finished bracket produced by computer-assisted design and manufacturing system. Innovations such as this CAD/CAM system are increasing demand in manufacturing sectors for computer specialists, engineers, technicians, and managers with basic technical skills.

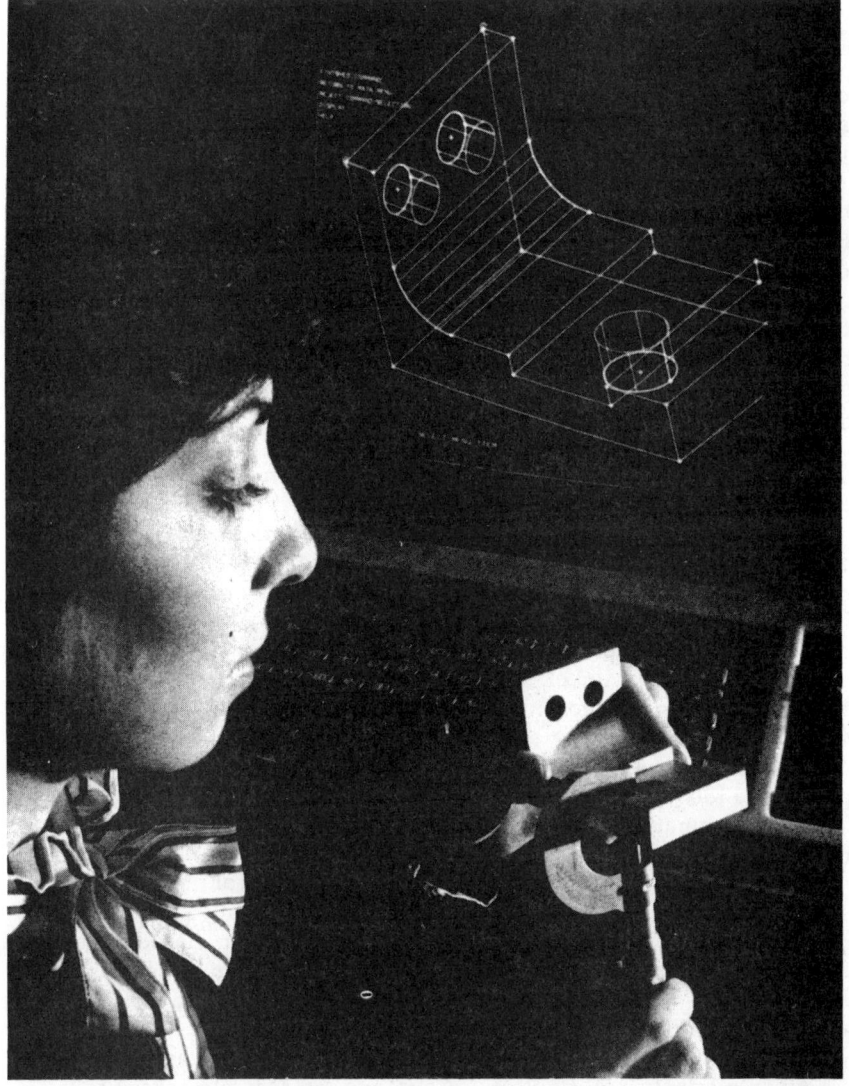

Technological innovations will also profoundly affect the nature of work in both office and service occupations. Just as we have moved from manual typewriters and carbon copies to memory typewriters and photocopy machines over the last few decades, newer technologies will vastly increase the efficiency and output of information processing.

Dramatic reductions in the cost of computers, the development of user-friendly software, and the availability of high-speed printers and telecommunication systems will create a fundamental shift from paper to electronics as the main medium of operation. Typewriters, file cabinets, and mail systems will increasingly be replaced by word processors, computerized data retrieval systems, and video transmissions between computer terminals.

As in the case of manufacturing and material processing, many jobs will become unnecessary. Demand will gradually disappear for mail deliverers, file clerks, stenographers, and other workers. Familiarity and skill with computers will become essential to all office workers, from manager to secretary.

Displacement and Realignment

National Cash Register reduced its U.S. work force from 37,000 to 18,000 between 1970 and 1975 because of productivity gains from using microelectronic rather than mechanical parts. The General Motors plant in Lordstown, Ohio, reduced its work force by 10% after increasing productivity 20% through the introduction of welding robots. In Providence, Rhode Island, the *Journal Bulletin* cut its printing staff from 242 workers in 1970 to 98 in 1978 as a result of new typesetting technology. These examples underscore the fact that workers have indeed been displaced by technology; however, the question remains as to how extensive such displacement will be in coming years.

Concern over job loss due to the higher productivity of machines has historical roots, beginning with Luddite resistance to industrial mechanization in early-nineteenth-century England. However, despite isolated cases of worker dislocation, most experts believe that technological advances have generally fostered economic and job growth by increasing the quality and quantity of products while lowering the costs.

Because costs are lower, producers can afford to sell at lower prices, which in turn commonly causes consumers to buy more. As a result of increased demand, producers generally employ as many or more workers than before technological innovation began to increase output. When this process occurs throughout the economy, the result is economic growth, with higher real wages and an increase of employment.

Two historic examples illustrate this process. First, during the early stages of the Industrial Revolution, the introduction of the Hargreaves jenny in 1770 ultimately allowed one worker to produce as much as 200 spinners could without the jenny. Yet employment in Britain's textile industry increased from less than 100,000 in 1770 to about 350,000 in 1800 because productivity allowed major reductions in price, leading to even more dramatic increases in market demand for textiles.

A second example is the introduction of the assembly line by Henry Ford. As a result of this combination of machinery and in-

The Evolution of Work

The social, institutional, and human roles associated with work have changed dramatically as human civilization has evolved. The work of antiquity was essentially direct physical toil, required for immediate survival. For primitive peoples, "work" and "leisure" were almost completely integrated. As civilization developed, work and nonwork activities continued to be integrated within families and tribes.

With the emergence of agriculture, economic surpluses, and culturally transferable knowledge, work became easier and more distinct as a social activity. Specialization and individual roles and responsibilities began to emerge as key elements of human existence.

As economic surplus, development of productive tools, and specialization continued to grow, the goals and conditions of work continued to change. Work became increasingly oriented toward the improvement of the human condition rather than bare survival. The resulting surpluses gave rise to increasingly productive tools, and ultimately machinery, which correspondingly allowed and required further refinement of skills and increased specialization.

While work dominated life, the concept of "leisure" as distinct from "work" began to crystallize. Industrial society was a natural outgrowth of these trends. As machinery became increasingly important and sophisticated, work became progressively specialized and oriented toward the use of tools and capital within the context of complex human organizations.

Organizational interdependence and division of labor gave rise to the ultimate predominance of employment. While productive human activity continued to be performed outside the context of employment, work became commonly viewed as an activity performed by "holding a job."

These dramatic shifts have caused a near inversion of the concepts of "work" and "leisure." As defined by classical philosophers, leisure was restricted to reflection and the fine arts; it was commonly viewed as nonmanual activities within preindustrial societies. Commerce, science, politics, writing, and all arts came to be viewed as the freely chosen "leisurely" pursuits of the elites.

Today, as progressively larger proportions of the work forces in advanced industrial societies become employed in "white-collar" jobs doing "knowledge work," the work activities of today are increasingly like the "leisure" activities of the past. While contemporary work conditions are commonly far from utopian, today's jobs tend to require more autonomy, creativity, freedom of expression, and skill than that required during the pre-industrial and early industrial eras.

While the work of the foreseeable future is likely to resemble much of what we do today, historical perspective suggests the importance of keeping an open mind to the possibility of radical changes in the medium- and long-range future. Just as the all-encompassing struggle for physical survival that commonly epitomized primitive humanity has little resemblance to "jobholding" within the offices of today, the nature of work in the future may take on new dimensions that we can scarcely perceive.

—Fred Best

---

dustrial organization, it took 56% fewer hours to produce the average car in 1920 than it did in 1910, leading to a 62% reduction in the real dollar price of an automobile. Consumers who previously could not afford a car began to make purchases, sales increased tenfold, and Ford employment rose from 37,000 to 206,000 in just 10 years. Workers may have been shifted to new assignments, but there was no overall loss of jobs.

From the standpoint of preserving and creating jobs, there appear to be few alternatives to technological innovation. While these changes are likely to cause considerable displacement and reassignment of workers, failure to modernize will cause affected industries to lose pace with national and international competition and ultimately cause even greater loss of employment and economic growth.

Technology and Non-Job Work

There are increasing signs that technological change may also alter the balance between job activities and our personal lives. If we define work as "productive human activity," it is clear that work has never been confined to "holding a job." There have always been people who are self-employed, who build their own houses, raise children, provide voluntary social services, and perform countless other productive actions outside the context of employment. The balance of productive activity inside and outside the workplace has undergone many changes in recent years and will probably change considerably in the future.

Just as the development of heavy machinery drew work out of the home and into factories and offices during the Industrial Revolution, new technologies may cause households and neighborhood groups to become more self-sustaining and to abandon institutional settings for many productive activities. Harbingers of such realignments are suggested by the emerging uses of many new technologies:

• **Home and personal computers.** The potential of home and personal computers, which didn't exist 15 years ago but now are an increasingly common new "home appliance," has scarcely been explored. This technology, which is greatly expanding in power and diminishing in price, is already being used for home entertainment centers, long-distance communication and mail systems, cookbooks, medical advisors, high-speed typewriters, portable offices, family business and tax filing systems, art and graphics devices, educational tutors, library reference services, financial planning, and control of other household appliances. Countless new uses, many of which are integrated with other new technologies, are being developed daily.

• **Video recorders.** Like home and personal computers, video recorders and disc players have emerged from nowhere in the course of only a few years. As archives of television and motion picture entertainment are rapidly transferred to video tapes and discs, a progressively larger portion of entertainment is likely to be pulled back into the home. The use of video recorders as substitutes for home movie cameras also affects the entire film development and processing industry.

• **Decentralized energy production and conservation.** A variety of new, improved, and rediscovered technologies are being developed as alternatives to centralized energy sources. Photovoltaics, solar heating, windmill generation, a variety of conservation measures, and other energy-related technologies are replacing or reducing dependence on central energy sources. These devices are likely to become more attractive as prices decline and the costs of central energy increase.

• **Decentralized medical care.** A number of affordable devices and services are being developed that provide patient-utilized and home-based medical care. For example, new technologies make it both desirable and less expensive to undertake sophisticated "do-it-yourself" medical treatments such as kidney dialysis, cancer chemotherapy, and intravenous feeding.

• **Decentralized and interactive communication systems.** Home-linked and controlled communication technologies are being developed that greatly expand the choice of information and provide options for interaction and local control. Cable and satellite television greatly enhance viewer choice, provide the potential for two-way communication, and open the option of local and neighborhood stations. Teleconferencing expands the concept of conference calls on the telephone to include visual communication. Satellite and microwave transmission greatly reduce the cost and difficulty of long-distance communication. When these communication systems are used with other technologies such as personal computers, work tasks that formerly had to be located and coordinated at a central location can be decentralized.

While the ultimate impact of these and other technologies is uncertain, their utilization will

COURTESY OF DIGITAL EQUIPMENT CORPORATION

Computer terminal and telephone allow office work to be done at home. Individuals can move work activities out of formal organizations and create new balances between their jobs and personal lives.

dramatically change the activities and skill required for work. They might significantly alter the timing, location, and organizational context of work in the future. These same technologies will increase self-sufficiency, open new options for individual business ventures, and generally reduce the need for "holding a job."

An Exploratory Scenario: Toward a Home-Based Economy?

Many novel developments are emerging that might make it desirable, efficient, and necessary to reduce traditional jobholding as the focus of "purposeful and productive human activity." High unemployment and growing job instability suggest the need for individuals to find backup modes of activity that are economically and psychologically rewarding.

The emergence of relatively inexpensive and user-friendly technologies may make it economically efficient and personally rewarding to move both job and non-job work activities out of formal work organizations. Greater flexibility in work arrangements could allow many individuals and groups to meet personal and economic needs through a better balance of job-linked work and other productive efforts.

There are already countless jobholders with computer-based home businesses and flexible worktime and workplace arrangements that allow them to perform job responsibilities without having to be "at work" in the usual sense of the term.

If such conditions become more prevalent, the average worker of tomorrow might work "full time" for six or seven years within a traditional work environment. Then, in order to better handle family responsibilities, the worker might arrange to perform most job responsibilities at home using information technologies. He or she might then reduce worktime given to employment and develop an auxiliary business enterprise, perhaps to increase home-based self-sufficiency. Ultimately, the worker might return to work on a part-time or part-year basis while retraining for new skills.

Without doubt, such arrangements would pose some costs and dangers to individuals, employers, and the economy. For example, the worker might worry about being able to return to suitable employment after an extended period away from an organization. Organizations might have trouble de-emphasizing and re-emphasizing the roles of individual workers. There might also be concern with the loss of social-professional networks, problems of maintaining income during de-emphasis of employment, and discontinuance or reduction of fringe benefits.

Certainly such a system would entail individual responsibility, initiative, and accountability. However, more people might be willing to confront the costs and dangers if recurrent unemployment and job insecurity make it necessary, if individual preferences for more autonomy within work settings increase, and if institutional and social policies provide the necessary options and resources.

While new balances between household- and employment-based economies may emerge primarily via individual initiative, they could be encouraged by a number of institutional and social policies. Policies that might support such developments include:

• Tax incentives to defer use of earnings for utilization during periods of de-emphasized employment.
• Guaranteed credit and loans.
• Individually vested retraining vouchers.
• Guidelines for job-return rights.
• Subsidies and tax incentives for the purchase and use of home-based technologies.
• Options for flexible worktime arrangements.
• Financial incentives to encourage use of homes as offices and to reduce job-related travel.
• Standardization of selected information technologies.
• Options for selecting and continuing fringe benefits during de-emphasized employment.
• Options for using income maintenance payments to start small business enterprises.

The costs of such policies are not likely to be undertaken unless private and public expenditures for other policies such as income maintenance, retraining, public transportation, public service employment, and general social services are reduced. Clearly, the political consensus for such a tradeoff is not likely to emerge until a significant number of individuals have developed nontraditional home-job work patterns on their own.

Although jobholding will probably continue as the prevalent pattern of work for the immediate future, ongoing transitional instability, shifting human preferences toward work, and new technologies may foster continued growth of hybrid balances between job and household activities. We can only speculate on whether such patterns will develop into a major trend or prevalent pattern; however, private and public policy makers must begin now to think about the implications, costs, and benefits.

About the Author

Fred Best, president of Pacific Management and Research Associates (1208 Seventh Avenue, Sacramento, California 95818), has written extensively on management and human resources, economic development, and the impacts of new technologies. His books include *The Future of Work*, *Flexible Life Scheduling*, and *Work Sharing*. This article is excerpted from his report *The Future of Work: A View from the United States*, prepared for the Swedish Secretariat for Future Studies.

Tammara H. Wolfgram

WORKING AT HOME

The Growth of Cottage Industry

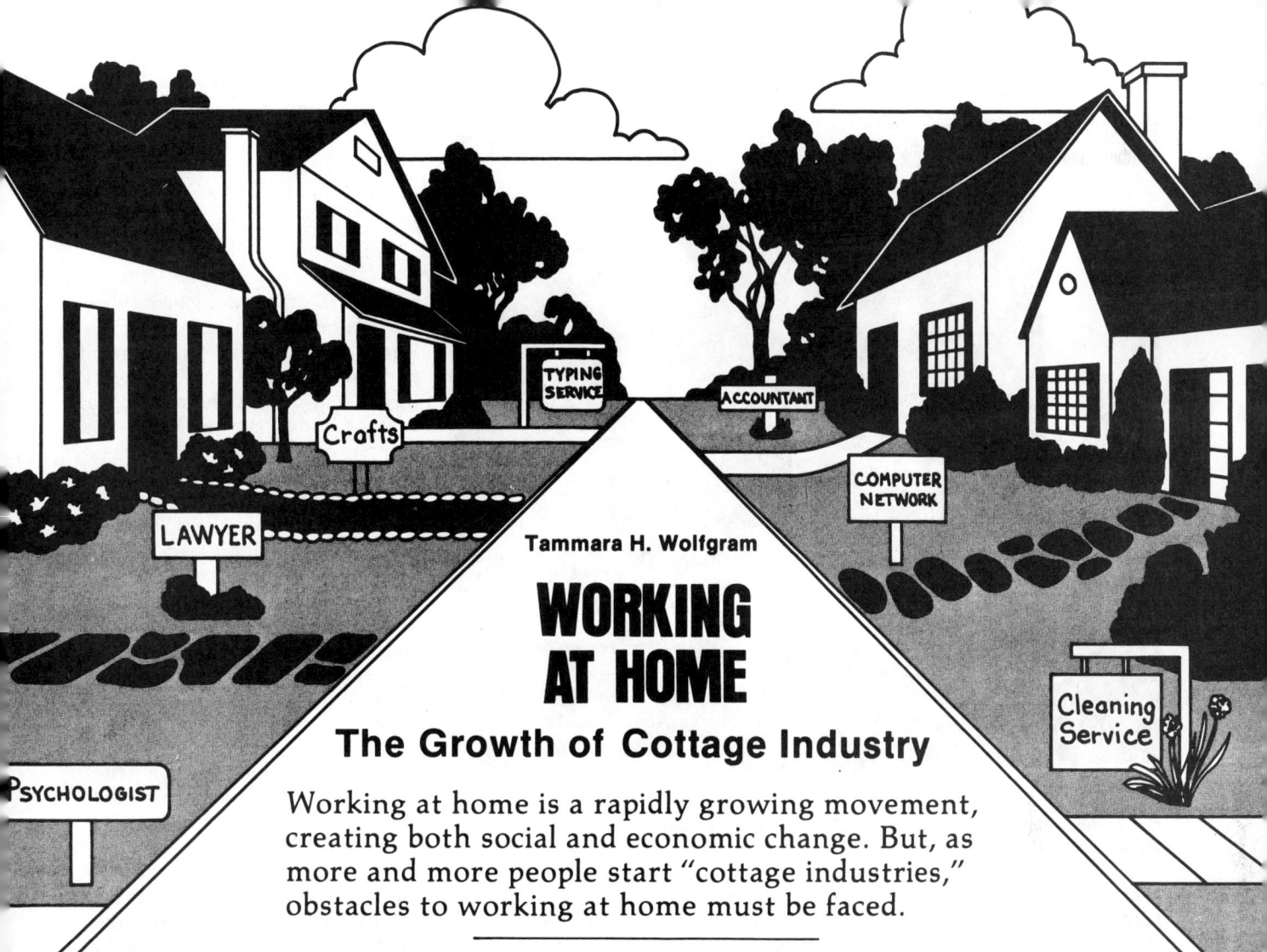

Working at home is a rapidly growing movement, creating both social and economic change. But, as more and more people start "cottage industries," obstacles to working at home must be faced.

A typical example of the home worker is Coralee Smith Kern, founder and executive director of the National Association for the Cottage Industry, who started her own home business nearly 12 years ago. According to Kern, she was actually ashamed to tell people that she worked from home when she started her business. She went so far as to rent downtown office space, which she never used, in order to have a "legitimate" business address. "Now," she says, "I hire a public relations person to publicize the fact that I work from home!"

Five years ago, a chance conversation with a repairman changed her thinking. After the repairman had fixed her typewriter, Kern commented that he was no doubt headed back downtown. He told her that he was staying right in the neighborhood, because there were over 200 typewriters like hers within walking distance of her home. Amazed by that fact, she began to wonder about what was really going on in her neighborhood.

The people she approached didn't want to talk about their businesses. It became evident that concerns about zoning laws, the underground economy, and fears of jeopardizing their conventional jobs were among the reasons for this reluctance. But Kern eventually learned enough to make her realize that the United States was experiencing a rebirth of the cottage industry. As she began to speak publicly about working from home, the mail she received reaffirmed her belief that a nationwide movement was under way.

Reasons for Working at Home

While there are no hard statistics, the U.S. Chamber of Commerce reports that 10 million businesses list home addresses as their place of business. Jack Nilles of the University of Southern California predicts that by 1990 as many as 15 million people will be telecommuting. And Nilles's figure doesn't include the people working with products and services not involved with electronic communications. These figures indicate that, without question cottage industries in America have not only reached significant proportions but will continue to expand.

The size and impact of the work-at-home movement has been largely overlooked, possibly because cottage industries have been lumped together with other small businesses. As a result, their importance in the economy was mistakenly viewed as insignificant. Only in the last few years have cottage industries received serious attention from government and the media.

Many people assume that the recent growth in the number of home businesses is a result of high unemployment. It is certainly true that many jobs in industry have been eliminated through more ex-

THE FUTURIST, June 1984

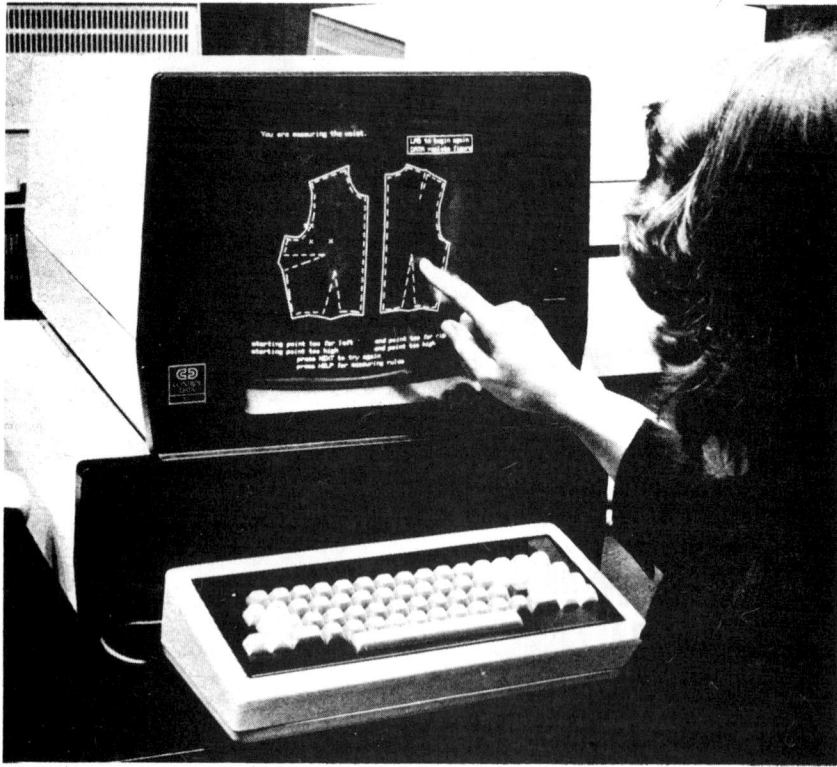

Computer technology helps make working at home more feasible for many professions. This woman uses her computer to design a dress pattern—something that previously would have required special drafting equipment and drafting skill.

tensive use of robotics and other technical advances. A portion of the displaced workers who must retrain and find other lines of work no doubt end up in some type of cottage industry. But unemployment is not the sole reason for the rise in cottage industries.

Who, then, are these people? What types of work do they do, and why are they choosing to work at home? Home workers are people who have made decisions regarding their careers and lifestyles. Tired of wasting time commuting, they want more time to spend with their families. Many want to take a more active role in raising their children. Others are disenchanted with big corporations and their way of doing things.

Home workers speak of many advantages to working from home. They save money on clothes, gasoline, parking, restaurant lunches, and other expenses associated with working in a traditional setting. Childcare is less of a problem. They have more freedom to arrange their own schedule and more time for the things they really want to do. And for many, the responsibility and challenge of being one's own boss is the most rewarding aspect.

One of the most frequently cited problems of working from home is the psychological problem of isolation. There are simple things one can do, such as going out to lunch, scheduling meetings outside the home, and joining professional organizations, to alleviate this isolation. For some, the isolation can be seen as a benefit, since one has fewer interruptions and one's time can be more productive. But clearly, not everyone is cut out to work from home.

Cottage Industry Trends

Although many people believe otherwise, the work-at-home movement is not a woman's movement. Certainly many women are working from home, but a large portion of home workers are men. And all ages are represented in the movement, from young adults to retirees.

Many "traditional" types of cottage industries exist, such as making crafts or running beauty salons, funeral parlors, or kennels. But they represent only a small percentage of the types of work now being done at home. Today, cottage industries include such diverse occupations as psychologists, lawyers, consultants, accountants, fabric designers, vehicle testers, publishers, and upholsterers. The increased demand for services has spurred the growth of all types, from cleaning and secretarial to exercise instruction and pet grooming. In addition, advances in microcomputers have opened information-related fields to home workers.

In fact, nearly every type of work is now being done from home. While one might think that there are a number of constraints that would make many jobs unsuitable for home business ventures, there are very few insurmountable obstacles to working from home. Cottage-industry experts have compiled a list of over 300 jobs that are currently being done from the home. And new titles are being added to the list regularly.

An interesting development is the growth of cottage industry buildings and communities, where people both live and work. For example, in Oak Creek, Wisconsin, there is a small shopping center called Market Place, which consists of about 20 homes that were specially built to accommodate cottage industries. People live and work in the same buildings. Shop entrances all face a common pathway, and the residents provide a variety of goods and services, from dentistry to handmade pottery. There are other similar types of buildings, villages, and communities springing up across the country.

The Electronic Cottage

Most futurists recognize that technological advances in mini- and microcomputers and telecommun-

"In an age where time and fuel are both precious commodities, telecommuting makes sense."

ications are revolutionizing work. Microcomputers and telecommuting will no doubt prove to be the most significant factors in the work-at-home movement. Until now, decentralization of business was simply not a practical alternative to centralized worksites; effective communication was seriously hampered. Now, it is not only possible but economically advantageous to have workers at decentralized work stations. In an age where time and fuel are both precious commodities, telecommuting makes sense.

Corporations in various parts of the country have initiated telecommuting test programs in which they have installed computer systems in employees' homes. Rather than commuting downtown to work each day, telecommuters send in their work via telephone modems to a company's central computer, saving time and money in the process. Most of these test programs have proved quite successful; productivity is often higher for telecommuters than for more traditional office workers. Moreover, the employees working at home find that there are many personal advantages in not having to make the daily commute. Unquestionably, there will be growth in this area of home work as test programs become a permanent part of corporate operations and more companies become involved.

Another development related to the electronic cottage is the emergence of electronic "halfway houses," which are beginning to crop up across the country. Located near residential areas, these centers have various types of computers and other office equipment not practical to have in one's home. Instead of commuting all the way downtown, workers drive a few miles to a "halfway house" and rent the necessary equipment at an hourly rate. Kern predicts the development of many of these centers across the country. Such centers may well play a part in greater use of flexitime or flexiplace, as future workweeks are divided between home, office, and electronic "halfway house."

Issues of the Eighties

Some of the problems faced by home workers deserve special attention. The most basic issue concerns the right to choose one's workplace. For people working from home, the major issues of the 1980s will be zoning, labor laws, and licensing. As the number of people who work from home continues to increase, some government and business factions are showing resistance to these changes. The political climate of some cities and some organized labor organizations is anti-home business. An example is Danville, Illinois, where a recently passed ordinance makes it illegal to store any kind of merchandise in one's home. Ordinances of this sort, coupled with outmoded zoning laws in many cities, make working at home difficult legally. Some labor unions perceive home business as a threat to job security and other gains they have made. They fear that the current growth of the work-at-home movement may undermine union strength or signal a new era of sweatshop labor. Consequently, they have become a primary force behind legislation aimed at making many types of home labor illegal.

On the federal level, the 40-year-old Industrial Home Work Act of 1943 is still in force, making it illegal to make belts, buckles, jewelry, and gloves, do embroidery, or sew women's clothing at home. Knitted outerware, which was originally outlawed by the Act, is now legal because a group of knitters from Vermont fought the issue. The Department of Labor recently lifted the ban on knitted outerware but otherwise left the Act intact.

A number of states have laws that make it illegal to run crafts businesses from the home. Further, many states and cities that have such laws are beginning stricter

A farm safety consultant, working at home, arranges slides for workshops he will conduct throughout the state of California. Cottage industries today include such diverse occupations as psychologists, lawyers, consultants, accountants, and publishers, in addition to such "traditional" cottage industries as crafts.

> "A groundswell of support is developing among home workers to end overly restrictive legislation."

enforcement. Some cottage industries have already been shut down. A groundswell of support is developing among home workers to end overly restrictive legislation. But instead of meeting in a combative atmosphere, governments, labor unions, and home working groups should cooperate to assure both workers' welfare and the right of individuals to choose their own workplace.

Because of the difficulty in monitoring home businesses, government officials fear that many home businesses will not pay their share of taxes. While the "underground economy" no doubt exists, more and more home businesses are run above ground, paying their taxes and taking their legitimate write-offs. Licensing of home businesses will become a greater concern as a larger percentage of the gross national product is generated by people who work at home.

There's No Place Like Home

Despite the negative reactions of some in government, many see the cottage industry as an arena for economic growth and are doing whatever they can to encourage cottage industries in their states and communities. An excellent example is Oregon, which formed an economic commission to study possibilities for economic development in the state. Since the state's fishing and timber industries are in decline, the commission concluded that cottage industries are the state's most promising area for economic redevelopment. Consequently, Oregon is assisting residents in starting home businesses. The state is offering courses in marketing products and services, and an expert is to be appointed to assist home workers with problems they might come up against. Oregon is just one of a number of state and city governments working to protect cottage industries and to foster their growth.

Within the next 20 years, the work-at-home movement will boom. Today, federal study of cottage industries is needed, analyzing current size, potential for growth, and impact on society.

"The work-at-home movement is already much larger than most people realize," Coralee Smith Kern states. "We can expect cottage industries to have a far-reaching impact on our society in the next 20 years. How far-reaching? Well, it is highly improbable that businesses as we know them will cease to exist, but they may well change dramatically as more and more people discover that when it comes to working or running a business, there's really no place like home."

Starting a Home Business with a Computer

Thousands of people across the United States, armed with personal computers, printers, and word-processing software, have started word-processing businesses in their homes. And they are finding lots of customers.

Word processing is perhaps the most popular computer service being offered out of private homes and small offices. A competent typist with a fairly sophisticated word-processing system soon discovers that great business opportunities exist.

Any range of services can be offered, including straight typing (charged by the page or hour); whole newsletters; weekly or monthly bulletins from businesses, churches, or clubs; and product catalogs, handbooks, and pamphlets—whatever services there is a market for.

Specialized knowledge is highly useful in such ventures. Law firms or doctors' offices, for example, like to deal with people who are already familiar with the forms they use and the jargon they write.

One successful entrepreneur got all the work she could handle by advertising on cable television for a week, for a modest fee. She also bought local newspaper advertising at a cost of four dollars. She followed this up by preparing two sets of business letters—one for lawyers and courts and one for businesses—and hand delivered samples to law offices and business people in the community. The response was immediate.

Another beginner found that advertising in a large city newspaper prompted only a few customers to call. But when she put a notice in the local suburban "shoppers' weekly," she had to turn away business.

—Jessie Gunn Stephens

Jessie Gunn Stephens is a widely published freelance writer. Her start-up guide for home word-processing services, New Profits in Word Processing, is available for $19.95 plus $2.00 shipping and handling from J. Norman Goode Publishing, 4121 Buckthorn Court, Lewisville, Texas 75028.

About the Author

Tammara Hoffman Wolfgram is project director for the National Association for the Cottage Industry (NACI). She is currently attending graduate school at the University of Wisconsin in educational psychology. Inquiries about NACI may be sent to: NACI, P.O. Box 14460, Chicago, Illinois 60614.

Joseph J. Kroger

Artificial Intelligence

A New Reality

Artificial intelligence is already moving into the factory and the workplace and helping solve problems that until now were beyond the computer's range. It may be in widespread use by the year 2000.

Science writers love terms that connote mystery. "Artificial intelligence" is one of their favorites. It has a futuristic, Flash Gordon-ish ring to it. But AI — which can be defined simply as the capability of a machine to mimic intelligent behavior — is really neither far off nor far out. It's here, now, and it's beginning to change the way we live.

Artificial intelligence (AI) is beginning to offer business and industry a vast array of new tools. Already helping to uncover subterranean oil deposits and design computer chips, AI is expected to be in general use among companies and government agencies virtually everywhere by the end of this century.

Though AI may still be misconstrued by some as a dangerous toy, it is basically nothing more than sophisticated electronic circuitry rigged up to manipulate symbols in the same way that people do when they reason through problems and come up with feasible solutions.

For example, AI technology is now making possible a sophisticated type of problem-solving activity called rapid prototyping, which involves simulation based so closely on reality that users can visualize real-life implementation. NASA scientists turned to rapid prototyping after spending eight years trying to eradicate carbon dioxide from space shuttles and solved the problem in four weeks.

A major U.S. airline has developed an AI system that optimizes seat revenue by analyzing such factors as capacity versus tickets sold, allocation of full fares and discounted ones, number of days until departure, competitive airlines' seats available, and so forth. For the airline, the benefits are significant: increased profit, more efficient use of personnel and facilities, and a competitive advantage.

An AI system called "Just In Time Manufacturing" aims at reducing costs and improving quality on factory production lines by virtually eliminating the need for inventory and storage. The "Just In Time" system simulates a factory's entire production flow via representations of various workstations and tools that appear in "windows" on a video screen. It shows not only the functions and relative speed of each tool, but also how much lead time is needed to order parts for each step along the way. The system also suggests ways to correct bottlenecks by moving people and machines around to change the product flow, thus indicating which configuration is most productive.

Another AI system being developed takes aim at automating the diagnosis of printed-circuit-board failures. The system has already demonstrated its ability to pinpoint faulty devices with a minimal number of probes, while it frees up valuable human resources. The potential cost savings are dramatic: Conventional testing uses hardware that costs $1.5 million and is operated by a highly skilled technician, while the AI approach uses a program that costs less than $100,000 and can be run by someone with just two weeks of training.

Expert Systems

Programs like the ones described above are called expert systems — so named because they contain the

Computers with Emotions

Computers may express love, hate, and other emotions in the future.

Can computers be made to love, hate, show compassion, or be creative? Should they? Lawrence Stevens explores these questions in his book *Artificial Intelligence: The Search for the Perfect Machine*. The important task now facing artificial-intelligence researchers, says Stevens, is to produce machines that can duplicate the psychological activities that allow people to reason effectively.

The fact that many great leaders and thinkers are emotional, creative people lends support to the importance of emotions and creativity for problem solving. For a machine to make decisions on a par with those of leading thinkers, it must be programmed to make use of psychological factors, Stevens claims.

Computers will interact more frequently with humans in the future, so emotional understanding by the computers will be necessary, says Stevens. A computer may need to make decisions for its human master based on emotional responses of love, hate, or compassion.

Stevens writes that emotions are based on rules — certain things make us happy, while other things make us frightened, depending on the situation. For example, a person would probably not be afraid of a nip from his own dog, but he might be afraid of a nip from a strange dog. Stevens writes that these situational factors can be converted into a series of rules — if/then statements — that can be programmed into a computer.

"Ironically, here in the emotional center of man, in the one area that many people predict no machines can imitate, is a behavior source that is very closely related to a computer program," says Stevens.

Stevens also writes that there is no evidence that even sudden personality changes — such as those brought on by prayer or meditation — are not also rule-based (though governed by rules not yet understood). These rules, once understood, presumably could be programmed, so that an intelligent computer might undergo a similar transformation.

Another possibility is programming imagination. Stevens writes that the ability of programs to make guesses about what would occur under a given set of circumstances can be viewed as rudimentary imagination. For example, a computer program on architectural design could "imagine" how a particular structure might be built, finding shortcuts and pitfalls before construction begins.

Computer programs could even use "pleasure" or "satisfaction" as a means of determining what to do, says Stevens. The computer could exhibit pleasure by exploring imaginative possibilities in detail and by working out possible variations and ramifications. If a ramification produces a negative emotion, the program would — as a human would — explore another possibility that might have more "satisfying" consequences. A program with "imagination" could be said to be a very efficient daydreamer, imagining for the sake of pleasurable solutions.

Source: *Artificial Intelligence: The Search for the Perfect Machine* by Lawrence Stevens. Hayden Book Company, 10 Mulholland Drive, Hasbrouck Heights, New Jersey 07604. 1985. 177 pages. Paperback. $14.95.

collected, computer-stored knowledge of specialists in a given field. An expert system can draw on mountains of data to make a decision based on its stored knowledge about a given task. Industry insiders are so bullish about the future of expert systems that they're forecasting $1.2 billion in sales by 1990. And by 1990, the total market for AI applications will grow to $5 billion.

Artificial intelligence's scope also encompasses natural-language processing, robotics, and vision and speech recognition. But — at least for the moment — the most promising advances are in the expert systems area. Potential applications for expert systems are in such diverse areas as health and human services administration, communications systems simulation, electronic data processing audit, natural-language interface, and airline pilot assistance.

Pilot assistance, or flight management, offers another good illustration of AI's practicality. Think of all the cockpit gadgetry with which a pilot has to contend. Some newer planes have more than a hundred computers spewing information onto the instrument panel. It's all important, but it can also be pretty confusing when a sudden problem demands an immediate response. But AI programs now being perfected will someday, when presented with an emergency, significantly reduce the complexity of the data, isolate and display critical information, and tell the pilot what options are available for corrective action.

Ultimately, that is just what AI lets the user do: obtain useful information from huge data banks faster, perform certain crucial tasks better by precisely narrowing

The Implications of Super Intelligence

Will the widespread use of artificial intelligence bring a technotopia or an Orwellian nightmare? Derek Partridge, an associate professor in computer science at New Mexico State University, says that this new technology has the potential to cause cataclysmic social change.

For example, AI's boost to automation — with the robot takeover of hazardous, repetitive, and menial tasks — could bring increased unemployment along with increased leisure time. A new socioeconomic system might separate income from employment, with most income being derived from a return on capital investment. Alternatively, employers could shrink the workweek, or governments might develop more automation-resistant human service jobs.

Partridge foresees the possibility of human and artificial intelligence forming a "partnership to super intelligence," composed of "the global knowledge and broad association abilities of human beings, together with the exhaustive rigour and depth of machines."

Advanced AI systems will adapt to the user, Partridge claims. Thus, AI holds the promise of customized mass production, with a wealth of cheap expertise and assistance that also embodies a sensitive treatment of people as individuals. Computer-aided instruction, for example, could be responsive to a student's particular strengths, weaknesses, general level of competence, and preferred style of interaction. Each copy of the system could build up a "model" of each student that has interacted with it and treat each one as an individual.

An especially promising type of AI technology — natural-language processing — could make sophisticated computer technology readily available to almost anyone. Natural-language systems are computers that possess some understanding of, say, English in the same way people do. Thus, one could give commands to one's computer in conversational English.

Source: "Social Implications of Artificial Intelligence" by Derek Partridge in *Artificial Intelligence: Principles and Applications*, edited by Masoud Yazdani. 1986. Chapman and Hall, 29 West 35th Street, New York, New York 10001. Paperback. 348 pages. $22.

down the available options, develop rapid prototype solutions for complex problems, and improve the users' understanding of what their computers are doing for them.

Power Packs

Another promising development in AI is the creation of "power packs" — specialized AI tools, or system "drivers" — which contain generic knowledge that can provide solutions to specific problems found in particular industries or fields of endeavor. One such "power pack" is already helping the utilities industry to design and build new plants. What it does, in effect, is allow users to place simulated boilers and pipes and valves in various configurations on a video screen while a software program runs fail-safe checks on the design.

Any company serious about participating in the AI revolution must be willing to invest heavily in R&D to make sure that its expert systems and other AI programs operate directly with data already held in traditional information-processing systems and that the programs keep up with software innovations. In addition, such a company must be willing to initiate extensive training programs, increase support for university research projects, and team up with other companies to undertake joint ventures so that products can be delivered in a smooth, timely fashion.

Artificial intelligence is an exciting development with enormous potential. As it moves out of the laboratory and into the marketplace, AI is solving problems that until now were beyond even the computer's grasp.

About the Author

Joseph J. Kroger is vice-chairman of Unisys Corporation, P.O. Box 500, Blue Bell, Pennsylvania 19424.

Alexander Petofi

PIXEL

The Graphic Revolution in Computers

Computer graphics promise to speed up decision-making, enhance white-collar productivity, and help prevent industrial accidents.

As we advance into the information age, the most profound changes we see will be in the form, rather than the content, of our information. We are seeing the rise of men and women who can make facts and figures more interesting, memorable, and understandable. The tools of their trade are electronic graphics, computers, and devices for telecommunicating. These information gatekeepers will apply the principles of physics, physiology, and engineering with an aesthetic awareness to make information more appealing and informative.

Many people are working today to design tools, create slides for presentations, expand our vision through electron microscopes and satellite pictures, and otherwise make our mental pictures of reality more encompassing and relevant. But our so-called "information age" may become the "information craze" if people continue to be faced with increasing flows of irrelevant, uninteresting, or incomprehensible data. There are limits to each person's ability to accept and process information, and information overload can seriously impair an individual's ability to make decisions and take action.

But as our need for information increases, our "information infrastructure" of electronic tools is improving. Video displays with higher resolution; input devices like computer mice, digitizers, and light pens; and inexpensive output devices that print in color or make slides instantly are giving people more image-processing power. There are an increasing number of ways to apply graphics—for scientific, commercial, industrial, and global purposes.

Computer Graphics and Exploration

In the scientific arena, we are now able to probe the atom, the cosmos, and our own planet with the aid of image-related technologies. Recent applications include improved electron microscope resolution and digital transmission of spacecraft imagery.

Graphic applications will be coming soon from Lucasfilm, the company that created the *Star Wars* series. The company will soon market its state-of-the-art computer graphics to businesses. One system will be designed to perform seismic analysis and enable oil-well drillers to determine with greater certainty whether soil strata contain oil.

"As the cost of computing comes down and the cost of data increases, there will be opportunities to use high-quality imaging technology. Graphics can provide a very good way of accurately presenting large amounts of information," says Edwin Catmull, head of Lucasfilm's computer graphics division.

Other graphics applications for personal computers may improve white-collar productivity. Over the past three decades, there has been practically no increase in productivity for "information" workers. In the entire decade of the 1970s, office productivity increased by only 4%. Personal computers and word processors have automated clerical and secretarial tasks to some extent, and now that personal computers are on the desks of many managers, great potential exists to automate the most important use of executive time: communication.

Top managers spend four-fifths of their time in meetings, delivering or receiving presentations and reports, and gathering information for subsequent meetings. Further, the average manager engages in 150 to 300 "information transactions" daily. The results of a study by AT&T confirm the fact that, since white-collar workers spend 80% to 95% of their time communicating or managing information, improvement in communications can lower costs and improve management decision-making. Executives need more productive and effective communications tools, not more computing power.

Another recent study, conducted by the Wharton School of Business, confirms the value of graphics. Presentations with and without overhead graphics were made to 36 different audiences. The results showed:

• Graphics are persuasive: Presenters who spoke without visual aids received group agreement only 50% of the time, while those presenters who used graphics persuaded groups to agree with their views two-thirds of the time.

• Graphics speed decisions: Most of those who saw presentations with graphics claimed that they made their decisions "immediately after the visual presentation," while those in other sessions said they waited until after group discussions.

• Graphics shorten meetings by as much as 28% and thus can add weeks of productive time to busy schedules over a year.

• Graphics encourage consensus: Group agreement was reached 79% of the time in the graphics groups, compared with only 58% in the verbal groups.

In the past, presentations required art done by hand—often

THE FUTURIST, June 1985

POWER

costing thousands of dollars—and took weeks to complete. Now, some presentations can be done in a few minutes for less than $100.

In 1983, the market for presentation slides was over $4.5 billion for 330 million slides. Only 2% of these were made by computer. But consultants for Kodak and Polaroid estimate that computer-generated slides will account for 50% of the market by 1990.

Graphic Futures

Computer graphics will help us to design and communicate our visions of the future. Computer-aided design (CAD) turns the tedious work of redrawing an entire set of plans for a single change into a simple operation. Architects can redesign a building by entering the new data and watching as the computer recalculates all other factors, including material requirements.

Manufacturers of automobiles, airplanes, and ships are equipping their engineers with CAD workstations, not only to speed up the design process and reduce errors but also to perform simulated tests. Considering the expense involved in actual tests of equipment—such as the test crash of a Boeing 747 full of dummies into a California hillside—any improvement in modeling physical elements with graphics will make products cheaper and more reliable.

The industrial applications of graphics in process control are just becoming evident. Charles R. Berg, formerly of Du Pont, conjectured that if operators at the Three Mile Island nuclear plant had had a more modern graphics display, the operators might have realized that the destructive steam was forming. Display panels that make use of the new digital technology will replace the scattered and often wall-sized arrays of controls in chemical manufacturing plants. These displays, which once presented only dials

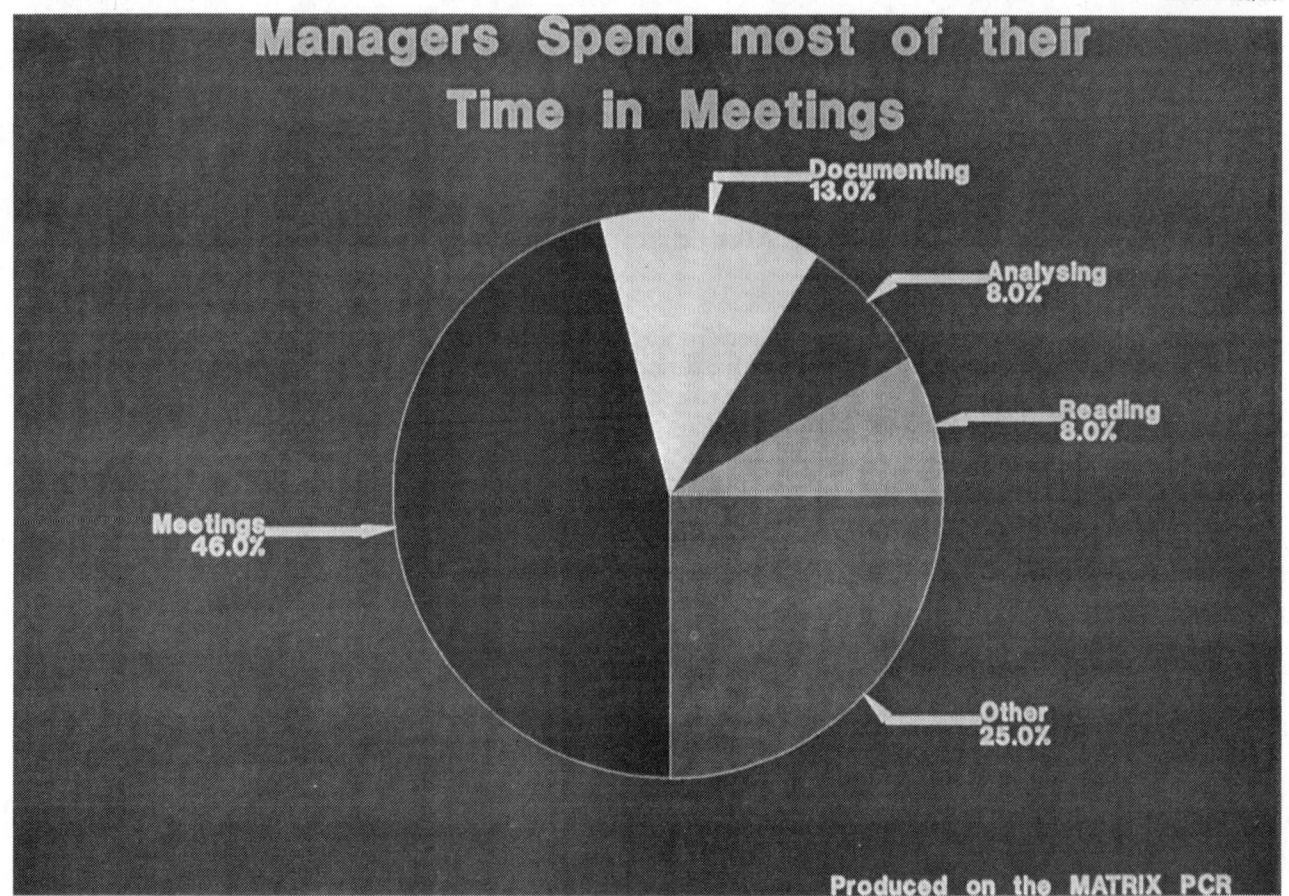

Cartoons by Computer

A cartoonist finds that the computer is no joke as an artist's tool.

Thomas Alva Edison and his groupies.

Artist Spyder Webb has made the jump from hand drawing to creating-by-computer.

With his Apple Macintosh personal computer, he explains, "I draw with a 'mouse' rather than with a pad/stylus arrangement. The results in black and white are excellent, and, by printing onto watercolor paper, I can paint color in the traditional manner, blending the most ancient and the newest technologies to produce something that for me is more comfortable, natural, and aesthetically pleasing than either alone."

Webb doesn't see computer-aided drawing as a substitute for the "real" thing. "Creating art with a personal computer is not better or worse, faster or slower, than drawing with conventional media," he says. "Neither should it be approached as a means of imitating traditional media. It is something different."

Once mastered, a computer can make the creative process less tedious. "I can try a series of steps, and if I am displeased with the result, I can revert to an earlier version of the drawing, which I've saved in the computer's memory. I can try several versions, all branching from a particular point in the development of the drawing, and save each version, without having to do the entire thing over again each time."

Webb doubts that computer-drawn art will replace art drawn with traditional tools; rather, it will add to the methods available to artists to create images. "Is it the wave of the future? Well, it's at least *a* wave of the future," he says. "One thing is certain, at least for me—it's not just a new way of doing old things, it's a way of doing new things."

Source: Spyder Webb Cartoons, 8637 Liberia Avenue, Manassas, Virginia 22110.

and tabular lists of numerical data, can present data in pictures, charts, and diagrams.

Increasingly powerful graphics software and electronic "libraries" of graphic images will become commonplace, ushering in a new era of business communications. "The 50-page marketing plan that takes all night to read will boil down to a 15-page graphics-intensive document that you can digest in five minutes," says a senior executive of a major computer company.

This increase in electronic communications will generate new software. Some of the changes we are likely to see include:

• A more "iconic," or symbolic, interface. Text will be replaced by little pictures of file cabinets, arrows, or waste baskets. Apple's pioneering use of icons and "pop-up" menus will become widespread.

• The Media Disk will replace printed catalogs and advertisements. These floppy-disk catalogs will contain colorful, animated descriptions of hundreds of products, along with an automatic ordering form. The personal-computer owner can type the number of each item desired and generate a complete order form.

• Project-management software, another rapidly growing area, will become illustrated. Construction supervisors, for example, will see a computer-generated image of what a site should look like at any stage, with the next phase of work identified by a different color or blinking dots. Computers with digitizing camera attachments can make quality control easier; as each person finishes a task, a picture will be sent back and compared with a control image for logging.

• Business people will be able to enjoy the "high touch" of personalization by keeping "knowledge frames" of clients in their data base.

The *Leonov*'s Ballute heat shield inflates in preparation for aero-braking maneuver in *2010*. Computer graphics can display a large amount of important information in colorful form.

Three-dimensional graphs such as this present information in a more dynamic way than traditional bar charts.

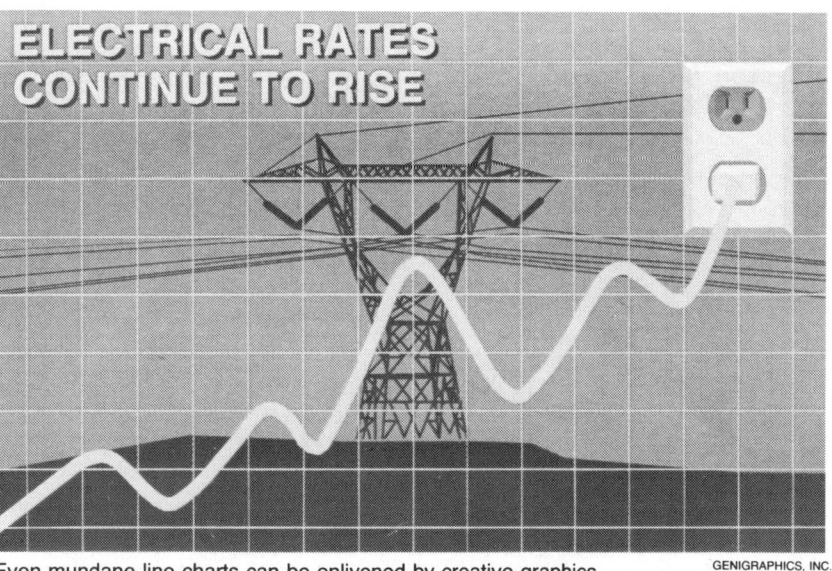

Even mundane line charts can be enlivened by creative graphics.

Bob Balaban, playing Dr. Chandra in the motion picture *2010*, converses with HAL's earthbound partner, SAL 9000. Author Petofi says that computer graphics will play a large role in how we communicate in the future.

Present data bases include only text and numbers. But data bases in the future might include a picture and personal information about various clients.

Global Trends

Given that only one out of every eight people on earth can read and write, and that an even smaller fraction can communicate in English, perhaps the greatest task will be the development of a universally comprehensible hyperlanguage. This language could be taught easily, could convey vast amounts of information quickly and unambiguously, and would not have the partisan taint of a foreign tongue.

An iconic language that uses pictures and symbols is already to be seen on signs in Europe. The Oxford-Duden Pictorial English Dictionary, published last year with over 28,000 illustrations, may be the watershed in the transformation of language reference from words with occasional pictures to illustrations with titles.

Japanese information theorist Yoneji Masuda foresees a time when "a Global Information Utility Network will make its appearance and ordinary citizens all over the world will have easy access to such a network and be able to exchange information and ideas related to global problems." A symbolic language, along with networks of videotext graphics, could make this system an equally accessible source for all mankind. The highest potential of computer graphics may be to promote global unity and understanding.

Computer-aided design (CAD) gives architects the freedom to experiment with a variety of forms before developing a final design.

About the Author

Alexander Petofi is vice president of Creative Business Ideas. His address is 8747 Baird Avenue, Northridge, California 91324.

F.D. Barrett

THE ROBOT REVOLUTION

RB ROBOT CORPORATION

The robotization of business is proceeding like a juggernaut, driven by soaring labor costs, the plummeting price of high technology, and the increasing intelligence and versatility of robots.

The modern robot may be viewed as a computer to which limbs, organs, tools, and other equipment have been attached. The computer is to the modern robot what the brain is to the human. This "brain" allows the limbs, organs, and tools to vastly broaden the range of occupations robots can engage in. And the number and variety of such attachments are growing: Already there are robots with eyes, ears, touch, smell, voices, arms, legs, wheels, wings, and fins.

Robotics is still in its infancy in North American business but has been making inroads in automobile manufacturing and in other industries, particularly those in which high wages and repetitious, low-skilled work are found together.

In addition, robots are being applied to many other tasks, including some that are quite com-

THE FUTURIST, October 1985

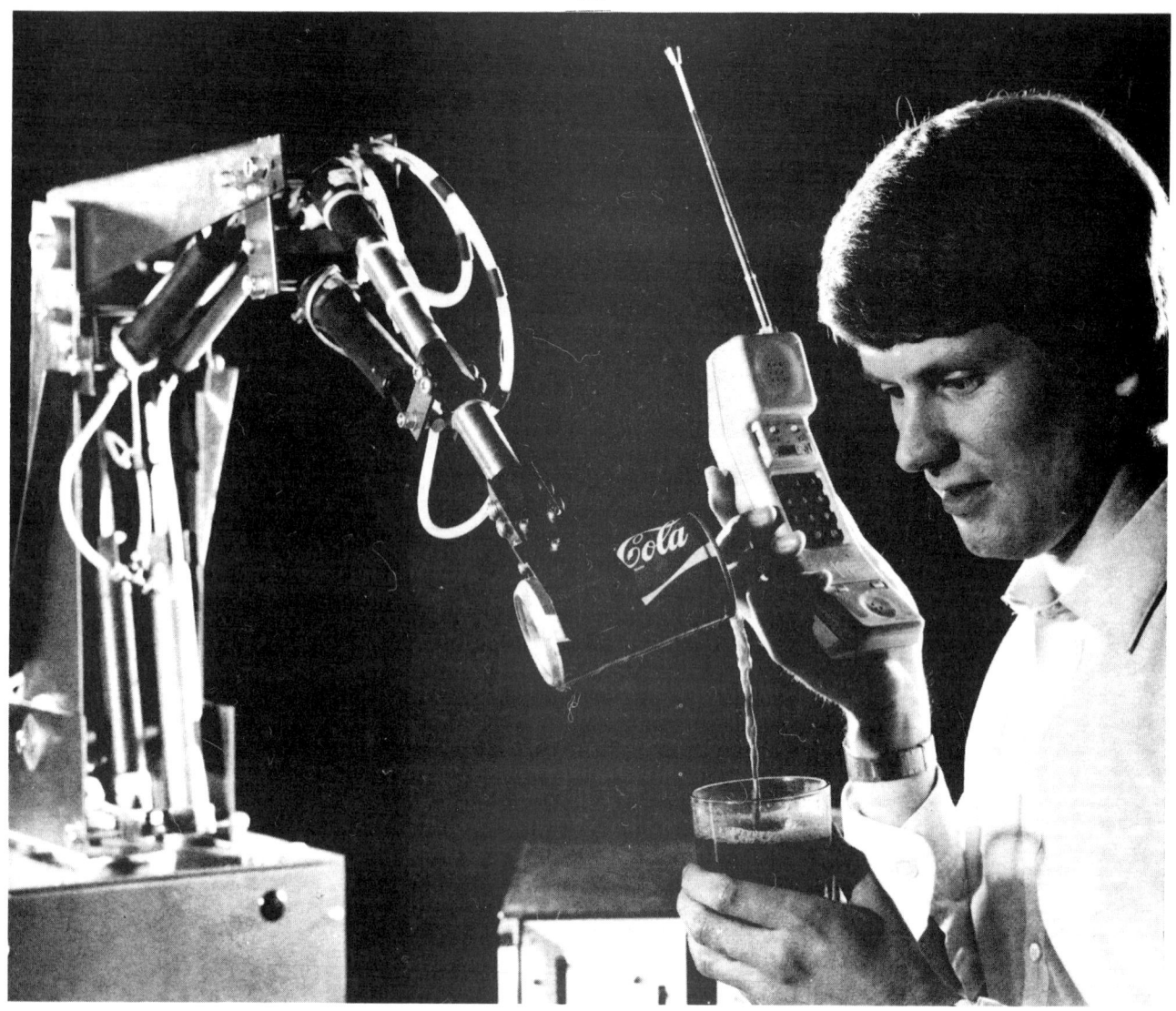

Robot named "Genesis" serves a soft drink, responding to voice command of operator Peter Vaughan, a member of a team of researchers at Nottingham, England. New skills such as the ability to recognize and respond to voices are enabling robots to do jobs they have traditionally been thought too "dumb" to do.

plex and skilled; to business fields other than manufacturing; to some nonbusiness, public-sector fields; to tasks formerly done by other machines; and, interestingly, to tasks made possible by the robot itself.

Robots work in food-testing labs, cleaning tubes and preparing samples. One retail grocery store in Japan has a robot butcher that slices ham to the customer's requested thickness and weight, wraps it, weighs it, and gives it to the customer with the charge slip all made out for the laser-scanning machine that will charge the customer at the checkout counter.

In Japan, robots soon will be spraying insecticide, spreading fertilizer, and handling cargo, according to *Industrial Automation Reporter*. And in Australia, robots are being developed to perform the backbreaking work of shearing sheep.

Equipped with camera eyes or optical scanners, robots can perform such tasks as the selection, inspection, assembly, and placing of parts or products on machines, trolleys, or warehouse shelves. Robots equipped with vision can be used for many purposes in many types of businesses. The National Bureau of Standards forecasts that 90% of all industrial inspection will be done by robot vision rather than by human vision by 1994.

Optically equipped computer-robots in Japan are used both to inspect and grade agricultural produce. An optically-equipped robot is being developed by Martin Marietta in Florida for picking ripe oranges from the trees while leaving the unripe. A robotic palletizing system at the Toronto margarine plant of Nabisco Brands will employ optical sensors that permit the robot to decide which pallet to load which boxes onto and then to do so.

Professional Robots

Robots differ from other automated machines and equipment in possessing the ability to "learn" or be programmed for a wide variety of things and, to a degree, adjust their behavior in response to changes in their physical environment. Some extremely advanced computer-robots are even capable

"It is hard to understand why the 'automated tellers' now so widely used in banking are not referred to as 'robot tellers,' since that is what they are."

of learning from their experience; they can, for example, come to play an ever better game of chess.

While the first generation of robots was designed to do physical work, the new robots now coming along are capable of doing such human work as interpreting documents, planning sales programs, and diagnosing physical or mental illnesses. Since such capabilities are not usually what we associate with robots, it is becoming increasingly necessary to define the robot.

"Robots" are machines that operate autonomously and are capable of behavior that can be adapted to different circumstances or functions. The automatic dialer on your desk is a robot that is programmable and that is capable of remembering and redialing a busy number. It is hard to understand why the "automated tellers" now so widely used in banking are not referred to as "robot tellers," since that is what they are.

Artificial intelligence is slowly adding inferring, reasoning, knowing, judging, and deciding abilities to the computer, giving the robot more humanlike qualities. With artificial intelligence, robots will have an enormous range. Those who associate robots primarily with unskilled manual work are also mistaken: Both existing robots, called "expert systems," and those still on the drawing board have the capability for doing certain kinds of skilled work—including work previously regarded as professional.

In some cases, the robot professional is no better than the human but has the ability to make professional or technical judgments and decisions 10, 20, or 100 times as fast. Some expert systems are now doing the work of geologists, physicians, mathematicians, and maintenance planners, to name only a few jobs normally done by professionals.

Robots on the Move

A robot with fins—a robot submarine—is being used by the U.S. Navy for underwater exploration. A Canadian robot sub is mapping the ocean floor near Halifax. The Southeastern Fruit and Tree Nut Research Laboratory in Byron, Georgia, has designed a computer-operated crop-spraying robot plane that may be in operation within a year.

Modern airplanes—essentially capable of taking off, flying, and landing themselves—come close to being pure robots. And robotic trains about to come into operation in Toronto will use humans only to open and close the doors at each stop.

Instead of walking on legs, most robots move on wheels. Such robots take form as robot-trucks, robot-forklifts, robot-trolleys, and robot-trains, but they are usually referred to as automatic vehicles rather than robots. One wheel-equipped robot is designed for bomb removal by bomb squads. Still another is used in nuclear-power damage control.

Robots on wheels can deliver mail or coffee. Robot delivery of the office mail is now quite commonplace. According to *Supermarket News*, a retail grocery store in Yokohama has 30 robot vehicles that automatically emerge at night from an adjoining warehouse and place containers of goods beside the appropriate shelves, ready for shelving by human clerks when they arrive in the morning. Other

Prototype of pilotless crop-spraying plane developed at Agricultural Research Service's Southeastern Fruit and Tree Nut Research Laboratory, Byron, Georgia. The plane is currently controlled by radio, but research is under way for computerization within a year, making it truly a "flying robot."

USDA-AGRICULTURAL RESEARCH SERVICE

> "Robotized factories need no parking lots, cafeterias, or washrooms and can operate in the cold and in the dark."

robot vehicles come out during the day and move about displaying special goods or special sales.

One of the most important robotic developments has been the Automatic Guided Vehicle system (AGV). Although AGVs are not usually called robots, that is what they are. Transport vehicles or forklift trucks and the like run along electrical or optical tracks under the direction of a central computer. An estimated 200 AGV systems are currently installed in U.S. industry. Some new AGVs can leave the track to come and go on their own for short distances.

Super-Big Robots

Robots are now built that are the size and shape of buildings and warehouses. These are integrated systems of specialized robots such as AGVs and optically equipped robots. A few of these "robot-factories and warehouses" already exist, and more are coming. The "factory-sized robot" is run by an administrative computer, a design computer, a production computer, and an automated warehouse.

For example, Giant Food, Inc., in Landover, Maryland, has robot "stacker cranes" (a kind of large forklift truck) that move manlessly around a huge freezer warehouse raising and lowering—by computer guidance—designated boxes of frozen food to heights of eight stories. These huge robot cranes are linked to an automated case-selecting machine capable of selecting 3,600 cases of frozen food per hour.

The system will likely be expanded to include other robots of the pick-and-place type to unload and load the conveyors that connect to the case-selecting machinery. A distant computer tracks each case from the time it is received at the warehouse until it is delivered to one of 131 stores in three different states.

Although the Giant Food freezer covers 22,000 square feet, it requires only 10 humans to service it. At times, the warehouse and all its vehicles and cranes operate busily without a single living being inside the bone-chilling $-10°$ environment. And robotized factories need no parking lots, cafeterias, or washrooms and can operate in the cold and in the dark.

A factory-sized robot, operated by Fujitsu, Ltd., outside Tokyo, has smaller robots working in it. These robots are busily manufacturing other robots. A hundred workers keep an eye on the robots, and the robots make a hundred new robots every month. If the workers themselves had to manufacture the robots, it would take 500 of them rather than the present 100.

Robots will eventually occupy a large place in all parts of all businesses. Robotics is moving into warehousing, shipping and transportation, and retailing. The robotics revolution is even moving into offices and service industries such as hotels, hospitals, restaurants, and landscaping. It is moving into medicine, human care, education—even entertainment: A robot called "Andy Warhol II" is about to go on the night-club circuit. Robots will move into housework. By 1995, robots will be found wherever people and machines are present.

Giant Food Inc.'s freezer-warehouse is a huge computer-integrated food distribution system. This robot warehouse, located in Jessup, Maryland, includes tall stacker cranes—automatic-guided vehicles that move merchandise around the eight-story storage facility. The system has improved inventory control, reduced damaged goods, and provided an uninterrupted supply of merchandise to stores while minimizing the need for employees to endure the harsh freezer environment.

About the Author

F.D. Barrett is president of Management Concepts Limited, 31 Pine Ridge Drive, Scarborough, Ontario M1M 2X6, Canada. He has conducted numerous international seminars on management, corporate strategy, policy planning, and management of change. His article "Tomorrow's Management: Creative and Participative" appeared in the February 1971 issue of THE FUTURIST.

James R. Metts

The Police Force of Tomorrow

The "supercops" of the future will be highly trained caretakers who may not carry guns. They will travel about in "space buckets" that will allow them to hover over the scene of a fire or accident.

The police force that will emerge in the years ahead will be markedly different from today's military-model structure. Future police officers will be extensively trained and qualified professionals. Well educated, certified in their trade, qualified in their job tasks, they will be tomorrow's "supercops."

Tomorrow's professional cop will have to be educated and educatable. As a minimum requirement, a bachelor's or master's degree in the social sciences will be needed. A law degree may also be deemed necessary for police officers by the early twenty-first century. Recruitment will take place at the best college campuses. Tomorrow's supercop will have to be bright, resourceful, and versatile.

The supercops of tomorrow will have to make complicated decisions and handle a variety of tasks not even envisioned by today's police officers. Obviously, such "full-service" officers will have to be better paid; salaries will have to be made commensurate with the responsibilities.

Along with the move toward recruiting better-educated officers, more and more women will be going into police work. Some studies show that women may be better than men at defusing family crisis situations, for example. And women may also be more suited to providing tomorrow's social service delivery job tasks. Tomorrow's police force will also include a growing number of minority members, as recruiting moves away from cronyism toward education and intelligence.

Tomorrow's law enforcement officer will have to be a true professional. The old adage that "anyone" can get a job as a policeman will have to be revised as officers deal with new crimes in a more complex and demanding society.

Today's specialization of public services is not cost-effective. Future police officers will have to be cross-trained in law enforcement, firefighting, and paramedical services. Where today three or more public-service agencies respond to a fire or accident, tomorrow's public-service officer will be trained to handle all emergency services and a variety of other needed tasks, such as traffic control or emergency escort.

Such training will have to be offered on the state and national level to be effective. Training standards will be raised significantly, as the job becomes more technical in nature. Tomorrow's supercop will have to meet vigorous pre-service

"Tomorrow's supercops will have an array of sophisticated devices with which to do their jobs."

certification standards and will have to undergo the periodic re-certification already seen in some professions.

Police training academies will become full-service training centers, offering courses in more technical areas, such as emergency medical diagnosis and care, as well as the standard full-service courses. These training centers will coordinate cross-training in police, fire, and paramedical services. Greater emphasis will also be placed on the social-services aspects of the job.

While "crime-fighting" training will continue, police officers will also be trained to investigate and settle cases involving areas such as child abuse and family crisis. Society will increasingly place the responsibility on police officers regarding juvenile and social-service cases. Tomorrow's supercop will have to be a bit of a marriage counselor, psychologist, sociologist, and lawyer.

As society becomes more and more technological, crimes will become more "white collar" in nature and more complex in means. Police officers will need to be trained to deal with crimes ranging from computer fraud to mercy homicides of terminally ill patients. The FBI's National Academy already offers training on computer fraud; such training will need to be offered at the state and local level.

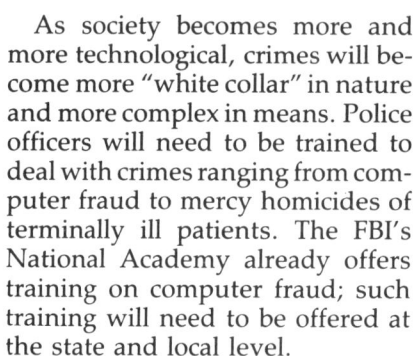

"Stun Guns" and "Jet Packs"

In the past, a policeman was given a badge and a gun and told to hit the streets. Tomorrow's supercops will have an array of sophisticated devices with which to do their jobs.

Police are already using new nonlethal weapons such as the "taser gun," a weapon that stuns its victim with an electrical shock without causing permanent injury. New weapons and devices will include laser guns, light guns, and electronic restraints, as well as newly developed surveillance equipment.

Robots are already being used by police in a few cities for such activities as traffic control. In the future, we will see robots being used in such crime-fighting situations as storming barricaded criminal hideouts or dispersing tear gas at riots, reducing the risk to human officers.

In the transportation department, "space buckets" and "jet packs" will allow the officer to soar above and around congestion or to hover a few feet above the scene of a fire, accident, or disaster.

(continued)

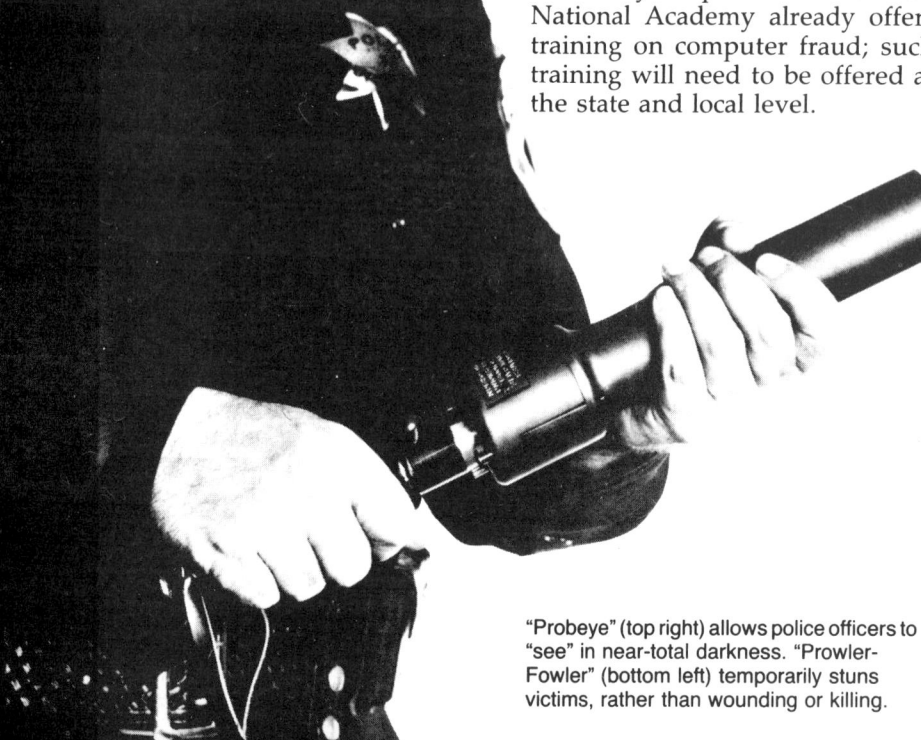

"Probeye" (top right) allows police officers to "see" in near-total darkness. "Prowler-Fowler" (bottom left) temporarily stuns victims, rather than wounding or killing.

A Police Officer's Day in 2001: A Futuristic Scenario

A police officer in the year 2001 will have different duties, track different criminals, and have different tools. This scenario follows a sheriff's deputy through a typical day's work.

Deputy Sam Browne of the Redrock County Sheriff's Department was assigned to the 4:00 p.m. shift on a Friday afternoon. He didn't need to go to roll call, since roll calls had long ago been eliminated in favor of teleconferencing using the home viewphones of the deputies. So Browne merely dialed the phone number for main headquarters, and a lieutenant's face soon appeared on the screen of the viewphone.

Roll-call teleconferences were about the only contacts that deputies now had with main headquarters. Mostly they worked out of their homes or out of one of the four substations in the various quadrants of the county. Many calls could be handled by viewphone, with the results reported to headquarters from computer CRTs at the substations. Some officers, such as Deputy Browne, even had CRT hookups to headquarters from their personal computers at home.

When all other members of the shift had called in, the lieutenant started roll call. The biggest item of discussion during roll call was a series of bank robberies. Someone was stealing electronic bank cards from careless or unsuspecting citizens, and the thief was apparently receiving the secret computer code numbers for those cards from a computer operator at the central office of a large bank in Capital City. The thief would then use the cards and the code numbers to make withdrawals from the bank at a suburban branch depository near Deputy Browne's residence.

Careful monitoring at the bank had led investigators to suspect a particular computer operator. Her boyfriend, who lived in Deputy Browne's quadrant, had become a suspect when Browne noticed that he had purchased an expensive new car despite being unemployed.

The plan for catching the bank robbers was simple. The bank created a computer file consisting of the names, ages, etc., of customers whose bank cards had been reported missing or stolen, along with the electronic code numbers of the missing cards. This information, along with the two suspects' names, addresses, phone numbers, license numbers, photographs, etc., was then programmed into the Sheriff's Department's central computer.

Foiling Computer Criminals With Computers

It was just a matter of time before the two bank robbers decided to strike again. They usually hit on Friday evenings, so a surveillance detail was set up. On this particular Friday, Deputy Browne volunteered for the surveillance detail and drove his department-issue propane-powered three-wheeler to the substation to pick up a "smart" patrol car.

One reason Browne enjoyed the surveillance assignment was that this was one of the few ways he could get to drive a regular-sized four-wheel patrol car. The patrol division consisted mainly of three-wheelers and mopeds assisted by the department's four helicopters. Each substation had a helicopter and several "smart" patrol cars. The latter, however, were rarely used for routine patrol duties. In fact, patrol as such was rapidly becoming obsolete except in a few remote areas.

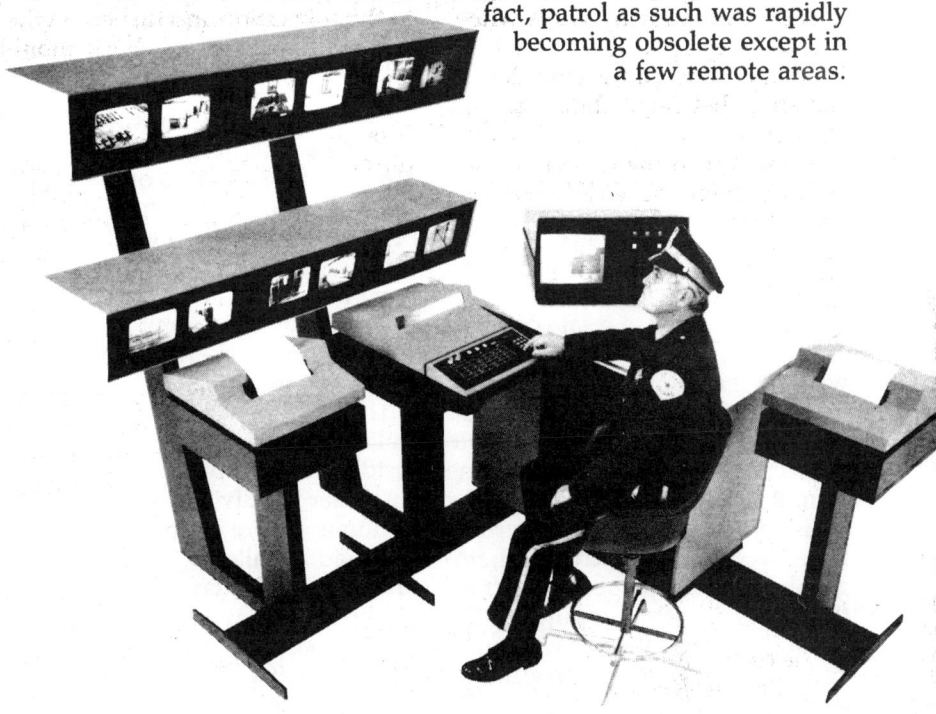

Closed-circuit television and display screens allow policeman to "patrol" an entire area without leaving headquarters. Such electronic monitoring of residential and business areas may make up a large portion of police duties in the future. HONEYWELL

Browne parked the "smart" patrol car behind a warehouse a block from the branch bank depository. He turned on the car's telescreen and its other computerized monitoring devices, hooked in with the computers at the bank and at main headquarters, and programmed the monitor to seek out the suspects' photographs and the numbers of the missing bank cards.

Before long, he heard a warning beep and saw a red warning light come on. The telescreen showed that the suspects were both at the branch bank, and the computer monitor revealed that they were using one of the stolen cards. Neither suspect even remotely resembled the card's owner, an elderly female. So Deputy Browne alerted the helicopter at the substation to be ready. The helicopter was already aloft when Deputy Browne pulled up behind the suspects' car as it was leaving the bank's parking lot.

As Browne expected, the pair tried to run. After all, they were used to laughing at the department's slow-moving three-wheelers. So they sped down the highway and soon put a considerable distance between their car and Browne's.

Although Browne could have outrun them, he didn't seriously try to chase them, since the helicopter was already following the suspects, unseen, from the air. Browne followed at a safe distance and kept in constant radio contact with the helicopter.

Soon the suspects slowed down. Browne used this opportunity to contact a magistrate by viewphone from the moving patrol car. On the basis of Browne's computerized transfer of two matching photographs of each suspect, one from the department's computer memory and one from the photo-monitor at the bank, along with an affidavit that Browne delivered orally by viewphone to the magistrate's remote recording device, the magistrate issued two arrest warrants. Browne had obtained printouts of the warrants on the electronic printer in his car by the time the suspects turned down the winding road leading to the woman's house.

The suspects drove into the driveway and got out of the car, laughing about their getaway. They had barely gotten inside the house when the phone rang. The woman answered and was asked by the lieutenant calling from headquarters to listen for a helicopter flying overhead. She was then told that the Sheriff's Department had warrants for the arrest of herself and her companion and would soon have a patrol car on the scene.

Meanwhile, if they wanted to give up, they should walk out into the yard and the helicopter would pick them up right then.

Both suspects decided to give up and went into the yard to surrender. In a matter of minutes, Deputy Browne drove up with the warrants. Soon, the suspects were taking a helicopter ride to the county jail. The lieutenant had been monitoring the chase and came on the viewphone to offer his congratulations.

Patrolling by Camera

Deputy Browne still had half a shift left to work, so he went back to the substation and turned on the commercial property check monitor. It showed sequential moving pictures of all the businesses in Browne's quadrant, with several different-angled shots of the inside and outside of each business. Browne studied the monitor's pictures carefully but saw no signs of any break-ins. In fact, since the installation of the monitor system, commercial break-ins had been reduced to almost zero.

This system had not yet been installed in very many of the county's residences, except in a few of the wealthier subdivisions and condominiums where a private security firm had installed a similar system on contract. But criminals were already getting the message. With modern communications technology, break-ins just didn't pay anymore, compared with computer crimes and other clever types of fraud.

After a few hours on the monitor, Browne claimed his special bonus time for participating in a successful arrest and went home early. A mandatory training class was scheduled at main headquarters, but Browne caught it on his home viewphone. He took the test on the training material by punching in the answers on his home computer and having them routed to headquarters.

In a few minutes, his home computer printed out his score on the test. He scored 100%, but that was hardly surprising since the topic was the legal basis for the use of computer-printed photographs and affidavits in obtaining probable cause for warrants printed out at remote computer terminals (such as in patrol cars). The laws on that subject had recently changed, but Browne was studying criminal law through a home viewphone/computer course offered by the law school in Capital City. He enjoyed local police work, but he was still hoping to get a law degree to go with his computer science degree and perhaps qualify for the FBI.

A Note on the Scenario

All the events described above could happen today, in principle. However, some of them would be prohibitively expensive and others would be questionable as to their legality. But by the year 2001, this should be a fairly realistic description of police work in a reasonably progressive suburban or rural police agency.

The only obstacle to the realization of this type of scenario, other than some relatively minor changes in the law, will be the attitude of the police themselves. But since most cops are "gadget freaks," that will probably not be as big a problem as one might anticipate.

By the year 2001, the cost of information-related technologies will probably have come down to the point that the average person—as well as the average police department—will be able to afford them. Police departments will soon realize that it is not only faster and cheaper but also more effective to move information than people. Information can travel faster than any fleeing felon, so there is just no need to worry about whether we can chase criminals down with patrol cars as long as we have computers, telephones, and an occasional helicopter. The police officers of the future will be at home with all types of technology and will use it as a direct extension of themselves.

—**Tom Cook and James Metts**

Tom Cook is head of the Criminal Justice Department at Southside Virginia Community College, Route 1, Keysville, Virginia 23947. James Metts is sheriff of Lexington County, South Carolina.

> "Tomorrow's police agencies will little resemble today's rigid, military-like models. The role of the police will be more 'caretaker' and service delivery in nature, and less 'lock 'em up.'"

Border police examine birth certificate of illegal alien working in Florida. Police officers of the future will have to deal with an increasingly diverse population, including more legal and illegal immigrants, and greater numbers of non-English-speaking citizens.

Computers are already common in law enforcement. Tomorrow's police officers will have a computer in their automobile for immediate retrieval of criminal-history information. Computer networks will provide birth-to-death dossiers, giving officers immediate field information.

With modern forensics, a strand of hair or a drop of blood can lead to the identification of a suspect. Highly qualified technical supercops will be recruited to run the police laboratories of the future. Each police agency will need a team of forensic pathologists, computer programmers, and crime scene technical experts.

Today, many police officers represent the state at preliminary court hearings. Tomorrow's police officers may be called on to assist with the actual court prosecution, as caseloads continue to grow and as police officers increasingly enter the profession with law degrees.

A New Society To Serve

In the near future, police officers will serve a much different society than that of today. With more elderly people, the police will need to deliver a full complement of programs geared to serve the aged. For example, tomorrow's supercop will need to be an expert in the paramedic services needed by these elderly citizens.

Increasing numbers of citizens will live in suburbs and in smaller communities, fewer in large cities. Fewer children will grow up with both natural parents in the household. Minorities will be a growing proportion of the population—one in four in the United States by the year 2000—and will represent a higher proportion of young people.

The supercop will need to be flexible enough to deal with many divergent ethnic and social groups. There will be few easy answers in tomorrow's diverse and protean society. Police officers may be called upon to deal with crimes as diverse as illegal-gene threats, computer theft, and nuclear terrorism.

Tomorrow's police agencies will little resemble today's rigid, military-like models. The role of the police will be more "caretaker" and service delivery in nature and less "lock 'em up." Police will take on a more "public safety" context of professionalism.

Advancement within a police agency will depend more on one's qualifications and education and less on seniority. Promotions will be based on performance in simulated role-playing and scenarios and not on years of service.

Administrators will care less about marksmanship and physical size and more about mental capacity and diplomas. Law enforcement, as a vocation, will no longer attract the "Wyatt Earp" types.

Police forces will be hard pressed to keep up with the increase in litigation against officers. As social-service responsibilities increase for officers, so will the opportunities for litigation. This will, in turn, increase the importance that administrators not hire hotheads who want the job only to "bust heads" and "lock 'em up."

In-house police agency standards will become very tough. If police are being paid as professionals, the public will demand the very best. The public will demand that police turn to performing human services. Thus, fear of the police

> "As our society becomes more mobile and more transient, there will be more uniformity in local laws."

Helicopter operated by the Baltimore Police Department flies out on assignment. Helicopters will increasingly be used by police to track and apprehend criminals.

CITY OF BALTIMORE POLICE DEPARTMENT

will end. The public will turn to the police for help because the police will be well educated, highly trained, and very professional.

As our society becomes more mobile and more transient, there will be more uniformity in local laws. Jurisdictions will need to establish uniform sentencing guidelines and uniform statutes.

Society will frown on any duplication of services by public-service agencies. There will be one police agency with local jurisdiction over traffic; local and state criminal violations; wildlife and marine resources; alcohol, tobacco, and firearms regulations; fire fighting; and paramedical services. Unneeded and wasteful specialized agencies will be disbanded, and a single localized agency will handle all complaints and emergency services.

Administrators will need to be experts in personnel management, budgeting, personnel motivation, planning, and organization. They will need to reorganize police agencies from quasi-military models to effective, versatile human service delivery institutions. Police chiefs will cease to exist: They will become public-service administrators.

Toward a Profession

Doctors, teachers, lawyers, and other professionals spend years in college, specialized schools, and training to join their chosen profession. These work groups are well respected, well paid, and are perceived as public "caretakers." The public turns to them for help or advice. Their skills and abilities are well tuned. They stay where they are by keeping informed, staying updated, and getting recertified. Their responsibility is great. Their margin of error is slim.

Policing will, in turn, become a profession during the next generation. It will have to: Society will demand a respected, qualified, well-trained supercop.

Police work, as we now know it, will cease to exist. Public-service officers will be society's "caretakers." They will still be the first line of public defense, but their role in society will be largely a matter of human-resource delivery. If they still carry guns, those guns will be loaded with "shock" bullets. Police use of deadly force will be nonexistent.

People will call the police for help, as always, but they will demand and receive the services of professional "caretakers," whose primary tools will be their legal, social, and technical expertise.

About the Author

James R. Metts is sheriff of Lexington County, South Carolina. In 1979, he became the first sheriff in the United States to earn a doctoral degree. His address is P.O. Box 639, Lexington, South Carolina 29072.

PRIVATE DISOBEDIENCE

The New Militancy

Randall L. Scheel

"Private disobedience"—acts of protest against the private sector—is a growing phenomenon in the United States. Unlike civil disobedience, this new militancy is uncompromising, direct, and frequently violent.

We are witnessing a new form of militancy in the United States. It can be called private disobedience and is characterized by deliberate acts of protest, sometimes violent, directed against the private sector. Many driving forces will support the growth of this new phenomenon in the next 15 years. Perhaps most alarming is the willingness of many practitioners of private disobedience to undermine the spirit of compromise so valuable in a rapidly changing society.

Consider these examples:

• Unemployed steel workers place dead fish in their banks' safe-deposit boxes. The stench is the workers' protest against the banks' unwillingness to continue support of financially troubled local steel mills.

• Anti-abortion activists picket and bomb clinics and harass their staff and patients.

• Recipients of "junk mail" return empty business-reply envelopes, knowing that the companies must pay postage to receive them.

• Environmental activists pound nails into trees designated to be harvested. The nails will ruin chainsaw blades and endanger loggers.

• Disgruntled employees sabotage their employers' electronic information systems by causing computer programs to self-destruct.

These examples of militancy may be called "private disobedience." It is different from civil disobedience in that it is directed against the private sector rather than the government. And it is sometimes violent.

Future Disobedience

Demographics, economics, and other "tools" can help predict who will be likely to protest private sector policies.

For example, as the baby-boom generation enters mid-career in unprecedented numbers, competition for certain kinds of jobs will be fierce. The curtailment of upward mobility will lead to rising worker frustration, alienation, stress, and more private disobedience.

Another demographic factor is the aging of American society. By the year 2000, more than 13% of the U.S. population will be over 65 years old. This represents approximately twice as many as there were in 1940. Retired people today are more active and are taking an increased interest in social change. As their numbers increase, so will their influence in such areas as Social Security, mental and physical health care, housing, legal services, nuclear energy, and employment. Older people have, more than any other demographic cohort, the discretionary time to act on these vital concerns, and it is not unlikely that they will resort to private disobedience to accomplish their goals.

Social and Economic Driving Forces

The shift from a manufacturing economy to a service economy is contributing to a shrinking middle class in America. Cities such as Johnstown, Pennsylvania; Akron, Ohio; and Gary, Indiana, are polarizing into two fairly distinct groups of residents: Relatively well-off retirees and a growing number of the poor and recently unemployed. A similar situation is occurring in major cities such as New York and San Francisco, where the middle class is being forced out by higher costs of housing. As the numbers of poor increase, retaliation against perceived oppressors becomes more likely.

Those who are employed in the newer high-tech and service industries tend to be paid substantially less than their manufacturing forerunners. In these companies, the polarization is internal. Income distribution in high-tech companies, for example, tends to be high for management and engineering and low for assembly workers. Certain consequences seem inevitable. The lower-income workers, including secretaries, will be persuaded to unionize, and increasing competition for high-paying jobs will lead to conflict, tension, and frustration. For many, the only outlet will be direct and deliberate acts against the organization perceived as responsible for their plight.

Shifting our view further to the future, we can identify other groups that may not share in the general well-being of society and strike out at U.S. business in the 1990s. These include semi-skilled blue-collar workers, many of whose jobs will be replaced by automation; immigrants with few skills and little knowledge of English; and youth in disadvantaged public schools, where overall performance levels are well below national norms.

Less obvious but perhaps more serious is the large mass of people who will not derive the full benefit from the shift to the information/communications era. For example, Congress has debated over whether, in the face of increasing rates, every American has the right to a telephone. Phone companies report that they are disconnecting more residential phones for nonpayment than at any time in decades—perhaps since the Great Depression. To be unable to afford a telephone today may not seem extremely serious, but, with the coming of the "wired society," lack of a telephone reduces a person's access to the rest of the world.

The next debate in the information society might be whether every American has the right to a home computer. Some people contend that computers are already driving a wedge in U.S. society, separating the country into classes of information rich and poor. A Louis Harris poll indicates:

• Sixty-eight percent of college graduates say they know how to use a computer; only 16% of those who didn't finish high school are computer-literate.

• Sixty-seven percent of those with incomes above $35,000 can operate computers, compared with 23% of those making less than $7,500.

Is owning a telephone and a computer a right or a privilege? This question will be at the center of one of the most critical issues of the next 10 years. The resolution of it will answer an impending question the government and the private sector are anxious to have answered: Which will contribute more to public militance—greater access to information or more restricted access to information? Since the start of the Industrial Revolution, some groups have consciously rejected the modern world and chosen to live without the latest technology: for example, the Amish people of Pennsylvania. Will the techno-peasants of the future do something similar?

Workplace Driving Issues

Computer and communications technologies are increasingly being used to monitor employees in the workplace. Computers could even be used to analyze employees' brain waves to determine whether they are keeping their minds on their work.

Not surprisingly, a number of unions, including the Newspaper Guild, the United Auto Workers, and the Communications Workers of America, have insisted on anti-monitoring clauses in their contracts. Among the several states with pending legislation to regulate VDTs, seven have included prohibitions against monitoring. But no state has yet passed VDT legislation.

Privacy in the workplace may also be invaded by biometric security devices, which are activated by fingerprints, voices, or the shape of one's hand. Companies are interested in high-tech security partly because employees are growing more hostile, but the devices themselves are often a focus of rebellion. Acts of sabotage include cigarette packs and ashes jammed

ART BY LAURA COSTAS

"Computer and communications technologies are increasingly being used to monitor employees in the workplace."

into the card slots of locks that read specially coded cards.

Another workplace issue ripe for private disobedience is the use of genetic testing to detect occupation-related diseases. Genetic screening could conceivably be used to justify denial of employment, job transfers, or even dismissal—none of which sits well with the public [see "Medical Discrimination in the Workplace," THE FUTURIST, March-April 1986].

Alienation and Protest

Citizen confidence in American institutions has been on the decline at least since the 1960s. For most people, though, "institutions" are distant and alien, and the fact that many of the people who run them seem incompetent or corrupt is more likely a source of irony than outrage.

But this attitude may be changing. Acts of private disobedience are manifestations of outrage. Private citizens do not commit dangerous and felonious acts out of a sense of irony, but out of genuine anger and frustration.

Even more disturbing is the likelihood that declining confidence will make the public more susceptible to demagogic persuasions, creating support for movements seeking to change the system in a fundamental way.

We are seeing this now in the plethora of activist groups composed of people who view themselves as reformers with higher and more enlightened values than others. They believe that opposition to their principles stems from selfishness, ignorance, bigotry, or even evil. Many see themselves as the "progressive" force overcoming the "oppressive" dominance of "selfish" profit-oriented business values, "dehumanizing" corporations, "blind" technology, "crass" materialism, and "commercialized" vulgarity. They turn issues into ideological, spiritual, or moral imperatives, or they treat these issues as too important to be subjected to compromise or cost-benefit analysis.

A large proportion of people who become activists are those who easily find fault and do not adjust well to living and working with others. They lack the sense of compromise that successful life in our complex society requires. As our world becomes increasingly complex, the art of compromise becomes more and more essential for progress, if not survival itself.

Many of the major driving forces that are shaping, and will continue to shape, our future have serious negative implications. Even more serious, however, is the prospect of growing numbers of people practicing private disobedience, for in this type of militancy there is no room for compromise.

About the Author

Randall L. Scheel is issue research supervisor in the Public Affairs Planning Department at Southern California Gas Company, 810 S. Flower Street, Suite 1033, Los Angeles, California 90017.

J.H. Foegen

THE MENACE OF HIGH-TECH EMPLOYMENT

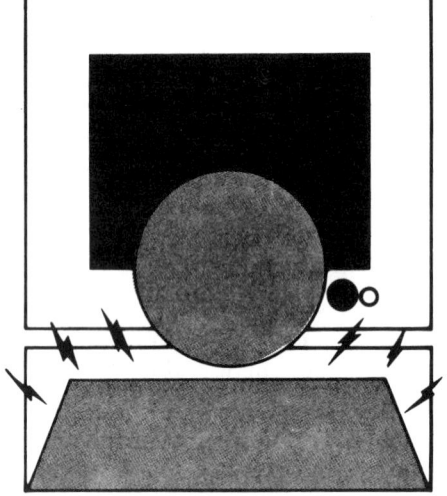

The office of the future could resemble yesterday's factory as high technology erodes working conditions and job prestige.

The awesome accomplishments and potential of today's electronic technology grow daily. Unfortunately, there is a growing suspicion that both working conditions and skill levels are deteriorating for many of the people who use the new equipment.

High technology poses a special threat to the growing white-collar work force. According to the Bureau of Labor Statistics, white-collar employees made up 53% of all workers in 1981; five years later, in 1986, the percentage had jumped to 65%. By the year 2000, white-collar workers are expected to be 90% of the work force.

Capital investment per worker in white-collar occupations is predicted to rise to as much as $10,000 per worker by 1989, up from only $2,500 in 1981, according to the American Productivity Center. The Office of Technology Assessment predicts still more small computers and networking in the office, more reliance on off-the-shelf rather than custom-made software, continuing decreases in unit costs of computing power, and optical scanning replacing rekeyboarding.

While apparently increasing productivity, high technology has also been changing white-collar work to parallel more closely the earlier factory situation of repetitive, tedious, unchallenging tasks, uncontrollable by individuals. Years ago, an office job was considered the height of middle-class respectability, head and shoulders above working in a factory, and worth bragging about. Today, working conditions have deteriorated even though the superficial "glitter" of carpeting and Muzak remains.

A shift toward more part-time and home-based work has become pronounced, facilitated by the proliferation of personal computers. Telecommuters were estimated to number at least 7.2 million in 1985; of these, the self-employed outnumbered employees five to one. IBM alone has put more than 8,000 terminals in employees' homes to facilitate working there.

The advantages of such "cottage industry" situations are savings in time and gasoline, but employers may seek to reduce health insurance, sick leave, and pension costs for such workers, who essentially become independent contractors. The result is a growing proportion of workers without basic protections, reversing a long-established trend.

More "Working Poor"

Wages as well as benefits have seen inroads. Ongoing loss of relatively high-wage manufacturing jobs to overseas competitors and the simultaneous growth of relatively low-wage, service-sector jobs are leading to increasing numbers of "working poor." Congress is addressing the situation by trying to raise the minimum wage once more. Overall income for American families has remained constant over the past 15 years, something never before experienced for that long a time.

Physical problems are also surfacing. With the rapid increase in the number of personal computer terminals, much attention is being given to potential eyestrain and musculoskeletal problems among video display terminal (VDT) operators, as well as to the greater stress induced by office automation in general. Japan's Ministry of Labor found that eyestrain caused by frequent shifting from manuscript to VDT screen and back again resulted in complaints approximately 20% higher among staff using terminals than among other office employees. These problems may just be starting to surface.

A more insidious threat to quality of worklife, one illustrating regression to earlier factory practices, is close computer monitoring of office work. White-collar employment was once characterized by lack of close supervision — no time clocks were punched, and missing a day of work now and then did not reduce pay. But now, Eastern Airlines monitors the number of calls taken by its 6,000 agents, the number of seats sold, and average call-handling time; failing to meet group goals can result in suspension. Norwegian Caribbean Lines gets printouts assessing the work of its reservation agents every half hour. The Southern Bell Telephone Company monitors its operators' calls.

A four-month investigation among 23 firms of a major U.S. company group showed that constant supervision, automatic computer monitoring, and elaborate productivity indices have made job-related stress pervasive. In an ultimate scenario, computers could even be used to analyze employees' brain waves to determine whether they are keeping their minds on their work! [See "Private Disobedience: The New Militancy" by Randall L. Scheel in the May-June 1986 issue of THE FUTURIST.]

Some major unions, like the United Auto Workers and the Communications Workers, have already insisted on anti-monitoring clauses in their contracts, and some states are considering prohibitions on prospective VDT-regulating laws, but recognition of computer monitoring has really only begun.

Job Downgrading

Traditional office tasks are being simplified, merged, and eliminated by the new technology. Word processors are downgrading secretarial skills. People no longer are valued for the ability to produce error-free typing, correct spelling, and grammatical accuracy, now that machines have these capacities. Likewise with programming: Humans increasingly need only supply data and select options, and software does the rest. According to a Stanford University professor, the principal impact of microprocessors and robots on traditional occupations will be to replace workers and reduce skills.

Stenographers are expected to be the fastest-disappearing occupation during the coming decade. The 1984 total of 239,000 may shrink to 143,000 by 1995, a 40% decrease. The number of typists is expected to grow only 1% during the next 10 years, secretaries by only 10%, as still more computerization occurs. More professionals and managers are using desktop personal computers and executive work stations to do work previously delegated to support staff.

U.S. Department of Labor studies show that only 15% of all jobs in

"The typical occupational middle class . . . is disappearing."

firms making electronic components, and only 25% in computer and data-processing firms, are technologically oriented. No high-tech occupations are among the top 18 categories in projected job growth, and, overall, only around 6% of all new jobs will be in high-tech areas.

Not only is the once highly valued skill of taking dictation in shorthand giving way to computerization, but keyboarding in general is on the way out. As computers have continued their rapid evolution, the classic IBM card has largely disappeared, and the typewriter-like keyboard of today's terminals is likely to follow shortly. Voice recognition in a rudimentary form is here already, and it is likely to become more sophisticated, economical, and practical.

Some experts predict that no fewer than six kinds of voice-based systems will appear within 10 years. Speech-to-text systems that are "natural" — without inter-word pauses — are already being developed, with vocabularies of 10,000 words and targeted 95% accuracy. Language translation from spoken word to text, optical character recognition of intermixed type styles, videodisc storage, and electronic blackboards are either already in use or will be before long. When all who have use for the hardware can make it work merely by talking to it, hordes of clerical support people will head for the unemployment offices.

The white-collar work force is increasingly bipolar. The typical occupational middle class, in other words, is disappearing. The "good" jobs — computer expert and upper-level manager — cluster at one end of the continuum; jobs that are relatively de-skilled and closely monitored are at the other end. In addition to the gender gap in wages and a rapidly widening information gap, a middle-job gap is growing also, with unknown but widespread implications likely.

Unions and Management

Despite all of these problems, technology and labor-force changes are nothing new; they are inherent in a still-vibrant U.S. economy. The challenges are great, but an intelligent and imaginative combination of assertive unions and sensitive management could translate current difficulties into productive outcomes. Both labor and management have begun to address the problems of high-tech employment.

Union membership has been declining as a percentage of a growing labor force — membership declined 1.5% among 25- to 35-year-olds in 1985 alone — but some union officials think the trend is "bottoming out." As working conditions in the computerized white-collar office deteriorate and office skills are robbed of their prestige, workers may become more susceptible to unionization. Many bank employees, doctors, and government workers have already joined unions, contrary to the assumption that such workers are immune to organization.

Even some telecommuters have been unionized. A pioneering group of home-based workers in Madison, Wisconsin, has joined AFSCME, the large public-employee union. The workers transcribe medical records for the University of Wisconsin hospitals and — unlike some remote-location employees — receive the same wages and benefits as on-site colleagues, not piece rates. This success comes in the face of general AFL-CIO opposition to telecommuting.

For management, the challenge is to take full advantage of the new technology's productivity potential while avoiding the inherent physical and psychological pitfalls. The common denominator of new and old remains the human element. Whether sitting before a machine, typewriter, or screen, the employee still responds to supervisors' sensitive, empathetic recognition of work-situation difficulties, open communication about real and perceived problems, and basic fair treatment. Given an enlightened management approach, whether technology is high or low becomes relatively less important.

About the Author

J.H. Foegen is professor of business at Winona State University (Winona, Minnesota 55987), where he also teaches courses in future studies.

Sar A. Levitan

Beyond "Trendy" Forecasts

The Next 10 Years for Work

"Trendy" forecasts of the American workplace for the next 10 years see radical changes — some good and some bad. But the American workplace is very slow to change, cautions a research professor of economics.

Will there be radical changes in the American workplace by 1997? Perhaps. It is a tribute to the richness of statistics published by U.S. government agencies, and the masses of data spewed out from private computers, that enterprising researchers can find evidence for all sorts of propositions by using data selectively. Before we turn to the crystal ball to fathom what is in store for American workers and labor markets a decade hence, let us first examine some trendy ideas that are currently receiving attention.

Four Trendy Forecasts

To achieve some balance in a review of misconceptions that dominate current labor-market analysis, I will select two predictions of gloom and doom and two that are full of promise and hope — for those who believe in the tooth fairy.

1. The Declining Middle.

One trendy idea holds that America is facing a polarization of society through the erosion of the middle class. According to this argument, foreign imports and changes resulting from new technology are causing sharp reductions in middle-management ranks as well as a shift from well-paid manufacturing to low-paid service employment. The conclusion is that an increasing proportion of workers is concentrated at the extremes of the earning-distribution curve. The facts are that even in

Modern Times revisited? Inspector checks automated gearbox. Automation will certainly affect the future workplace, but *how* has been the subject of "trendy" myths.

LONDON PICTURES SERVICE

THE FUTURIST, November-December 1987

manufacturing — where most of the fat was supposed to have been cut — executive, administrative, and managerial positions rose by 15% between 1983 and 1986. This is almost three times the growth rate of total manufacturing employment.

Prognostications about the middle class have come full circle over the past 30 years. For example, three decades ago, *Fortune* magazine pronounced that the United States was undergoing a revolution. Groups "hitherto identified as proletarians" were rushing into the "huge new monied middle-income class." In 1983, *Fortune* reported that the revolution had ended and that the middle class "is gradually being pulled apart [as] economic forces are propelling one family after another toward the high or low end of the income spectrum."

A more realistic and careful investigation would have shown that relatively few "proletarians" were joining the middle class in the 1950s. Similarly, we're likely to find that the more-recent gloomy prediction of the erosion of the middle class is no more accurate. Depending on the statistical series used, an analysis of the data during the past 10 or 15 years leads to diametrically contrary conclusions.

Government data on the earning distribution of year-round full-time employees — where middle-income workers are concentrated — show that since 1970 the share of the earnings of the top third has declined while the share of the bottom and middle earners (the middle class) has actually risen.

On the other hand, an analysis of family income shows that the share of the bottom and middle thirds has declined while that of the top has risen. But adding the variable of family size would lead to a different conclusion. On a per capita basis, the income of the middle third has remained stable. In addition, the role of the tax collector should not be ignored. The share of the middle third after taxes increased, while that of the bottom third also rose, and the top third declined.

There is no solid evidence that the middle class is shrinking. The Census Bureau has consistently found remarkable stability in income distribution despite the profound changes that have taken place in the economy and the labor force since World War II. There appears to be little reason to believe that middle America is about to become an extinct or even an endangered species.

Marketing manager goes over map for distribution of his product. Despite gloomy projections for the future of middle-level occupations, jobs for managers, executives, and administrators are growing at almost twice the rate of total employment, says author Levitan.

2. The Future Belongs to Robots.

Another gloomy prediction suggests that not only is the middle class eroding, but there will be no work for an increasingly large proportion of all persons seeking work. There is nothing new about the prediction that labor will become less important as new technology replaces human labor with machines — this prediction has been heard repeatedly since the beginning of the industrial age. It can be asserted with some confidence, however, that this forecast is no more true today than it was a century ago. On the contrary, the overall employment-to-population ratio is now at a historical high.

Computers and robots are definitely here, but it does not follow that the future belongs to them. Robots may be getting smarter and cheaper, but they are hardly likely to replace humans at work in the foreseeable future. Computers may spit out loads of data, but humans are needed to make judgments about the data retrieved from the computers.

Granting that the workplace is changing at an accelerated rate and that computer technology is becoming increasingly sophisticated, changes in the workplace will still be painfully slow and evolutionary in nature. As computer-driven machinery is introduced to ensure more-stringent quality controls, the factory and the office will become increasingly capital-intensive; the replacement of existing technology will be slow due to the cost of the newer equipment.

We should expect, therefore, that the workplace a decade hence is not going to be much different from what it is today. Even if the 15,000 robots in operation today increased by twentyfold in the next decade, their work will be confined primarily to repetitive and hazardous work now being done by humans and will replace only a tiny fraction of the estimated 131 million people in the labor force by 1997. For every "working" robot, there will still be more than 400 people in the labor force.

3. Eliminating Government Regulations Will Boost Productivity.

Now to turn to two more-hopeful notions. One fashionable idea is that government regulation has stymied productivity growth. Pre-

> "There is every reason to believe that women will continue to flock into the labor market, although not necessarily at the rate experienced during the past decade."

sumably, if government ceased to interfere with free markets, productivity would take off again and return to the levels the economy enjoyed in the 1950s and early 1960s.

There is no question that government regulations have reduced measured productivity growth. Achieving clean air, clear water, and safety in the workplace has its costs. However, even if we ignore the benefits to society, the best available estimates about the impact of regulations upon productivity suggest that, at most, measured productivity has declined by a fraction of 1% as a result of governmental regulations.

During the Carter and Reagan administrations, much governmental intervention has been reduced, but, so far, productivity has not responded to these changes. Indeed, productivity growth during the past four years has been below that of other post-recessionary recoveries since World War II. In 1986, the fourth year of recovery from the 1981-1982 recession, there was even less room for optimism — productivity per work hour increased by less than 1%. We must conclude that governmental intervention in the free market, whatever its merits or faults, has hardly been the culprit for the declining growth in productivity during the past decade.

4. Labor–Management Cooperation.

Another trendy idea is that the United States is about to enter a new era of labor–management harmony. As a response to foreign competition and threatening trade deficits, the concept of labor-and-management cooperation in the national interest is certainly appealing. It is reminiscent of Benjamin Franklin's warning: "We must indeed all hang together, or most assuredly we shall hang separately." Unfortunately, clarion calls alone do not resolve the age-old conflicts between labor and management.

One popular suggestion to iron out labor–management differences is the establishment of quality-of-worklife programs. Advocates have also placed much reliance on the increasing prominence of quality circles. But it is not clear who is going to run circles around whom.

While paying lip service to cooperation, American management has often tried to undermine employee efforts to organize — the essential ingredient in giving employees a meaningful voice in the workplace. A few companies have established grievance procedures, which allow employees to air concerns. In most cases, however, management preaches worker cooperation but ignores workers' priorities if they conflict with immediate profit-maximization efforts. Employees are encouraged to participate in corporate decision making only if it does not infringe on management prerogatives. Such efforts differ little from traditional management attempts to secure the voluntary cooperation of workers and to encourage identification with management goals.

There are persuasive reasons to encourage participative-management techniques. By increasing worker involvement, management can tap new ideas and enhance employee dignity. But the hope that purely cosmetic changes will radically alter the work environment or transform labor–management relations is likely to result in frustration. The traditional adversarial relationship between labor and management is, for better or worse, resistant to change.

A View of 1997

The rejection of the trendy ideas suggests that we should not expect radical changes in the workplace by 1997. Accurately forecasting overall labor-force demand and supply a decade hence is not as speculative as it might appear. About five of every six persons who will be in the labor force in 1997 are already working or looking for jobs.

On the demand side, if history is any guide for the future, the American economy will experience at least two business cycles within the next decade. Of course, we all hope that future recessions will be milder and shorter than the last one. But hope is not a prediction. Unprecedented federal-budget deficits, the disturbing trade imbalance, and the uncertain state of recently deregulated financial institutions all require action and wisdom on the part of policy makers if the United States is to avoid other deep recessions.

Given these assumptions, loose labor markets may be in the offing for the balance of this decade. The supply-side economics championed by President Reagan has not yet had any perceptible impact upon savings. Because of large deficits, the federal government will be forced to compete more vigorously with business for the limited available capital. This will slow down private investment and job expansion.

Labor Supply Will Grow

The supply of labor during the next decade will continue to increase despite reduced birthrates in the 1960s and 1970s. While the total supply of teenagers will decline, it is probable that the labor-force-participation rate of young people will increase, either because they will not be able to pay for higher education or because the attractions of further education will diminish. Cutbacks in federal support for youth attending college may discourage some from enroll-

New secretary is trained on word-processing equipment. Many of the basic skills of secretaries, such as typing, will be little changed by new technology. The secretary's ability to plan and organize will retain its value in the workplace of 10 years hence.

ing, particularly as the cost of a college education — whether public or private — continues to rise more rapidly than inflation.

At the other end of the age spectrum, it is likely that older employees will stay in the work force longer and that early retirement will become increasingly unattainable. The federal government is already taxing the Social Security benefits of more-affluent retirees. As Congress continues to look for revenue enhancement, it may tax all Social Security benefits. Full indexing of Social Security benefits may also be ended, as it has been for retired federal employees. The high cost of pensions and retiree benefits will induce employers to discourage early retirement. The federal government is already trying to do that for its employees.

There is every reason to believe that women will continue to flock into the labor market, although not necessarily at the rate experienced during the past decade. Women continue to acquire more education, postponing marriage and children, to prepare themselves for lifetime careers. While the divorce rate has stabilized, at below five per thousand population, the number of female-headed families continues to rise. In 1985, households headed by women accounted for one of every five families with children under 18 — nearly double the proportion in 1970. And for married couples, the wife's earnings are increasingly important to continued financial well-being. In light of these circumstances, few women are likely to withdraw from the labor market for more than short periods of time.

Even if the labor-force participation of the native population does not rise as anticipated, immigration may continue to swell the supply of labor in the United States, since the United States offers extremely attractive opportunities to immigrants. Even as the new immigration law goes into effect, farmers are successfully fighting restrictions on Mexican laborers, and other employers are likely to attain similar results if labor shortages develop. Moreover, international events may mean that the United States will have to accept additional political refugees.

Changing Nature of Work

The overall supply and demand of labor will change slowly, as will the occupational composition of the labor force. New technology will generate both mundane, low-paying jobs and sophisticated, high-paying jobs, just as mechanization and automation have done in the past. The Bureau of Labor Statistics has estimated that, by 1995, for every computer specialist, operator, or technician added to the work force there will be three additional unskilled laborers, three salesworkers, and seven clerical workers.

No doubt the content of many jobs will change. But these changes will not substantially alter the basic skills required for work. The most widely held occupation in the American economy is that of secretary and office clerk. Today, there are some 7 million individuals performing these duties.

Despite the introduction of new office equipment over the past century, intrinsic secretarial skills have changed very little since the typewriter was introduced. Whether secretaries operate a manual typewriter or a word processor, carbon paper or a photo-offsetting machine, the skills necessary to perform the job remain essentially the same: an ability to type and to spell correctly. But the work of the secretary does not end, obviously, with the ability to type, and the many other administrative and related tasks that

> "Even if changes in the workplace are accelerating, as some observers suggest, a decade is too short a period for radical changes."

secretaries perform will persist. Technology may have changed *how* the secretary works, but there is little prospect that the secretary's administrative and planning duties will change in the foreseeable future.

In sum, the evidence seems overwhelming that in the next decade the economy is not going to generate an extraordinary demand for new skills. Computer technology may appear to us — the first generation of observers and participants — as a promising (or threatening) revolutionary transformation of work and society. It does not follow, however, that users will have to be familiar with the mysteries of computer technology. We all know how to operate a telephone, but very few of us fathom the technology that makes it work.

Whatever wonders computer technology may spawn, the production managers will simplify work. Just a decade ago, few people could locate the "on" switch of an IBM PC. Today, "user friendly" computers require only marginal changes in skill requirements.

Adjustments to Change

While the nature of work has evolved only gradually, the character of the labor force has changed at a much faster rate. These changes — all too often missed by the forecasters of trendy ideas — will require adjustments in the treatment of employees and in labor–management relations.

The most significant development has been the rise in educational attainment of American workers. In 1940, the median American worker acquired slightly more than a grade-school education. Today, more than half of all workers have a smattering of college, and three of every four new employees in American industry are high-school graduates.

The changing structure of the family has also had a major impact on the workplace. Most American families no longer depend on the earnings of one breadwinner because married women with spouses present — to use the government statisticians' phrase — are now in the work force. The proportion of two-earner households is likely to increase during the next decade. With fewer mouths to feed — because of anticipated low fertility rates, together with postponed marriage and childbearing — American families should experience continuous boosts in discretionary income.

Higher educational attainment and greater affluence among employees will call for greater sensitivity and attention by management to the concerns of their workers. So far, there has been a great deal of rhetoric but, with few exceptions, no overall change in labor–management relations. Questions about the optimal amount of delegation of authority and control have been debated at least since Jethro advised Moses on the organization of his chain of command. The latest pronouncements by management and their consultants have not shed much light on the subject.

No Radical Changes

The twentieth century has experienced a significant cumulative transformation in the workplace, and changes are likely to continue in the next decade. But even if changes in the workplace are accelerating, as some observers suggest, a decade is too short a period for radical changes. Managers and workers in the labor market will continue to face the same problems.

Given present technology, it is easy to envision cataclysmic changes within a short period, but vast capital expenditures would be necessary to radically transform the workplace. Because the populace is unlikely to drastically reduce its demand for government services, government responsibilities will not decline in the years ahead. A rising share of the gross national product will be needed for defense and to support social programs. To pay for these outlays, the government will continue to tax and borrow. This will reduce the share of the GNP available to savings and investment and limit capital available for investment in new technology. The capital necessary to fuel a short-term restructuring of the economy is not likely to materialize.

We should not expect, therefore, any radical changes in the workplace. The robots may take over some of the more unpleasant and repetitive work, and computers may perform some jobs now performed by humans. People will, however, continue to work not only for the pay, but for many other reasons.

Most of us are destined to be neither poets nor philosophers, and we get our satisfaction in life by creating things or performing services. As Sigmund Freud said, "Man's work gives him a secure place in a portion of reality in the human community."

About the Author

Sar A. Levitan is a research professor of economics and is director of the Center for Social Policy Studies at The George Washington University, 1730 K Street, N.W., Suite 701, Washington, D.C. 20006. He chaired the National Commission on Employment and Unemployment Statistics and has acted as a consultant to several governmental agencies and private organizations. His latest book is *Protecting American Workers: An Assessment of Government Programs*.

David Macarov

Overcoming Unemployment

Some Radical Proposals

None of the solutions thus far offered to overcome unemployment has worked. What is needed is a new perspective on a workless society—one in which automation allows people to do what they want and still receive a decent income.

One of the most ubiquitous and persistent social problems in the Western industrialized world is that of unemployment. Despite continuing and massive efforts of various kinds to reduce the number of the unemployed to acceptable proportions, in most countries the problem of unemployment remains

Reducing Unemployment: Does Anything Work?

In two decades of the "war on poverty," the U.S government has tested a number of policies aimed at either reducing unemployment among the disadvantaged or reducing poverty itself. No policy has yet emerged as a completely effective weapon, says Brookings Institution economist Gary Burtless, who recently made a study of these programs. Burtless concludes: "Residual poverty can be eliminated only if society is willing to change the distribution of economic rewards, either in the labor market or by reform of the tax and transfer system."

Here are a few manpower programs that have been tried in the United States, along with their advantages and disadvantages, as indicated by Burtless's survey:

Program	Pro	Con
Classroom training: Provides skills for specific occupations in which plenty of job opportunities are expected.	Raises subsequent earnings among women, new entrants, and reentrants, who have little recent job experience.	Works less well for men who have held steady but low-paying jobs. Jobs may not actually exist in the areas that the participants train in, and participants may miss out on valuable work experience during the months of training.
Comprehensive training (Job Corps): Offers a comprehensive set of health, educational, and vocational services to low-income youth.	Leads to higher wages and reduced crime.	Costs are substantial: about $14,000 per participant per year—more than three times as much as any other type of training program.
On-the-job training: Private employers provide entry-level jobs to disadvantaged workers and receive subsidies to cover some of the added costs of training.	Trainees are more likely than classroom trainees to get permanent jobs, and their earnings are higher.	Employers are reluctant to hire disadvantaged workers, and the trainees who are hired usually succeed because they were more employable (than classroom trainees) in the first place.
Wage subsidies: Government pays employers to hire disadvantaged workers.	Employers can recover all or part of the wages of "hard-to-employ" workers and need not provide training to qualify.	Employers are reluctant to hire job-seekers who are labeled "disadvantaged," despite the tax advantage.
Work experience as training: Places disadvantaged workers in government agencies and nonprofit institutions, where their wages are subsidized.	Workers receive experience that improves their employability, even if in menial occupations.	Tasks performed may have little value, and the wages can be viewed as a form of income redistribution.
Job-search training: Disadvantaged workers are shown how to find jobs for which they are already prepared.	Far less expensive than other training programs.	Many of the jobs found are low-wage, dead-end situations that do little to end poverty.

Source: "Manpower Policies for the Disadvantaged: What Works?" by Gary Burtless in *The Brookings Review* (Fall 1984). The Brookings Institution, 1775 Massachusetts Avenue, N.W., Washington, D.C. 20036.

and—with current advances in technology—may become a permanent feature of society.

Long-term unemployment, particularly among youth, now commands the attention of many national and international bodies. Conventional methods of attempting to overcome unemployment are becoming more and more ineffective. Consequently, this article proposes some more radical attempts to overcome the problem of unemployment.

The Future of Unemployment

The likelihood of growing permanent unemployment is becoming more accepted as a reality among social planners as figures mount and as palliative measures fail. The AFL-CIO's Committee on the Evolution of Work, for example, foresees a persistent job shortage, consisting of 4-6 million Americans unemployed at all times.

A careful perusal of such options as tax cuts, wage subsidies, reduced worktime, public-works projects, public-service employment, and macroeconomic changes reveals that most of these "solutions" don't work. In addition to simply cutting work hours directly and through increased vacations, holidays, and so on, devices that have obscured the extent of unemployment include:

- **Job creation.** The direct creation of jobs, although much discussed and recommended, is too costly to be feasible. With about 10 million people unemployed in the United States, creating jobs for them would cost $171 billion. Providing them with construction jobs—often cited as the most socially necessary jobs—would cost $416 billion. This option is obviously not open for any large number of people.
- **Subsidized jobs.** Under this plan, employers are subsidized by government grants to offer jobs. The expectation (or rather, the hope) is that the employee will then become permanent. Rarely does this happen. For example, in the Comprehensive Employment and Training Act (CETA) program in the United States, subsidized people were substituted for regular employees for as long as the subsidies lasted, so there was no net gain in jobs created.
- **Work relief.** This is a method of making relief payments through the mechanism of work. Indeed, work relief is not designed to overcome unemployment but to get some return for welfare expenditures. Inasmuch as most of the work done under such programs is make-work, of little intrinsic value, it has little employment potential.
- **Public works.** Public-works projects differ from work-relief programs in that workers are usually picked for competence (at least to some degree), paid according to a standard scale rather than according to individual need, and usually do work that has some intrinsic social value. Such programs suffer from a number of limitations, however. For one thing, unions often insist that if there are jobs available, their own unemployed members should get them; they also object to pay scales established within public-works programs that are below union scales. Nor do commercial firms want goods produced or services performed at prices lower than they charge. Hence, both relief work and public works tend to be marginal jobs that nobody else will do for the money paid.
- **Work-sharing.** Work-sharing divides a job (and its salary) between two people. If the participants work in this manner for lack of alternative, then what actually exists is part-time work used to conceal the extent of unemployment. And since the participants are sharing one salary, rather than earning a full salary, it increases poverty while decreasing unemployment—a doubtful gain.
- **Universal service.** Voluntary or compulsory national service, similar to the Civilian Conservation Corps of Depression days, is offered as a way to take large numbers of people out of the normal labor market. Military service sometimes serves this purpose. The details of such plans are usually vague and bear the earmarks of hopes rather than of programs.
- **Reducing retirement age.** The removal of older workers from the labor force through a lowered age of mandatory retirement frees jobs for younger people. However, as technology decreases the need for human labor, such attrition might reduce the labor force in the aggregate, without opening up job opportunities. And reducing the retirement age goes counter to the entire trend of present social movement toward abolishing mandatory retirement.
- **Government as employer of last resort.** Using this method, the government would employ everyone who cannot otherwise find work. In no known case has this been tried as a general solution, although Egypt, for example, guarantees a government job to every university graduate who cannot find one otherwise. The result is a horde of overtrained government clerks with absolutely no work to do.

Public Works Administration workers construct a school destroyed by fire in LeRoy, Michigan.

PHOTOS COURTESY OF FRANKLIN D. ROOSEVELT LIBRARY

Public Works

In the 1930s, the Public Works Administration and Civilian Conservation Corps were set up to help Americans recover from massive unemployment. Today, similar programs are frequently proposed as cures for the growing unemployment of the 1980s.

Civilian Conservation Corps youths build tiny dams to halt water runoff that causes erosion.

"In short, the goal should be full *un*employment."

Some Radical Proposals

None of the proposals put forth to date can overcome mass, permanent unemployment. Human labor is not only increasingly unnecessary but is beginning to be seen as an inefficient substitute for advanced technology.

The failure of current attempts to do away with unemployment, or even to reduce it, arises from unwillingness to recognize that the amount of human labor available is much greater than that needed for the production of goods and services. The assumption that there is work for all if only the right formula or combination could be found leads to the promotion of labor-intensive industries and services, even though machines could do the job better, faster, and cheaper. People are condemned to difficult, demeaning, unsatisfying work as a condition for financial maintenance, and those who don't or can't work are stigmatized.

What is needed is a planned, conscious movement toward the highest technology possible, replacing human effort in every area for which changes in methods, machines, and materials can be found. In short, the goal should be full *un*employment. Paradoxically, the elimination of unemployment requires that it be widened to include the majority, if not nearly all, of society. This way, it will be seen as a social good rather than a social ill. When only 10% of the population produces all the goods and services needed, the remaining "unemployed" 90% will look at unemployment in a much different light.

We must cease trying to find work for people to do; instead, we must bend every effort to replace them with machines. Then we can pose new questions: Assuming a society in which automation has taken over the bulk of work (and therefore jobs), through what mechanisms will people be supported? How will their situations be defined so that they will feel free of stigma? What activities will structure their time, give them identity, cause them to feel needed and wanted? These are the questions that proposals to eliminate unemployment must seek to answer.

Guaranteed Incomes

A guaranteed minimum income for everyone, whether they work or not, was originally conceived as a method whereby social workers could avoid inflicting the presumed stigmatizing "means test" on their clients. It was later proposed as a simplified method of aiding those who could not, or should not, work—the aged, the handicapped, single parents of small children, and the unemployable.

The basic difficulty in adopting a guaranteed-income plan is the fear that people would not work if they were given money. But in an almost completely automated society, work incentives would not be an issue.

There are other questions that must be resolved, however. First, how would income be distributed? One possibility is for the kind of family or children's allowance that is common in almost every Western country. Instead of paying the money based on number of children, or to a legally defined family, however, grants would be made to every individual—a personal-allowance scheme, so to speak.

Second, how much would each person be paid? If everyone is given the same amount, in accordance with the theory of equality, then people with special or additional needs would suffer. If payments are made on the basis of categories of people—the aged, parents, middle aged, etc.—the question of special individual needs remains. If payments are to be based on individual need, in accordance with the theory of equity, then need determination may be extensive, expensive, and complicated.

Third, how would society acquire and distribute the fruits of automated production—via taxes, insurance, nationalization, or some other means? Finally, how will people spend their time? This is not just a matter of avoiding boredom, which may require an enormous expansion of leisure-time skills and activities, but has to do with what will replace work in terms of prestige, time-structuring, personal identification, and so on. People are already increasingly identified by their leisure-time pursuits rather than by their work.

These are difficult, but solvable, problems. In fact, devising answers to the questions will be the simple part of the problem; finding methods of implementing them in a manner that will not create social unrest and upheaval is more difficult.

Redefining Work

A simple way of arriving at a satisfactory "workless" society is to redefine work, paying people to engage in activities that are currently unpaid. The most obvious example is paying housewives for what they do. A less obvious example is to pay people for engaging in socially desirable activities, such as studying, playing games or sports, entertaining others, playing musical instruments, and writing, or for activities such as parenting, neighboring, tutoring (including one's own children), gardening, and exploring.

In this way, people could be given income for a wide variety of desirable activities and could avoid the stigma and other consequences of being unemployed. Payments could be scaled to performance, such as good students being paid more than poor ones. Not only could musicians be paid according to ability, but also composers, conductors, and even those who tune musical instruments, print the music, and turn the pages.

Although at first glance this proposal seems fanciful, if not fantastic, a moment's reflection will indicate that society already pays certain people to engage in just those activities. Baseball, football, and basketball players are well supported, but only when they have achieved a certain level of skill. Why can't everyone who wants to play ball be supported by the fruits of automated production, even if the level of skill determines the level of support? Musicians are certainly paid in our society, and entertainers of various kinds are not only paid but paid lavishly, as are those who write for them or do their clothes and make-up. Students are supported by stipends, and some of these already make academic attainment a condition of continuation.

Since foster parents and child-care professionals are paid to take care of other people's children, why shouldn't natural parents also be compensated for their time and ability?

Similarly, helping one's neighbors is not necessarily restricted to unpaid activities. Many countries use "paid volunteers" on a community basis to bring services to those needing them. Israel's "Aged Helping the Aged" program supplements the income of elderly helpers, gives them the feeling that they are useful, and provides services that the social-welfare system is not large enough to offer. Community health aides are used in other countries, as are agricultural assistants. Other examples of paid neighboring abound.

Canada supports aspiring writers through direct grants and grants to supporting agencies. In many countries, grant organizations fund a variety of careers, from artist to researcher. This could be extended to many other kinds of consultants, counselors, advisors, and others who now act on a volunteer basis.

In short, the automated society would pay people for doing what they enjoy, within the limits of socially approved behavior. Such a program overcomes the problem of time-structuring, since the activities undertaken would clearly require some sort of time commitment. Similarly, with payments linked to achievement, it would be a spur to ambition. With special payments for creativity and originality, many wellsprings of progress might be uncovered. Positive self-images and social identity would be linked to the activity performed.

There might remain the problem of those with neither interests nor skills. For these, a basic payment might still be provided, even if their activities consisted of watching television, drinking beer, and playing cards, as long as it was not anti-social.

Cooperatives

One method of overcoming unemployment, or its effects, is through ever-widening circles of cooperatives, in which the income is divided among all members, including those not working. With the merging of co-ops, ever-larger units can be included, until income from all work done is shared equally among everyone.

Even when the co-op members have little to do, they are not considered unemployed as long as they are members of the group, and they are supported by the income of the total cooperative. Widespread ownership of automated industries and services by co-ops would, in a sense, make the members owners and thus not unemployed even if they do no work.

This is not outside the realm of the possible. Workers could purchase robots to replace themselves and then lease these out to employers, living on the profits of robot labor. A $41,000 robot, lasting eight years, will cost less than $5 an hour to buy and operate, as compared with $15 per hour paid one employee in the auto industry. In Japan, a robot leased for $90 can turn out work that would cost $1,200 if done by humans. By the turn of the century, robot labor may be down to about 70¢ an hour. The purchase of several robots by co-ops of (former) workers may be

Tenor Luciano Pavarotti sings in the San Francisco Opera production of Verdi's Un Ballo in Maschera.

"Full Unemployment"

An opera star and a pro basketball player are paid handsomely for doing what they do, even though it is not "work" in the traditional sense. In a society of "full unemployment," people could earn a living income for a wide variety of activities, suggests author Macarov.

Boston Celtics star Larry Bird handles a rebound during the 1983 NBA All-Star game, of which Bird was named Most Valuable Player.

more feasible than on an individual basis, while owning several kinds of robots might avoid seasonal or employment fluctuations.

Cooperatives are not a dream. A number of countries, notably in Scandinavia, have used cooperative industries extensively, with good results. Indeed, the spread of cooperatives until they encompass the total economy is not even dependent upon the advent of the technological society. Co-ops, by their nature, obviate unemployment as it is now understood.

Collectives

Going beyond cooperatives, which divide proceeds among members, there is the possibility of collectives, which provide for all their members' needs (and many of their wants) from the income of the group. Perhaps the best-known example of the large-scale permanent collective is the Israeli kibbutz. Kibbutzim are voluntary collectives in which all of the property is owned by all of the members in common, and in which all of the members' needs—including child care, education, health care, housing, necessities, amenities, vacations, and care of parents—are taken care of by the group.

Perhaps the most salient difference between the kibbutz collective and other social forms is that the type and amount of support are in no way linked with the kind or amount of work done by the member. Income is based purely on need.

Although kibbutzim were originally founded as agricultural communities, with a very heavy emphasis on human, or individual, labor, many have recently made great strides in technology. Thus, finding work for all the members has become a problem for some of these collectives. Accepting life without work as it is currently defined has been difficult for them, but kibbutzim have always supported members who paint, make music, sculpt, and—to a lesser extent—write.

Overcoming Unemployment

Overcoming unemployment will require a basic change in current

Kibbutz Dance Company of Israel in rehearsal.

The Kibbutz Solution

In the Israeli kibbutzim, technology has greatly reduced the need for human labor, enabling members to pursue alternative forms of "work." Kibbutz members are supported on the basis of need rather than on the type or amount of work they do.

Combines harvesting on Israeli kibbutz.

societal values. Work will have to be dethroned from its present central position in the pantheon of values. Changes in societal structures, to achieve a basis for income distribution other than through jobs, will also be necessary. Paradoxically, these changes will probably come about only as the result of a massive increase in the number of the unemployed—a situation of "full unemployment," which technology is rapidly bringing into being.

If the experience of the past is any indication, the workless society is not to be feared. In ancient Greece, which was a complete welfare state for citizens, the work was done by slaves—free men were neither expected nor encouraged to work, since, according to Plato, Aristotle, and Socrates, work made a person a bad friend, a bad patriot, and a bad citizen. The result of such a "workless society" was the beginnings of modern drama, dance, philosophy, mathematics, geometry, astronomy, sculpture, and many other arts and sciences.

Freed from the day-to-day exigencies of making a living, people were able to be creative in widely different fields, enjoying life as they did so. There is no valid reason to believe that modern humanity will experience a different outcome. On the contrary, the workless society might usher in the most fertile period of imagination, creativity, and originality that the world has yet seen, raising mankind to a new threshold of self-fulfilling, happy lives.

About the Author

David Macarov, WFS chapter coordinator for Jerusalem, Israel, is an associate professor at the Paul Baerwald School of Social Work, The Hebrew University, Jerusalem, 91905, Israel. He is the author of several articles and books, including *Worker Productivity: Myths and Reality* (1982) and *Work and Welfare: The Unholy Alliance* (1980)

This article is adapted from his paper "Overcoming Unemployment: Some Radical Proposals," published in *Creating a Global Agenda: Assessments, Solutions, and Action Plans*, the WorldView '84 conference volume, which is available for $14.50 from the World Future Society Book Service (pre-payment required; please include $2 for postage and handling).

Lane Kirkland

Labor Unions Look Ahead

Changes in the economy, in the labor force, and in the types of work being done will bring changes for unions in the United States.

Despite what you may have read or heard, unions in America do indeed have a future.

Everything the crepe hangers are saying about the labor movement today we have heard before. In remarks to the American Economic Association some years back, a certain eminent professor said that trade unionism was of "lessening importance . . . in American economic organization. . . ." Trade unionists did not believe the professor's prognostications when they were uttered—in 1932, when unions had 2 million members. Today, their ranks number 13.5 million. But in deflating the doomsayers, we must not minimize the difficulties facing the labor movement.

At the top of the list is chronic, high unemployment. To some, it may seem strange to talk about high unemployment when we have seen the official jobless rate drop over the last few years, and when supply-side medicine men are boasting of having created millions of new jobs. But let's put the current employment picture in perspective.

Even today—at the peak of the supposed boom—unemployment is higher than at the very depths of the 1971 recession. The official unemployment rate doesn't count those who have become too discouraged to look for work. And it doesn't count part-time workers who want full-time jobs. Include them, and the real rate of unemployment jumps several percentage points.

A reserve army of the unemployed makes it difficult for unions to organize and bargain—and it always has. And it makes it tempting for employers to indulge their fantasies of getting rid of a union. Years ago, railroad executive Jay Gould claimed he could hire half the working class to kill the other half. Some employers apparently still believe that—and they see heavy unemployment as the ideal condition for testing the theory.

These employment statistics are evidence of other forces at work on the American economy and American society. The labor movement may feel their effects most acutely. But the problems they create are not only labor's problems: They will touch everyone.

Changing Employment Patterns

Three decades ago, a third of the work force was directly engaged in manufacturing. Today—as any visitor to Minnesota's Iron Range well

THE FUTURIST, May-June 1986

AFL-CIO members attend a regional conference. Changing union membership is reflected by the fact that over 40% of union members now work in white-collar and technical jobs.

knows—only a fifth of the work force earns its paycheck in basic industries. During the same period, the number of Americans in service jobs has nearly doubled, from 12% three decades ago to 22% today.

Some of this is the irreversible result of technological change. The steel mills and assembly plants that were the Second World War's arsenal of democracy can today be manned by fewer workers. In the last few years alone, more than 2 million jobs have been lost in the manufacturing sector. A great many of those lost jobs belonged to union members.

But technology is not the only problem. Many of the jobs that have been lost in America have turned up in foreign countries. Just five years ago, the U.S. trade *surplus* in goods was $40 billion. This year, the U.S. trade *deficit* will hit $140 billion. That deficit represents almost 4 million jobs that have left the country, possibly never to return.

What has happened to unions is a measure of what has happened to America. The steady erosion of America's industrial base is depriving millions of young American workers of the stable, well-paying jobs that sustain their standard of living and offer admission to the working middle class. Trapped in low-paying service jobs, they see the American dream fading fast.

For the first time, we have a young generation of Americans who do not expect to do as well as their parents. Their opportunities are shrinking, and so are their hopes. No one should believe themselves immune from the damage. Ask the shopkeepers of Johnstown, Pennsylvania, what happens when the steel mills close. Ask the realtors of Flint, Michigan, what happens when the assembly lines shut down; ask them how many homes they sell to people earning the minimum wage flipping hamburgers in fast-food franchises. And ask those who earn their living from high technology where they will sell their mainframes or their robots or their lasers when their biggest customers—basic industries—are forced to shut down.

All this is to say nothing about what will happen to the tax base that supports our public schools and universities, and the avenues of opportunity they open up for bright, young students, no matter what their circumstances of birth. Anyone who thinks he or she is immune from these changes is living an illusion.

The Future of Labor Unions

But while these trends would appear to bode ill for the labor movement's future, a close examination tells a different story.

Unions today have fewer steel and automobile workers in their ranks, because there are fewer of them. But at the same time, they have more than 11 times as many teachers; 10 times as many state, county, and municipal workers; 4 times as many pilots; 3½ times as many service employees; 3 times as many actors and artists; and more than twice as many postal workers, fire fighters, and communications workers as they did 30 years ago.

More than 40% of union members today work in white-collar and technical jobs. Another 23% are craftsmen and supervisors. Less than 40% of union members work in blue-collar jobs. And unions affiliated with the AFL-CIO have a higher proportion of members with college degrees and with graduate degrees than the population at large.

The labor movement is the first line of defense for all the plain people who have no desire to rule or live high on the hog at the expense of others—all the people who ask only for a decent job that will support a decent family and enable them to pay the bills, retire the mortgage, and give the kids a decent start in life.

That is not to say that the path for trade unionists will be free and clear in the future. Unions face changes—changes in technology, changes in the makeup of the work force, changes in materials and production patterns and job patterns, changes in relations with employers and government. A new labor force has grown up around them, and the trade union share of it has dropped. And unions are operating in a hostile political environment.

As Hubert Humphrey once said, "The future is all that is left." The labor movement has a future and will always have a future because at its core it stands for some fundamental American values.

About the Author

Lane Kirkland is president of the AFL-CIO. His address is 815 16th Street, N.W., Washington, D.C. 20006. This article is adapted from the annual Carlson Lecture at the Hubert H. Humphrey Institute of Public Affairs, University of Minnesota, delivered by Kirkland on November 18, 1985.

Cynthia Burton and Edward Cohen-Rosenthal

Collective Bargaining for the Future

Collective bargaining is usually viewed as a way to settle past differences between labor and management. But if bargaining is to succeed for both parties, it must be viewed as a method of shaping the future.

Collective bargaining can be a creative way to manage the future for employers and employees. Often, collective bargaining seems like a dry tug-of-war between warring factions. Yet behind the institutional struggles are people whose lives and families often depend on the quality of the outcomes. Rather than discuss trends in wages or benefits, we focus here on a new process for collective bargaining that alters both the content of agreements and the nature of the relationship between labor and management.

There are essentially two ways to conduct win–win negotiations: integrative bargaining and strategic bargaining. *Integrative bargaining* focuses on a particular problem and, through joint problem solving, creates new solutions in which both parties wind up further ahead than they would have through traditional, win–lose distributive collective bargaining. The process encourages creativity and discourages polarization. By turning today's problems into tomorrow's solutions, integrative bargaining provides a bridge to the future.

Strategic collective bargaining builds on integrative models by bringing to bear a holistic perspective to creating a common future. This article focuses on the strategic approach due to its possibilities for bringing future thinking into the workplace, though the more targeted and less encompassing integrative models will probably be used more frequently.

Labor and Management's Concern for the Future

For both labor and management, looking to the future is vitally important. Management predicts a demand for certain services and goods and then schedules the labor, provides the technology, and obtains the raw materials. All of these require foresight. For the overall organization, management must consider emerging markets, changing technology, manpower needs, shifting competition, resource availability, and other future variables. It is the ability to prepare for the future well that undergirds the management function. Attending only to the present leads to an unattended future. The past is a set of indicators and a potential resource for an organization, but its survival depends on how well it meets its future.

The union's major roles are to present the interests of its membership to management and the public at large and to protect the gains already made from erosion in the future. But if redressing past mistakes is all that is done, then there is little future for the union. People join unions because of hopes for a better future. They make a statement that together they have improved prospects for their future.

Collective Bargaining As a Common Forum

Too often, managers view collective bargaining as a drag on organizational performance, or — at best — irrelevant. But collective bargaining can be the forum where labor and management consider their future and order a relationship that best addresses their common desire for future success. Labor and management can determine their common future by employing more creative collective-bargaining strategies.

Traditionally, most collective bargaining is oriented toward the past. In other words, most contracts are responses to experiences in the previous contract period rather than anticipations of the future. Labor and management look at what has been done to them over the term of the previous agreement. They put together a list of all of the things that have gone wrong over that period and make demands to rectify those mistakes. If a supervisor engaged in a behavior that rubbed the membership the wrong way, a provision is put forward to prohibit that action. If union members "got away" with something in the past, then a new rule is proposed by management.

But a collective-bargaining agreement is fundamentally oriented toward the future. The agreement sets patterns of relationships and compensation for the next one to three years. It specifies what will be the relationship *after* the contract is ratified. Since collective bargaining inevitably shapes the future of each party, we ask, Why not use the agreement-making process as a way to deliberately examine and create a coherent common approach to the future?

Strategic collective bargaining goes beyond the traditional reactive bargaining found in most settings. The fact is that labor and management are tied together into the future. This means that, even if there are personality or issue conflicts, they need to cooperate to move forward. Strategic approaches enable the parties to leapfrog over past differences so they can focus on where they should be and avoid getting stuck on one or two issues.

The Strategic-Bargaining Process

Strategic collective bargaining can take place in the private or public sectors. In the private sector, the primary focus is on the relationship of the company to the marketplace and profitability. This allows the parties to share the financial and other results of success in the marketplace. In the public sector, strategic approaches encourage the bargainers to focus on public purposes rather than petty regulation of employee behavior.

Strategic collective bargaining begins with a scan of the common environment of the two parties. The parties are asked to look realistically at the past, the present situation, and their probable 10-year future for key variables affecting their organization. The key items are: product or service; market, including competition; natural, fiscal, and energy resources; technology; human resources; and economic and social trends. The gestalt of these variables affects bottom-line performance and work life.

For example, we worked with management and union representatives in a paper mill seeking to anticipate their future. They had to deal with changes in their customer base and use of their product, new product-quality demands, strong competition, growing foreign competition, the rapid pace and high cost of new technology, the availability of groundwood, and the possibility of more stringent pollution controls. We found that in a two-day session this process was eye-opening and mind-expanding for both parties.

General Motors management and the United Auto Workers have created the new Saturn division by working together to plan every aspect of its future course even before one brick was laid or any worker was hired to build the car. Technology, marketing, operations, and human-resource use were all considered as part of an overall package. They signed an innovative labor agreement that was both a reflection and a product of their joint effort.

The way the review is handled depends on the nature of the organizations involved and their resources. It can be a supplement or a spur to strategic planning by the employer and/or the union. It could range from simply sharing impressions by each party of opinions and presumptions to more in-depth reviews of each topic. If in-

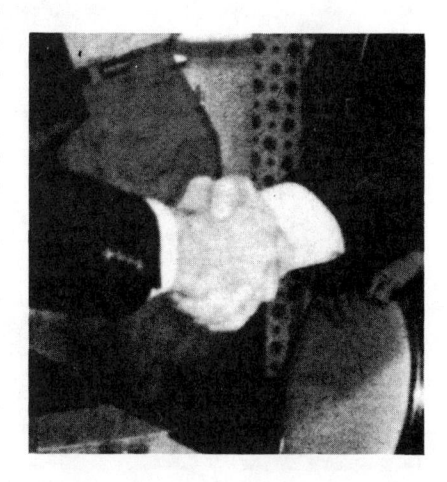

> "The fact is that labor and management are tied together into the future. This means that, even if there are personality or issue conflicts, they need to cooperate to move forward."

> "Joint teams should be set up to study each major objective and to propose specific actions. Issues that raise problems are flagged and brought to the bargaining table for resolution."

Union and management get down to business at bargaining table. Both labor and management have a strong interest in the future and can learn creative bargaining techniques for shaping that future.

ternal resources are available to the employer and/or the union, presentations could be made by one or both parties based on their data and analysis.

In some cases, outside experts could be used to inform and supplement internal resources and perspectives. It is not important at this stage that the parties agree with each other but that there is a full sharing of information and assumptions. Assumptions by either party should be questioned and challenged — not for adversarial scoring of points, but to help test their validity.

Common knowledge of the situations and the assumptions of both parties sets the groundwork for the development of joint strategic goals and objectives. When the parties make assumptions about the future of an organization, they consciously or unconsciously trigger responses to proposals on the bargaining table. Strategic bargaining makes these assumptions public, allows them to be tested, and provides a context for understanding them.

Joint objectives could include items such as maintaining profitability, meeting competitive pressures, pursuing modernization of technology, updating skills of employees, achieving maximum employment stability, improving market share, creating a safe and healthful work environment, establishing a positive image and presence in the community, etc. There need not be total agreement, but there should be an overlap of concerns. Each party may attach different weighting to objectives, but the bottom-line goal of strategic collective bargaining is to create a community of common interest.

Some objectives may be in conflict. So long as the objectives that are not in common do not threaten the basic survival of the other organization—e.g., establishment of

AFL-CIO

a union-free environment or elimination of the enterprise — then differences can be acknowledged and respected. For example, in some circumstances, the parties will agree that productivity increases are mutually desirable; in other places, this will not be an objective shared by labor.

Common objectives form the basis for strategic collective bargaining. At this point, the focus of the parties is on how to turn their common objectives into realities. The means of doing so may be the compensation systems, work classifications, grievance structures, work-time arrangements, and advancement mechanisms traditionally found in contracts. However, the common objectives may also focus on joint approaches to new technology, health and safety, resource use, education and training, marketing, quality, product development, and other critical areas of the organization's operations.

The parties can go directly into collective bargaining with each side presenting proposals designed to meet the common objectives and other particular concerns. The common understanding of the critical variables in the scan and the common objectives provide a basis for assessing proposals and a test for common agreement. Preferably, joint teams should be set up to study each major objective and to propose specific actions. Issues that raise problems are flagged and brought to the bargaining table for resolution.

Some strategies may not fit neatly within the term of one agreement, but future directions can be identified. The partners need to develop concrete plans for implementing their objectives and engage in ongoing monitoring to ensure that their plans are being implemented and their joint objectives are being met.

Outcomes of Strategic Bargaining

At the very least, strategic collective bargaining provides common understanding of the future. For many organizations, this spur to conceptualizing the future can be in itself critical to success. The process does not require that there be unanimity between management and labor.

There will be objectives in common and those that are not shared. Further, the parties may have very different perspectives on how to achieve common goals. They will be moving toward meeting their common concerns, which will help advance the interests of both parties. Where there are differences, they will thrash them out as they have done in the past, but the knowledge of the common possibilities should help moderate the intensity of disagreement and contain the conflict.

At best, strategic collective bargaining provides a community of interest in the future. The technique involves employees in long-range planning for the enterprise and helps to mesh labor–management agreements with a desirable future for everyone involved. It provides an orientation to the future that educates and motivates employees and their organizations to take concrete actions.

Because this process avoids reactive approaches to bargaining and substitutes anticipatory models, a new, more positive future opens itself to those at work. Collective bargaining is transformed from tactics of containment to means of common construction. It is no longer purely incremental but aims to be comprehensive. The real purpose of collective bargaining to help order the future can be more directed, more imaginative, and more successful when viewed strategically.

BURTON    COHEN-ROSENTHAL

About the Authors

Cynthia Burton is vice president and Edward Cohen-Rosenthal is president of ECR Associates, 2421 Everton Road, Baltimore, Maryland 21209. They are co-authors of *Mutual Gains: A Guide to Union–Management Cooperation* (Praeger, 1987).

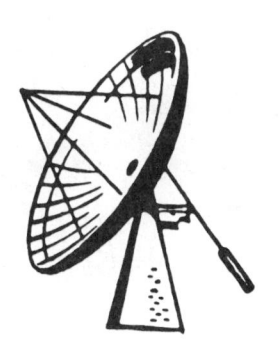

Labor Union Uses Satellite

Unions are becoming some of the fastest-growing users of satellite communications. The satellites are used to link together local and state branches of a union, to hold teleconferences, to deliver public-affairs and educational programming, and to transmit live or taped television signals to the news media. The Labor Institute of Public Affairs (LIPA), the media arm of the AFL-CIO, recently signed a multiyear contract with a satellite transmission provider, Washington International Teleport. According to the labor group, satellite communications will better link the scattered branches of the organization and will bring substantial savings in time and money for travel and management. LIPA's first video conference using the service will take place this year.

Right to Work Skills

Future labor negotiations may focus more on workers' rights to acquire work *skills* than on simply the right to work, says Robert Smith, president of The Futures Group, a management-consulting firm based in Glastonbury, Connecticut. Retraining is an ever more significant issue in occupations vulnerable to layoffs and displacement due to automation. In one agreement, between the United Auto Workers and GM and Ford, the companies set aside 5¢ an hour for each employee into a training fund.

Roger B. Smith

Creating A 21st Century Corporation

Now is the time to begin planning and building the businesses of tomorrow, says the chairman of one of the world's largest corporations.

Life today is more complex than ever before. We live now in an age of perpetual, unprecedented change. This makes planning for the future absolutely critical—and infinitely more difficult.

In his book *Future Shock*, Alvin Toffler gives a striking example of the accelerating rate of change. Toffler likens the past 50,000-year history of humankind to 800 lifetimes—a lifetime being a little over 60 years. He describes a progression that goes something like this:

The first 650 lifetimes were spent living in caves. That means we've been living in constructed dwellings for only the last 150 lifetimes. Only in the last 70 lifetimes has it been possible to pass the written word from generation to generation. The printing press was developed about eight lifetimes back. Accurate time measurement has only been possible for about four lifetimes. And only in the past two lifetimes has anyone, anywhere, used an electric motor. Toffler concludes that the vast majority of all the material goods and services we use today have been developed in the present lifetime.

Each of us has seen dramatic trends take shape in this present lifetime, including:
- The majority of American women now working outside the home.
- Radical changes in the family unit and in childbirth and divorce rates.
- Telephones and television sets in almost every room.
- The rapid growth in number and acceptance of VCRs, cable, and home computers.
- Greater personal travel, mostly by automobile and airplane, than ever before.

Clearly, change can no longer be considered an aberration: It is the norm.

Business Planning for the Future

In an age of perpetual change, planning presents a special problem for business. For example, how do you plan a product with a five-year lead time? And with markets changing and competition intensifying almost daily, how do you plan and develop systems to guide your company through the present and on to the twenty-first century?

Business's only answer is to plan for change as a way of life. Rather than making only occasional and drastic course corrections, business must now get out in front of the change curve and lead change rather than follow it.

Business must invent a whole new concept of itself. It must see itself not landbound by tradition and predetermined plans but rather flowing along with the river of change. It must work with nature, not against it. It must make progress by changing the very essence of the enterprise, by creating new opportunities, and by creating its own future.

Having an effective plan for crisis is usually about 90% of the solution to that crisis. But getting ahead of the change curve doesn't mean that business people must make advance plans for each and every contingency. You can go broke buying insurance. And you can paralyze an institution with too much planning. It's much more important to decide what steps you can reasonably take and what insurance you can afford to buy.

In General Motors' case, we've used such strategic planning techniques as competitive analyses, "environmental scanning" of pertinent issues, alternate-scenario studies, and computer modeling.

The Planning Process

It's important in the planning process to look far enough out to get an accurate perspective on your industry and your company's place in it. You then select a positive, long-term course of action for a plausible, possible, and desirable future—and you go with it.

That was exactly what General Motors did in the early 1980s. GM had just suffered a loss in net income of $763 million—its first annual loss since 1921. And the auto industry—and the nation—were still locked in a deep recession. Understandably, the first item of business was to organize a financial recovery plan.

Next, we took a long-term look at the future. The idea was to get ahead of change. We wanted to position ourselves so we wouldn't be playing "catch-up"—we'd be playing "leap over."

We started with the question of what we wanted to be in the twenty-first century. We wanted to offer the highest quality at the lowest cost. We wanted to be international in scope, and to make the most efficient use of our resources. We wanted the highest technology, the most innovative and creative people, and a very efficient supplier network. And we knew we would need new qualities of leadership—management with the vision to determine where the corporation should go, as well as the ability to involve the entire organization in that vision and to create enthusiasm and support for their ideas.

With our goals firmly in mind, the next step was deciding what it would take to get us there. We looked at what the competitive challenges would be and at our own strengths and weaknesses.

First, we saw that we needed to create a climate where employees felt free to contribute their knowl-

THE FUTURIST, November-December 1986

"In an era of perpetual change, even long-term strategies must be flexible."

edge and skills. We needed to build structures that fostered teamwork, innovation, and entrepreneurship. We wanted our corporate structures to encourage people to do what needed to be done and to do it on their own.

We also saw that we needed to broaden our business to counterbalance the severe cyclical trends of the automobile industry.

In our survey of our technological strengths, we saw great pockets of brilliance around the corporation. But we also saw pockets where the shine was not nearly as bright. It was obvious to us that, to get to the twenty-first century in the shape we wanted to be in, we would need massive help in several critical areas—robotics, machine intelligence, data processing, and systems engineering. The technology was just coming faster than we could adapt to it.

Becoming a Twenty-First-Century Corporation

At first, we thought we could contract out for help. But when we realized the size of the job, we saw that it wouldn't be practical to depend on outsiders for work that was integral to our operations. We needed somebody who could get inside our skin and be a part of us.

Ultimately—to address these several needs—we developed a strategy to make General Motors a twenty-first-century corporation. It had three major parts: reorganization, diversification, and acquisition.

The reorganization stretched from one end of the world to the other—from the top of the product line to the bottom. We restructured and rationalized our overseas business. We put our bus business up for sale and consolidated our truck business into a worldwide activity. And we reorganized our North American passenger car operations, creating two major groups out of eight separate divisions.

We even created a brand new organization, the Saturn Corporation, to develop not only a new car but a whole new way of making cars.

Altogether, these organizational changes moved the decision-making process closer to the marketplace and speeded up product development while reducing lead-time. The changes brought people closer together by eliminating unnecessary levels of management and by encouraging teamwork and participative management styles. And, by making the new units responsible for all aspects of their products, we fostered risk taking and entrepreneurship.

Through diversification, we were able to spread our risks over a broader base. For example, our financial subsidiary, General Motors Acceptance Corporation, entered the mortgage-servicing business in a big way. GMAC is now the second-largest mortgage-service company in the United States. It also offers homeowner's insurance to customers.

Our joint venture with a Japanese company created GMF Robotics, which now designs and produces robots for industry. And other new-business ideas, which might have been disregarded or given away in previous years, are now being explored and developed. One of these is a GM invention called Magnequench, a high-powered magnet that could revolutionize the electric-motor business. We are also moving into such areas as defense and space electronics and even artificial intelligence.

This is not to say we're heading for the exit in the car business. But we're becoming a more broadly based company, with diversified lines of business complementing and strengthening each other.

Another road to success in the twenty-first century is acquisition. For example, we knew we needed help in data processing and computer expertise. We got it by acquiring a computer services company, Electronic Data Systems, or EDS. We know General Motors can save billions of dollars with the right computer system, and EDS is working on that right now. Soon we will have an information-sharing network for employees, suppliers, plants, dealerships, and staff to draw on.

Complementing this capability is a major acquisition in the field of systems engineering—Hughes Aircraft. Systems engineering is what GM needs to create the factories of the future and the twenty-first-century car. Hughes is also an electronics company, and the car is well on its way to the day when all of its functions will be electronically controlled. In the works right now are electronically controlled anti-skid brakes, "active" suspensions, satellite navigation, collision

"People are a bigger part of the automation equation than anybody could have predicted."

avoidance systems, and electronic power steering.

Our needs in the machine intelligence area are being addressed through five new investments. These include four robotic-vision firms and an artificial-intelligence company.

We're also moving toward the twenty-first century via the joint-venture route. For example, we're learning many things from our joint venture with Toyota, New United Motor Manufacturing Company, which makes the Chevrolet Nova.

Overall, we think our strategy to become a twenty-first-century corporation is a sound one, and we're sticking to it. We think it has a long enough point of view to keep us ahead of most day-to-day developments.

Creating Flexible Long-Term Strategies

In an era of perpetual change, even long-term strategies must be flexible. They must adapt to new trends and changing conditions if they are to succeed.

For example, General Motors is making a substantial, long-term investment in automation. And each time we automate a plant, we'll probably do it a little differently—we hope with more sophistication and confidence—because of what we learned from the last experience. Each new automation project takes us—and our suppliers of high-tech equipment—that much further along the learning curve. Both of us are stronger as a result, and better prepared to meet the next challenge presented by the technological revolution.

One thing we've discovered, in almost every instance, is that people are a bigger part of the automation equation than anybody could have predicted. And much more up-front education and training of people will be required to reach the higher levels of automation. The joint-training centers we've established with the United Auto Workers and the educational programs set up at our plants and in community colleges have only begun to scratch the surface.

It's my own personal belief that with automation we may even have labor shortages—especially of trained people. It's true that the per-unit number of people required to make a conventional car may go down with increased mechanization. But we won't be building a conventional car—at least not by today's standards. We'll be building a much more complicated product with advanced electronic systems and other value-added items. That will potentially take more people. And so will the additional volume required by growing markets.

Our ventures into robotic-vision companies also demonstrate our efforts to stay flexible. The reason we invested in four robotic-vision companies is to have a sufficient number of options open—not only in robotic-vision companies but also in other major projects important to the business. The job is to track them and—precisely at the right time—to shed the ones that don't work.

Planning the future is still a very inexact science. And business is probably as prone as anyone else to making mistakes in this very gray and hazy area. But one thing I think we can say with certainty is that the future will not be like the past. It will be new. It will be different. It will be neither all good nor all bad. It will be what we make it by our actions today.

As Adlai Stevenson once observed:

There is a New America every morning when we wake up. It is upon us, whether we will it or not. The New America is the sum of many small changes—a new subdivision here, a new school there, a new industry where there had been swampland—changes that add up to a broad transformation of our lives. Our task is to guide these changes. For, though change is inevitable, change for the better is a full-time job.

About the Author

Roger B. Smith is chairman and chief executive officer of General Motors Corporation. His address is 3044 West Grand Boulevard, Detroit, Michigan 48202.

This article is adapted from his plenary speech at FutureFocus, July 16, 1986.

Management in the Third Wave

H. Alan Raymond

Western society has experienced three major waves of technological advances, each of which changed all aspects of living and working and engendered new challenges for world management.

As Alvin Toffler has pointed out, the First Wave developed when man discovered agricultural technology and switched to settlement from a subsistence and nomadic hunting and gathering society. In most areas of the world, this change began thousands of years ago. The Second Wave switch to industrial organization and technology began about a century ago for most of the world, though much of the world has remained in the agricultural First Wave. The Third Wave—the Information-Electronic Wave—began its major impact in North America and the world in about 1970, with the invention of the microchip.

Each of these waves required the demise of a previous social structure and its values, replacing it with new structures and values. Each shift was significantly wrenching and demanding. The United States, which shifted from a society based upon individual enterprise and localized markets in its agricultural period to one of mass markets, organization, and corporate enterprise, now appears to be shifting back to a period of individual enterprise and specialized markets based on information.

Businesses have been an integral part of the turmoil at each juncture. In the transition to the Third Wave, many businesses have apparently been unprepared or unwilling to confront the new demands for innovation, opportunities for creativity, challenges of constricting costs, and requirements for increased specialization and efficiency. Most businesses still view the world in industrial Second Wave terms of tight market control, employees rather than corporate partners, low cost inputs, simplified tasks and routine management, a slow speed

The revolutionary changes brought on by the microchip and information technologies caught many businesses off guard. Corporations that hope to be competitive in the Third Wave—and in the upcoming Fourth Wave—will have to be more flexible and human oriented, says author Raymond.

of business, giving the market (customer) what it will bear, and little or no innovation.

Many Western businesses found themselves in trouble as the Third Wave bore down on them. Some went out of business. Some asked the taxpayer for help. Some were absorbed in an acquisition or merger. Some limped along with their creditors and bankers, who were often reluctantly pulled into their difficulties. Others cried in their red ink that the competition, mainly the Japanese, had some kind of unfair advantage.

Some Western businesses have, however, made an effort to change with the times, transforming their organizational structure to one more suitable for this new period. Some have done this by copying the Japanese. General Motors, for example, has sent study teams to learn "how to do it right" from Japanese companies.

The Japanese and many other "new" competitors were forced to become more innovative, just as those in the West are now, in that they did not have any appreciable markets under control, and their supplies of raw materials and energy were relatively expensive. It is these "new" parameters of the Third Wave that many Western businesses are just now facing, to which the Japanese have already adapted.

Companies that chose reality recognized a world of accelerating competition, increasingly expensive resources, and increasingly demanding customers. The only

Female trainees line up for instruction at Boston Edison's Roslindale Substation during World War I. In the industrial Second Wave, businesses valued employee obedience and loyalty rather than individuality and innovation, and tasks were simplified to the lowest level so that workers could be as interchangeable as factory parts, says author Raymond.

way they could meet this challenge was to cut their costs, increase quality motivation, meet more specialized customer needs, and innovate faster than the competition. This process has been popularly known as "leaning and meaning." The process, however, also requires the cutting of corporate "fat," the accelerated introduction of technology (computers, robotics, and telecommunications), the continuous upgrading of personnel, and increasing dependence upon accurate "real time" information.

People in the Third Wave Corporation

Retraining and many education programs are often only temporary measures for displaced workers, as technology changes and labor becomes more easily and inexpensively replaced. The concept of employment is so central to industrialized society that we have never questioned it as a natural economic function. But for most of the first hundred years of the United States, employment was, except for small pockets, an anomaly. Most of the population developed their own enterprises in small farms or manufactures.

We may be entering another such era of individual enterprise. The need for labor as known during the industrial era is diminishing, and the basis of enterprise is shifting from materials to information. Information has become as widely available to the corporation as land once was. Third Wave corporations will invest in the workers and technologies that best extract and process this resource. This has already become apparent—not only to many workers, but also to many of their supervisors, the middle managers, who are also being displaced. Both groups will find that the only useful and profitable roles they can play are those they create themselves.

The New Social Structure And Economy

A premium was placed upon obedience and loyalty in the Second Wave industrial organizational structure. Thinking and innovation only upset rigid, planned structures and were not highly valued. Tasks including management were simplified down to their lowest level so that almost anyone could do them.

People, like parts, were interchangeable and standardized. Indeed, one of the proudest boasts of industrialist Alfred Sloan was that he had built an organization at GM that almost anyone could run. It may still be so at GM, but the probability is that it will not be so for much longer. Increasing competition will force the issue.

In contrast to the Second Wave, a new monetary premium is being placed on the individual, on thinking, on innovation, and on the speed and precision of execution. Decision making and responsibility are again required of the individual who may less easily pass the buck and must be financially responsible for his area or product, as the corporate pyramid flattens.

Decisions in a faster-paced economy cannot wait for endless committee meetings and analysis that would only allow the competition to win. Fast decisions require a maximum of information and instant and precise analysis. This, in turn, requires better and more highly educated personnel, who also must be innovative in using the new technology. At Honda, for example, all workers carry notebooks into which they enter ideas for technological and process improvements.

Individuals are becoming less easily interchanged and more intrinsic to the business. They are often given a "piece of the action"—shares in the company—to keep them. Workers at People Express, for example, all have a share in the company and thus have a stake in its success. Since they are all treated as managers, they all have input into the company's success or failure as well.

Companies in many sectors have come to recognize that each individual is becoming an entity of precisely applicable human capital that cannot easily be duplicated.

As decisions become increasingly made "where the action is," and personnel become better, the need for supervision, staff analysis, committee meetings, and reports lessens. The Third Wave organization begins to evolve into one that is less hierarchical, flatter, richer, faster, more precise, more information dependent, more innovative, more responsible, and interconnected through multiple electronic channels.

The role of the middle manager has changed, as a result, from a bureaucrat primarily concerned with the supervision of workers and business systems to an entrepreneur whose prime concern is motivation and project management. This trend has caused severe turmoil and stress among the ranks of middle managers who were used to administrating by formula and now find that they lack the

Managers gather to review videotapes at Seven-Up Company headquarters. Management in the Third Wave is moving beyond bureaucracies and toward democratization, with management by consensus and collaborative networks.

THE SEVEN-UP COMPANY

skills to manage and motivate. Many have been forced to find new careers or accept an early retirement.

The New Business Politics

There is a general feeling of anticipation and tension throughout the world, as the general population begins to sense the challenges and opportunities ahead.

Around the world, societies that for the last few decades have been building their social infrastructures have begun to shift toward a free-enterprise economy, recognizing that if they are to progress they need the energy and innovation of individual enterprise to take advantage of the new technology and compete effectively.

This trend has also had a marked effect on the workplace, as corporations progress toward increased industrial democracy. The worker-owned company, the union representative on the board of directors, and consensus management have become common. As these new energies and technologies are released and spread, they in turn increase the pressures of competition, forcing each government and economy further along this evolutionary route.

Bureaucratic politics of the Second Wave has begun to give way to the new collaborative networks of the Third Wave. Third Wave corporations must react with maximum speed, trust, efficiency, and effectiveness, and there is no room for the constant bickering that has characterized so many Second Wave organizations.

The way to advance in many Second Wave organizations was often to trip up someone else. But in the Third Wave corporation, since everyone is involved and responsible, the way to advance is to become as indispensable to people, networks, and the corporation as possible. This too rests upon having as much information and skill as possible, and in turn on having more technology. The technological-information edge and sharing it has become as important to the individual as it has to the corporation.

On the Horizon: The Fourth Wave

Using Toffler's framework, the Third Wave, based on information and electronic technology, will mature and become clearly dominant in the next 10 years. Another period of innovation and high growth will occur, lasting about 25 years. A third period of Third Wave innovation will take off and last us until about 2045, at which point (following the Kondratieff, or long-wave, cycle) the economy will decline until the next wave of technology comes into dominance in society and organizations: the Cybernetic Wave.

This Fourth Wave will be based on artificial intelligence and the application of human thought to electronic technology. Thought patterns will be read and linked into computer networks, creating unlimited global memory. This technology will also enable direct creation of products. Biochips, or some other technology, may connect the brain to computerized automated factories. As a result, products and services will be infinitely precise and individualized—"tailor-made."

Information will be interactive and generated continuously. Creativity will be instant, and innovation will be spontaneous. The corporation of the Fourth Wave will be integrated through computers and telecommunications and will be similarly linked with other corporations. Individuals will cross over the boundaries of such organizations, and each "employee" will be an entrepreneur with no strong ties to a single corporation. Linked into an international computer grid, all individuals will be able to benefit directly from their own productivity as well as that of the combined efforts of others in the Cybernetic Wave.

We are now in the turmoil of a period of rapid change. The United States, Japan, and some European countries will complete the transition into the Third Wave by early in the next century. The momentum of high-speed business and high-technology economies indicate that many developing countries now still in the First Wave will be pulled into the Third Wave, passing rapidly through the Second Wave.

Every trend, every significant event, contributes to the combined synergy of this momentum. Those corporations, nations, and individuals who would hope to survive and prosper had better run fast—and in the direction that the current is going.

Computer and information technologies allow Third Wave workers to maximize their individual potential for creativity and innovation. Advancement will come to those who develop their skills enough to work autonomously as entrepreneurs.

HEWLETT-PACKARD COMPANY

About the Author

H. Alan Raymond is executive vice president, Woodside Consulting Group. He is also adjunct professor at the University of San Francisco's McLaren College of Business Management Information Systems and teaches entrepreneurship at St. Mary's College in Moraga, California. His address is 7 Embarcadero West, #209, Oakland, California 94607.

Robert Rosenfeld and Jenny C. Servo

Business and Creativity

Making Ideas Connect

Many diverse skills are required in the innovation process. The organizations or businesses that succeed in the future will recognize and encourage these diverse skills in their employees.

Industry is interested in increasing the number of good ideas coming from employees. Attempts to do this have most commonly been made through investment in idea-generation systems. However, scarcity of ideas is not a problem with American industry. The failure of large organizations in America to innovate is primarily the result of a communication gap, not a decline in ingenuity.

Before elaborating on this point, some often misused terms need clarification. Creativity refers to generating new and novel ideas, whereas innovation refers to the *application* of an idea, leading ultimately to increased profit or improved services. Although creativity and innovation are temporarily and intimately related, they are distinct concepts. Creativity is an attribute that can be assigned to an individual. However, in today's complex society, innovation is almost always a collaborative enterprise, requiring the cooperation of numerous individuals.

Between the conception of an idea and the actual product lie considerable time, effort, and risk. Many good ideas never get beyond the originator's mind. The originator fails to connect with others who may possess the knowledge, tenacity, clout, or money necessary to transform the idea into a tangible process or product. Such unclaimed thoughts dissipate into thin air. Those that undergo a material transformation do so because of a tremendous investment of time and energy made by teams of individuals.

Material Transformation

Transforming an idea into a tangible product is a lengthy process. We will limit the discussion here to two types of innovation: those that involve evolutionary products/processes and those that involve revolutionary products/processes. The distinction between these forms of innovation is based on the degree of departure from conventional ways of thinking and the degree of organizational change that would be required for implementation.

Not every idea is worthy of transformation. However, for such a decision to be made, the technical feasibility and marketability of the

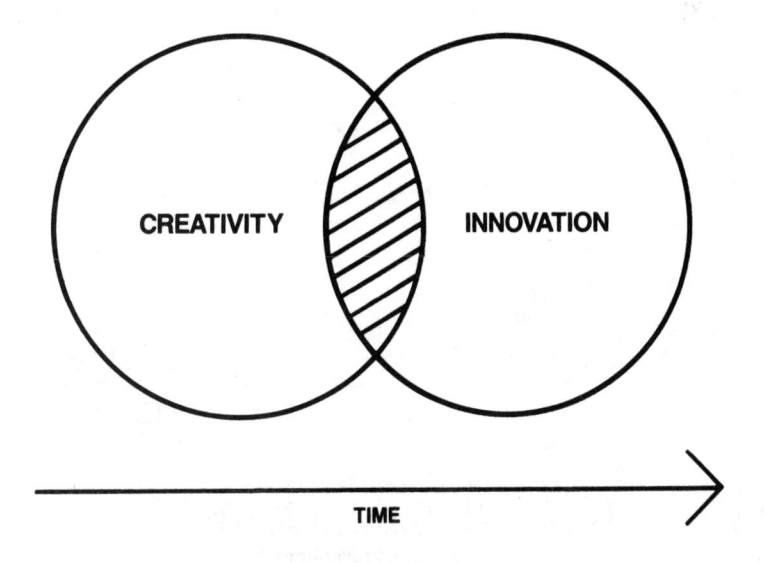

FIGURE 1: Relationship between the concepts of creativity and innovation.

THE FUTURIST, August 1984

idea need to be examined. In addition, consideration must be given to whether the idea fits a company's image or long-range strategic plans. Although this process sounds straightforward, it is actually quite complex. Numerous smaller decisions are made along the way, and greater reassurances are sought by the decision-maker as he or she makes the commitment to proceed. If the idea withstands careful scrutiny and a sponsor is found, it can then be introduced into the company's formal channels for development. However, the information needed to make such decisions may not be readily available to the "ideator"—the person who likes to generate ideas—or to first-line or middle management.

Communication Gaps

Getting an idea through an intricate corporate labyrinth is best likened to a relay race. If one does not appreciate the complexity of the process or does not know to whom the baton should be passed, ideas will falter. An idea may be dropped at various levels within a complex organization: (1) the originator, (2) middle management, and (3) across organizational boundaries.

Most originators are considered to be creative. Literature on creativity is replete with articles describing the personality characteristics of such people. In addition to having many positive characteristics, they have also been described as abrasive, hard to deal with, withdrawn, etc. One of the most valuable findings is that many creative people are ideators; that is, they are content with generating ideas but are easily bored with the long and difficult process of transforming ideas into something tangible. For some, generating ideas is a compulsion, a way of life over which they have very little control. Their minds are always buzzing with novel ideas. However, moving beyond the conception of the idea is something many of them are loath to do. They may mention the idea in passing to a colleague or may tinker with it. However, many creative individuals are unexcited by the idea-transformation process. "That's just straightforward engineering," they may say.

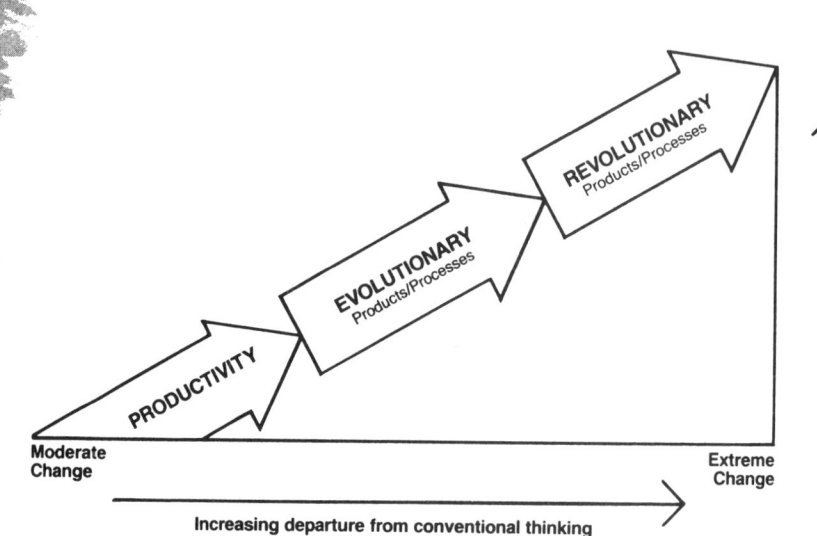

FIGURE 2: Innovation continuum of products and processes

Some management studies argue that failure to work on an idea is a form of irresponsibility and recommend that originators be provided with training on follow-through. However, there is often little incentive for the ideator to do so. Such individuals are commonly motivated not by money but by the intrinsic reward that comes with solving problems. Here is the first communication gap. The ideator may fail to bring the idea to the attention of someone else who has the disposition to follow through, or may bring it to a manager and expect that the idea will be pushed by him or her.

Even if the originator brings the idea to management, nothing may happen. Typically, managers are chronically overextended and may view a new idea that is outside their normal line of work as merely an annoyance interfering with as-

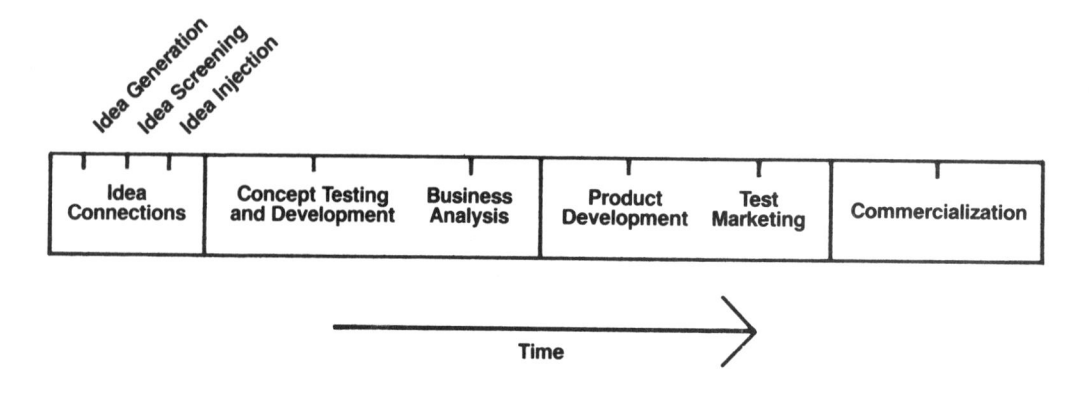

FIGURE 3: Stages in the Innovation Process

> "Creative style [can be defined] as the manner in which a person interacts with his environment when solving a problem."

signed objectives. Often managers simply do not know what to do with the ideas. As mentioned earlier, the information required to evaluate the potential value of an idea to the company is quite complex. It is unreasonable to expect that first-line or even middle management would necessarily have the perspective or information needed to deal effectively with such an idea. Clearly, ideas that would increase productivity in one's immediate area could be evaluated at this level. However, ideas that may turn into revolutionary products or processes most likely could not be evaluated at this level.

In addition to lacking the information required for such an evaluation, an increasing body of literature suggests that middle management is often selected on the basis of criteria that may preclude them from being good evaluators of such ideas at an early stage of maturity. Michael Kirton, director of occupational research at Hatfield Polytechnic in England, devised his Adaptation-Innovation inventory to measure just such differences in creative style. Kirton, along with psychologist Stanley Gryskiewicz, defined creative style as the manner in which a person interacts with his environment when solving a problem. According to their studies, there are "adaptive" and "original" styles of creativity. Adaptive people operate cognitively within the confines of the pattern in which they initially perceive a problem. They aren't likely to challenge the existing frameworks. On the other hand, individuals with an original style solve problems in a different fashion; they are more likely to treat patterns as a part of the problem. They redefine the problem, going outside of its original definition.

Studies suggest that individuals who submit ideas for evaluation have a creative style that is more original, whereas management tends to have a more adaptive style. Individuals with very different styles value characteristics that their opposites may not possess. Research done by the Center for Creative Leadership, located in Rochester, New York, indicates that those with a more adaptive style value precision, reliability, prudence, discipline, and conformity; those with a more original style, however, value tangential thinking, lack of structure, and challenge. One can see how individuals with such different styles of problem solving may find it difficult to work together or even to communicate effectively.

The second communication gap, then, occurs at the level of management. Management may not perceive the potential value of an idea, owing to a narrow perspective, a lack of information or vision, overextension, or differences in creative style. Hence, the ideas may not be passed beyond this management level to those who could evaluate the potential value of a revolutionary or evolutionary product/process idea.

In actuality, the expertise needed for such evaluations is housed in different sectors of large, highly bureaucratic, and mature companies: in reseach and development, marketing, manufacturing, administration, finance, etc. However, the physical separation, differences in jargon, and differences in mode of operation present a third barrier to communication: the fragmented expertise possessed by individuals isolated by organizational and cultural barriers.

Idea Connections

There are boundless opportunities for an idea to be dropped and few occasions for it to be carried through. Numerous approaches have been used either formally or informally in an attempt to prevent ideas from faltering. Tales abound of the heroic efforts made by inventors to push their ideas through bureaucratic mazes. Individuals such as Charles Kettering have taken it upon themselves to buck the system. They have bootlegged time, found contact people in various sectors of the company, and in general done outlandish things in order to get a hearing. However, not every originator has the drive or aggressiveness to do this.

Ideas can also survive if they are picked up by an internal entrepreneur ("intrapreneur") who, although not the originator of the idea, has the mettle required to fight for its implementation.

More recently, some formal approaches have been suggested by those aware of both the shortcomings and the strengths of originators and managers. Suggestions range from providing training for ideators on follow-through to providing incentives for management to push the ideas. Another approach has been tried at Eastman Kodak Company and is operating successfully in some sections of the company. At the suggestion of Kodak's Office of Innovation, this approach utilizes a "facilitator" with the responsibility to make idea connections. This responsibility is therefore not placed solely upon the individual ideator or manager, but the option to be involved is ever present. This approach is unique in its design, which allows workers to handle ideas that are outside their normal line of work.

The facilitator functions as a corporate ambassador, bridging communications gaps within and between organizational enclaves. He or she assists the ideator in elaborating upon the initial idea and in putting it into a form that can be readily communicated to others, and raises questions regarding feasibility, marketability, etc.

The facilitator, who is free to cut across the various organizational boundaries, sets up impromptu teams from various sectors of the

> "Too much emphasis has been placed upon ideas and individuals who generate them. But ideas lacking material form are of little value."

organization to serve as consultants. The facilitator also serves as a mediator at meetings between originators and consultants, attempting to anticipate the priorities and concerns of both sides. The facilitator should be aware of how to tailor issues, language, and presentation style to the various cultures existing within the organization. If the originator and the consultants feel that the idea is worth pushing, it may become the facilitator's responsibility to find a champion and perhaps a sponsor for the idea.

The Future

Organizational design for innovation is still in its infancy. However, some things are becoming increasingly clear. Too much emphasis has been placed upon ideas and individuals who generate them. But ideas lacking material form are of little value. Increased attention needs to be focused upon individuals who participate at various stages of the idea tranformation process: inventors, facilitators, "champions" (those devoted to a concept who will pursue it relentlessly), sponsors, and entrepreneurs.

Organizations need to make use of the rich diversity of human resources they contain. Those who enjoy generating ideas without following through on them should be allowed to do so. Those who enjoy taking risks and "bucking the system" should be encouraged and given guidance. Those who enjoy efficiency, structure, and routine should be steered into suitable jobs. We should delight in our differences and use them to organizational advantage, rather than insisting on sameness.

In the future, increased attention should be given to developing communication networks to facilitate idea evaluation and transformation. As organizations vary in their function and the nature of the people they attract, it is reasonable to expect that a diversity of communication networks will be required to meet the needs of different organizations. However, the goal of each of these networks will be the

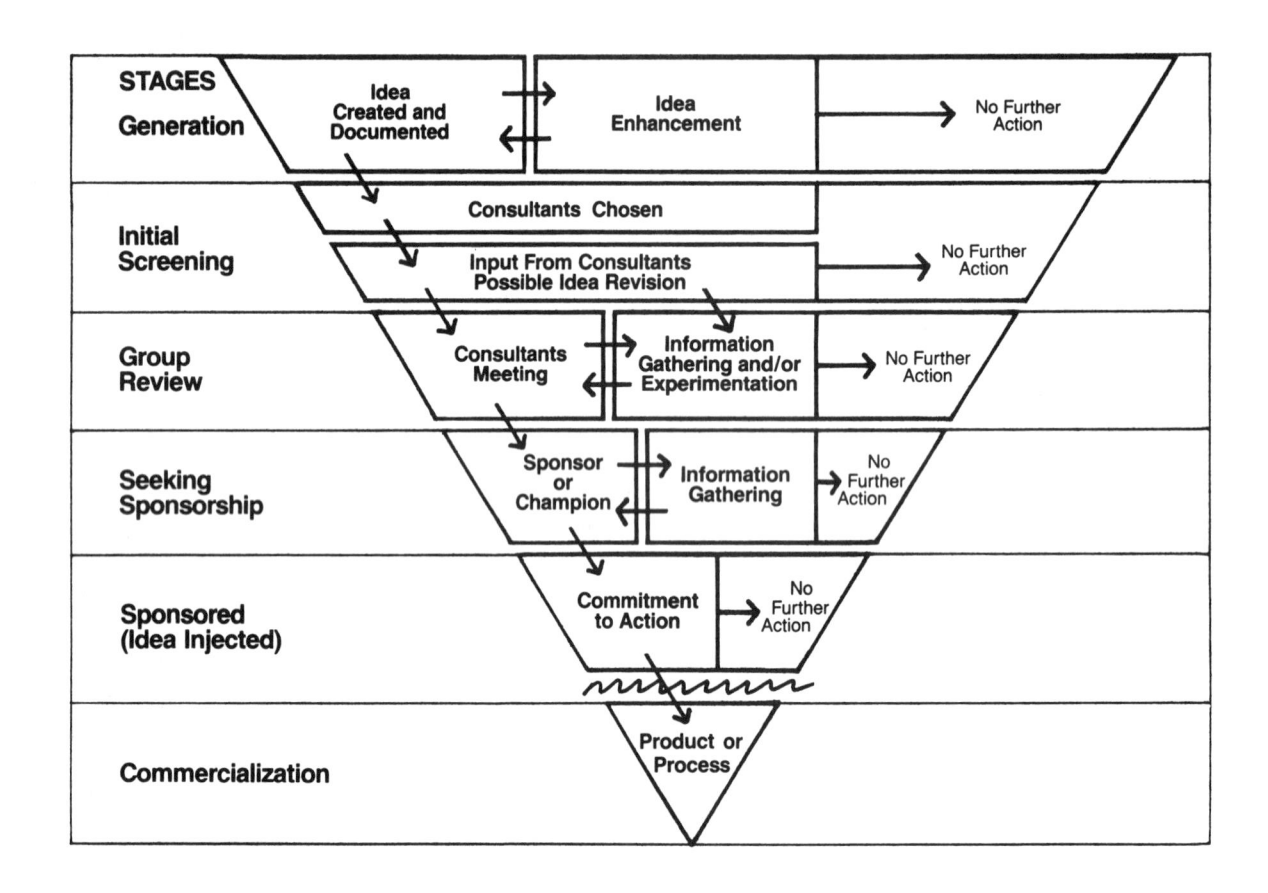

FIGURE 4:
Innovation/Idea Evaluation System
(Office of Innovation, Kodak Research Laboratories)

Putting square pegs into round holes is not the best way for a business to use the diversity of its employees, say the authors.

same: to assist the passage of an idea swiftly and carefully from the ideator to those individuals who have the expertise needed to determine the potential worth of an idea to the organization.

Also needed will be different types of internal organizational environments. These environments should be tailored to the employees' problem-solving styles and personalities rather than their job descriptions. In other words, many creative people work best in an unstructured environment and seem to be motivated more by problem solving and the satisfaction it imparts than by money. Other individuals who may serve as intrapreneurs might better be motivated by money or even the "thrill of victory." Still others involved in the later stages of idea transformation may prefer structure and precision. An organization, be it industrial, service, military, etc., should consciously strive to contain within it such diverse environments.

Organizations should know the strengths, weaknesses, motives, and needs of their employees. They should know which of their employees to call upon when different types of needs arise. Rather than throwing the whole organization into chaos when more innovation is desired, they should loosen up the reins in the areas that flourish under such conditions. Not all do.

Think of it as contained disorder, akin to what takes place within a nuclear reactor. Some individuals function better in unstructured environments (disorder) and can unleash creative energy under such conditions. However, unless this dynamic energy can be controlled and directed, it is destructive and will accomplish nothing. Likewise, other sections of the organization that are more structured, predictable, and proficient in money-making pursuits should harness ideas and turn them into innovative and productive products or processes. Both types of environment play invaluable roles.

How the diverse creative styles of individuals are used is reflected in corporate listening styles. Most of the time, organizations seem to be responsive to the suggestions made by individuals with an adaptive style. These individuals usually make suggestions that relate to increased productivity, efficiency, and slight variations in product lines. Clearly, it is advantageous to heed their suggestions, as this leads to reduced production costs and improved products. However, there is an upper limit to increases in productivity.

As productivity gains appear to be reaching their limits, the company must scout around for evolutionary and revolutionary

"As productivity gains appear to be reaching their limits, the company must scout around for evolutionary and revolutionary products or processes in order to keep its place in the market."

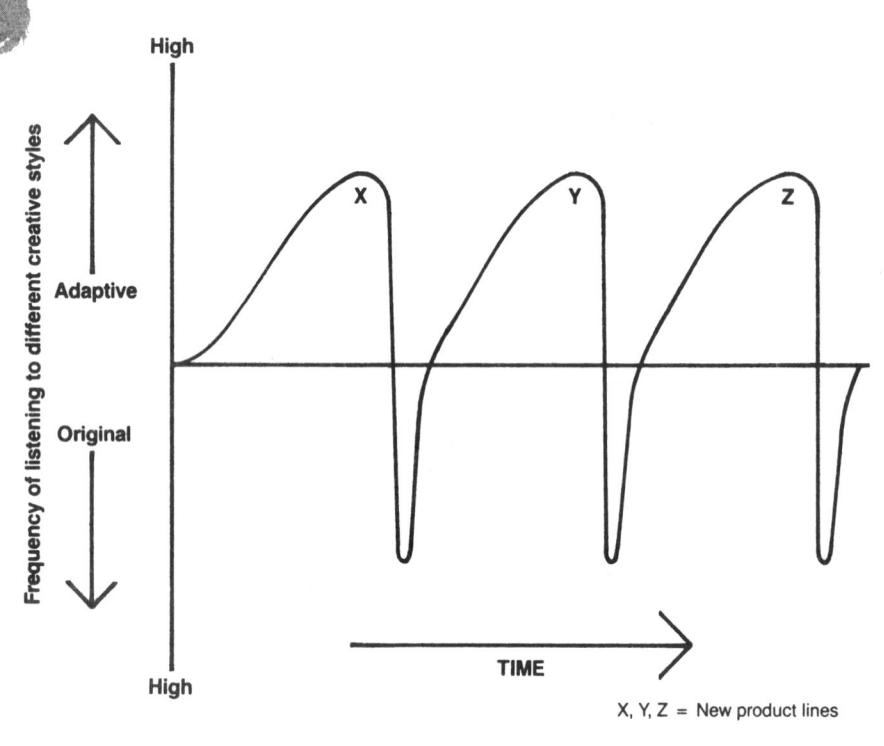

FIGURE 5: Model of Corporate Listening Styles

X, Y, Z = New product lines

products or processes in order to keep its place in the market. At such times, organizations seem to become more responsive to those individuals with an innovative style. However, attentiveness to such individuals is often short lived, as other skills assume a higher priority once an idea is transformed into a product. Another reason for this relatively short period of attentiveness is that those with an innovative style tend to "rock the boat." Most of the time they are merely tolerated by the organization, but when the need arises they are courted by their employers.

Creative style is only one human attribute that could be tapped for organizational advantage. Many diverse skills are required in the innovation process, such as risk taking, creativity, follow-through, and efficiency. Organizations should recognize these characteristics in their employees and develop communication networks to draw together their rich and diverse talents.

Glossary

Champion: A person (sometimes a group) who is devoted to a concept and pursues it relentlessly against all odds.

Entrepreneur: The person who pulls together all the elements of technology, manufacturing, marketing, and finance to make the product commercially feasible. In a large organization, this function is often divided among many people.

Facilitator: A person who facilitates or assists a process without taking a judgmental stance.

Ideator: A person who likes to generate ideas.

Intrapreneur: A person internal to an organization who acts as an entrepreneur.

Inventor: A person who discovers a phenomenon or dreams up an idea and then proceeds to transform it into a tangible product. This is usually done on a small scale, to meet a need perceived by the person.

Originator: A person who is responsible for the conception and documentation of an idea.

Sponsor: A person or group with resources and clout who is willing to support the development of an idea by providing resources at any point in the process of idea development to commercialization. The sponsor can also provide encouragement and protection.

ROSENFELD   SERVO

About the Authors

Robert Rosenfeld is a senior research chemist and head of the Office of Innovation at the Kodak Research Laboratories (1169 Lake Avenue, Rochester, New York 14650). He holds several patents in the field of photographic technology and has presented the concept of the "Office of Innovation" at numerous conferences.

Jenny C. Servo is assistant professor of psychology at the Community College of the Finger Lakes, Canandaigua, New York 14424. She has several publications in the areas of learning and social skills training.

The authors wish to acknowledge critiques of this article by Robert Tuite, Richard Vickers, John Thatcher, William Peters, Dwight Allen, and Robert Paine.

Denis E. Waitley and Robert B. Tucker

HOW TO THINK LIKE AN INNOVATOR

Innovators are a special breed who have a big appetite for information and the vision to recognize new opportunities. Based on their studies of some of America's leading breakthrough thinkers, the authors here provide some guidelines on how you can become an innovator.

We are living in a time when one of the most important skills you can develop is the ability to stay abreast of change. Trend watching, information gathering, "looking out ahead" — all are important survival skills in the new era. Those who have the insights about change will thrive and prosper; those who have an obsolete knowledge base will suffer the consequences.

In studying America's leading innovators — individuals who have themselves introduced a change in the form of a new product, service, method, or set of ideas — we were constantly struck by how well informed they were on a broad range of current events, issues, and trends, both within and outside of their particular fields. They had a "finger on the pulse" of a society in motion. This connectedness enables innovators to stay slightly ahead of their time. Yet, what passes for vision is often just an intense appetite to understand what's going on.

For example, Bill McGowan, the founder of MCI Telecommunications Corporation, reads four hours a day. Excessive, you say? McGowan doesn't think so. In 1982, he happened upon an article in the Stanford Business School magazine entitled "The Skunkworks." It told about a group of Lockheed intrapreneurs who, separately from Lockheed's regular design bureaucracy, developed the U-2 spy plane in record time.

As McGowan read, he became excited: The article expanded and reinforced theories he'd been thinking about. Maybe the same concept would work on a unique project he had in mind. As a result, he established a "skunkworks" task force down the block and away from headquarters. The result, only nine months later, was MCI Mail, the company's electronic mail service.

"That's a very specific payoff from my reading," McGowan reports. "I'm convinced that wide reading helps you make better decisions even though you might not specifically be able to say why."

Innovators don't look at trend watching as "one more thing I gotta do." They love it! They are dazzled by breakthroughs, interested in other people, and concerned about political issues. They believe there has never been a more exciting time to be alive!

A knack for trend watching, which precedes trend spotting, is one of the innovator's secret skills. It is one of the things innovators do to make their own luck. Innovators ride the wave of change because they constantly study the wave.

The knack for successful information gathering isn't something we are born with. Like the innovator's other skills, it is one that can be developed. What follows are several steps to becoming your own trend spotter.

Audit Your Information Intake

Become aware of the way you inform yourself. When you diet,

AUDIT YOUR INFORMATION INTAKE

you become conscious of your caloric intake. By monitoring your

THE FUTURIST, May-June 1987

Innovators also read intuitively. They are looking for what's different, incongruous, new, worrisome, exciting.

information intake, you can cut down on your consumption of mental "junk food" and start making more rewarding informational choices.

What newspapers, magazines, newsletters, and trade publications do you currently read? Do these publications provide you with the information you need to accomplish your objectives? If not, what must you add to the list?

How much time per day do you spend reading? Although quality is more important than quantity, absorbing new information takes time. Innovators often spend as much as a third of their day reading.

DEVELOP YOUR OBSERVATIONAL SKILLS

Develop "Front-Line" Observational Skills

Most of us have read a newspaper account of an event we saw firsthand, even if only a sporting event. When we read about it the next day, or saw it on television, we felt the report didn't accurately convey the essence of what happened. And that's the point: Nobody can do your observing as well as you can. You are your own best information gatherer. It is important to draw your own conclusions and to remain active rather than passive when absorbing information.

Try to "tune in" to your own observations of the world around you. For example, suppose you arrive at the airport to find your flight delayed an hour. Instead of digging into your briefcase and doing paperwork, watch the behavior of arriving and departing passengers. Eavesdrop on someone's conversation, strike one up yourself, or go scan the newsstand, not necessarily reading articles but just looking at what is available.

Listening in on conversations helps expand your world view by allowing you to follow the thoughts of people you might not ordinarily meet. What are they concerned about? How do they see themselves? What do their values seem to be? Rather than relying on television depictions, you are developing your own "mental files" regarding the ways people really behave, think, and feel.

Ask Questions

You can't get all your information simply through observation. Take the initiative to ask questions — even of perfect strangers.

Robert Hazard, president of Quality Inns International, formed

ASK QUESTIONS

his breakthrough idea of market segmentation from talking to a barber. While in Phoenix on business, Hazard struck up a conversation by asking, "So, where do you go on vacation?" He got an earful. In small towns, the barber stayed in moderately priced motels. He refused to pay more than $20 or $25 a night. But when he hit the big cities — Las Vegas, San Francisco — he always stayed in style; price wasn't a consideration. By leading with questions, Hazard obtained key information — information his formal marketing research hadn't revealed!

Adopt the Methods of Professional Trend Watchers

In recent years, professional trend spotters have multiplied

USE THE METHODS OF TREND WATCHERS

rapidly. In the race to predict what will happen in the near future, they scan newspapers, conduct polls, monitor bellwether countries such as Sweden, and pore over obscure trade publications — all with the goal of seeing the earliest signals of change.

John Naisbitt, author of *Megatrends* and chairman of the Washington, D.C.–based Naisbitt Group, employs a method known as content analysis. It is patterned after World War II intelligence-gathering methods: A Swiss intelligence team, for example, read the social pages of small-town newspapers smuggled out of Germany and figured out where German troops were massing by seeing which generals were in what towns.

The Naisbitt Group hires researchers who scan 300 daily newspapers from Toledo to Orlando,

Professional trend watcher John Naisbitt uses content analysis to spot what's happening around the country.

ROSS SUTTON

clipping articles on local concerns. They measure the articles for length, then sort them into dozens of topics. By monitoring increases and decreases in the amount of print devoted to various issues, Naisbitt is able to quantify society's changing concerns and priorities.

One way you can adopt the methods of the pros is by doing a content analysis of your "in basket." What is in there today versus this time last year? And what about the junk mail and advertisements you receive? A little scanning before you consign it to the wastebasket can provide valuable clues about developing trends.

Also, read the local newspapers when you're on the road and make inferences about the state of a region's economy. Or compare the job opportunities listed in your local newspaper with those of a year ago.

Florence Skelly, president of the Daniel Yankelovich Group, advises trend spotters to "keep your eye on the popular culture. Make an analysis — look at magazines, watch television, go to the movies, watch MTV. What themes run through current movies, books, magazines, videos? What values are portrayed? Once you get a handle on what everyone is singing about, you may find popular music very instructive."

Make Your Reading Time Count

Finding reading time is a challenge, but it doesn't stop innovators from keeping up. One surgeon who lectures frequently in different parts of the country uses flying time as reading time. He doesn't rely on what flight attendants might bring down the aisle; rather, before boarding a plane, he buys a dozen or so different magazines: business, computer, science, news, photography, and literary periodicals.

To make the most of reading time, read actively rather than passively. Look for the point the writer is trying to make. Innovators make the most of their reading time by sampling broadly and reading selectively. They skim over disaster stories in favor of articles that contain ideas, and these they read very slowly, stopping to take a note or two, or to jot down an idea.

Innovators also read intuitively. They are looking for what's different, incongruous, new, worrisome, exciting. You can read intuitively by tuning in to possible patterns, making inferences: "If this is true, then maybe that is true also." Look for information that

MAKE YOUR READING TIME COUNT

jumps out because it surprises you and challenges long-held assumptions. Look for articles reporting on new solutions to old problems, changes in people's values and lifestyles, new trends in business, breakthroughs in science and technology.

Innovators aren't just trend spotters — they're opportunity spotters as well. They are adept at sensing the direction of change.

In addition to sampling a broad range of publications, it is important to be open to whatever hits you. Scan everything, from advertising copy to flyers, matchbook covers to billboards, always looking for the unexpected, always broadening your world view. This is the mind-set of the innovator.

Monitor Other Media

Other information-rich media you should monitor:

• **Television.** Be selective in your viewing — tape good programs that air when you're not home, such as the news. Later, you can watch with fewer distractions — and zap through the commercials. But don't ignore commercials altogether: Commercials have become an important cultural barometer.

• **Radio.** Call-in talk shows can tip you off to what other people are concerned about. National Public Radio is a blessing to many commuters for news and features on "Morning Edition" and "All Things Considered." Try listening to a different station every day for a week: rock, all-news, all-talk, country, black, Hispanic, and so on. What perspectives do you pick up? What type of person does each program address? Who advertises on that station and why?

• **Cassettes.** Recorded "publications" such as the *Hines Report*, a monthly audiocassette service, provide brief updates on events in the business and financial community. Subjects are researched, written, and taped as short, fast-paced reports.

• **Lectures.** Broaden your informational intake by attending seminars and lectures by experts.

• **Books.** Keep a list of books you want to read. Cull new titles from newspapers and magazines and from asking others what they've read that influenced their thinking. When you go into libraries and bookstores, you'll know exactly what you're looking for.

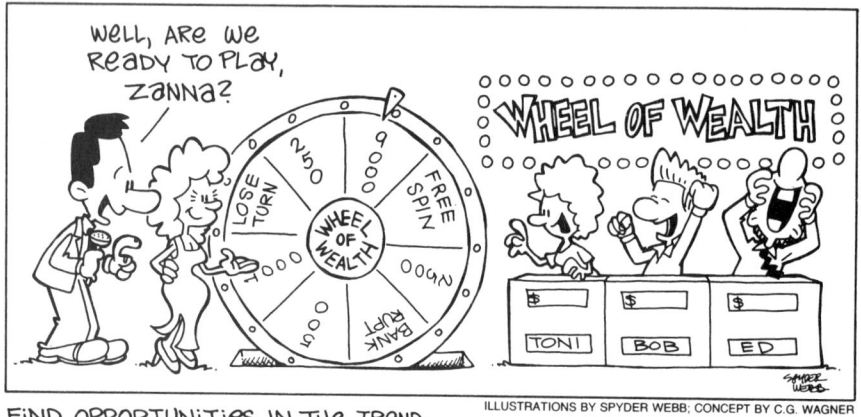

Find Opportunities in the Wave

The goal of trend watching is to discover opportunities for yourself. As you begin actively observing change, you'll become adept at distinguishing fads from trends.

There are no hard and fast formulas to separate fads from trends — the "hula hoops" versus the "baby boom," say. But by separating those things that are part of the wave from those that aren't, we begin to see patterns, and in seeing patterns we can begin to spot problems to solve and opportunities to create.

In most instances, innovators don't create the wave. They merely amplify it and help popularize certain products and services based on it. Look at the many opportunities created by the fitness trend: health-food stores, vitamin manufacturers, exercise equipment manufacturers, aerobic workout studios, health conference centers, health magazines, exercise magazines and books, specialized athletic shoes — the list is a long one.

Spotting Opportunities in Change

Innovators aren't just trend spotters — they're opportunity spotters as well. They are adept at sensing the direction of change. For them, opportunity seeking is an instinctive process. But even if this pattern recognition doesn't come to you quite so naturally, you can train yourself to see the patterns as you go about observing trends — patterns that can tip you off to new opportunities.

Here are five sources of innovative opportunities most often cited by the innovators in our study:

1. Observe a trend and come up with a way of exploiting it. For example, as the number of two-income households continues to rise, what opportunities might this change bring, and for whom?

The Campbell Soup Company saw that working couples have less time to spend in the kitchen. But they didn't necessarily want to eat the available TV dinners, either.

IN THEIR OWN WORDS...

"I'm convinced that wide reading helps you make better decisions even though you might not specifically be able to say why."
— Bill McGowan, founder
MCI Telecommunications Corporation

"Keep your eye on the popular culture.... Once you get a handle on what everyone is singing about, you may find popular music very instructive."
— Florence Skelly, president
Daniel Yankelovich Group

"I figured if you could make the stuff taste good, you'd have an idea."
— Mo Siegel, co-founder
Celestial Seasonings

Look at your worst problems for possible breakthrough ideas. Where have you noticed handwriting on the wall? What ideas can you come up with to counteract it?

They wanted a more nutritious meal, and they were willing to pay more for it. As a result, Campbell introduced its Le Menu line of frozen dinners.

2. Search for solutions to negative trends. If you can identify negative trends and come up with a way to counteract them, you may have a breakthrough idea. Pinpoint a negative trend and ask, What will happen if this continues? What can I do to provide the affected group with an alternative solution?

Consider the trend of growing budget deficits and rising pressure to cut government spending. One solution that has received an increasing amount of interest in the mid-1980s is privatization, whereby government services — garbage collection, emergency services, street maintenance, etc. — are performed by private, for-profit companies. Companies set up to provide these services are thriving because they can provide services for less than the government agencies. And, as government budget deficits continue to mount, the counter trend of privatization will probably continue. How might this become an opportunity for you or your company?

3. Look at your current activities, beliefs, and interests for ideas that might appeal to others. Some innovative ideas exploit change in an accidental way. Certain innovators start a business because it "feels like it might have potential" or because they believe in it themselves. Suddenly it takes off.

This happened to Mo Siegel, cofounder of Celestial Seasonings Herbal Tea Company. Celestial Seasonings capitalized on the health-and-fitness trend, appealing to growing numbers of people looking for a caffeine-free substitute for coffee.

The trouble was that herb teas then available didn't taste very good. Siegel began collecting herbs in the Colorado countryside, blending different herbs together in hopes of improving the flavor. "I figured if you could make the stuff taste good, you'd have an idea," he recalls.

Like Siegel, you may already be in the middle of an opportunity. Your next breakthrough idea may come from looking around at your current activities, interests, and beliefs. Ask yourself, What am I doing that could serve a larger group? What unexpected successes have I had? What might they mean?

4. When a present trend is running against you, come up with a new idea. Recognizing a threat is half the battle. It may also be the source of a breakthrough idea.

Al Neuharth, chairman of Gannett Company, Inc., observed the demise of several afternoon newspapers, recognizing that lifestyle changes were responsible. Instead of reading the afternoon paper,

USA Today founder Al Neuharth found opportunity in satellite technology, which allowed the development of a colorful national daily newspaper.

people watched television news when they came home at night. And a widening array of special-interest magazines gave readers in-depth discussions of the issues that most concerned them.

Looking at these changes, Neuharth discovered developments that could be turned into an exciting new opportunity. He noticed, for example, that millions of Americans were traveling by air and thus wanted to know how the weather was in other cities. And he saw that satellite technology would allow him to transfer color layouts less expensively and more rapidly than in the past. He put all of these factors together and came up with a breakthrough idea: *USA Today*, a national daily newspaper.

Look at your worst problems for possible breakthrough ideas. Where have you noticed handwriting on the wall? What ideas can you come up with to counteract it?

5. Watch what the competition is doing and do it better. All business innovators come to realize this idea.

Schoolteacher Sandy Gooch didn't set out to beat the competition or even to capitalize on the health-and-fitness trend. Her breakthrough idea came about as the result of a close brush with death. After a nearly fatal reaction to chemical additives in processed food, she adopted a diet of natural foods: No refined flour or sugar. No artificial additives. No artificial flavors, colors, or preservatives. No caffeine. No hydrogenated vegetable oil.

While shopping at health-food stores, she noticed that not all of them had the same standards. Some even sold products with sugar and other additives in them. In addition, the stores she shopped at were small, making it necessary to go one place for fresh vegetables, another for staples, another for meat, and to a conventional supermarket for light bulbs and such.

> ## Questions for Breaking Through
>
> 1. What can I offer that "they" aren't offering?
> 2. How can I position myself in a way that is different?
> 3. Where's the niche that hasn't been developed?
> 4. How can I add value to the service or product I now produce?
> 5. Where is the market inefficiency?
> 6. What would make this process or procedure more convenient?
> 7. How can I do this less expensively?
> 8. What would people pay for that isn't available now?
> 9. What might my customer group want if it were available?
> 10. What do I really enjoy doing that I'd like to do more of?
> 11. How can I make a living from doing what to me is fun, challenging, and never boring?
> 12. What trends will change the assumptions my colleagues and competitors are now making in my field?
>
> — **Denis E. Waitley and Robert B. Tucker**

It was then that Gooch's breakthrough idea occurred to her: Why not start a natural-food supermarket, with everything else offered by regular grocery stores available as well? In 1977, Sandy Gooch opened the first Mrs. Gooch's Natural Food Store, which now does over $40 million in sales annually.

Discovering Your Breakthrough Idea

Breakthrough ideas are most likely to occur when you are actively, confidently searching for new opportunities. They often appear after lengthy periods of thought and consideration. They occur to those who are prepared to *act*. Rather than experiencing a single magical moment in which the idea arrives, fully developed, you may find that your next breakthrough idea comes to you in pieces — pieces you will gradually put together.

However they come to you, all breakthrough ideas "feel right" in various ways: They solve someone's problem; they satisfy a want; they are right for *you*. A breakthrough idea must align with your values. You will recognize it intuitively.

WAITLEY    TUCKER

About the Authors

Denis E. Waitley is a consultant on high-level performance and personal development. He is author of the books *Seeds of Greatness*, *The Double Win*, and *The Winner's Edge* and of the audiocassette album *Psychology of Winning*. His address is Box 197, Rancho Santa Fe, California 92067.

Robert B. Tucker is president of Innovative Resources, Inc., an executive-development firm. He is a speaker on innovation, creativity, and managing change and is author of several trend-spotting articles in such publications as *Esquire*, *INC.*, and *Success!* His address is 4360 Allott Avenue, Sherman Oaks, California 91423.

This article is adapted from their book, *Winning the Innovation Game*, Fleming H. Revell Company, Old Tappan, New Jersey 07675. 1986. 256 pages. $15.95.

Jay W. Forrester

Economic Conditions Ahead
Understanding the Kondratieff Wave

Current economic conditions are a result of the economic long wave. By understanding the long wave, we can anticipate what lies ahead.

For the last decade, several of us in the MIT System Dynamics Group have been applying "system dynamics" to achieving a better understanding of the behavior of national economies. The system dynamics approach builds up a model from the microstructure of an economic system with the expectation that, if the perception of structure is correct, the parts of the system will interact with each other to produce the kinds of macroeconomic behavior that have been so puzzling in real life.

The System Dynamics National Model is built up from the policies followed by the Federal Reserve, corporations, and banks. It also reflects the economic habits of the population as well as the mobility of people from sector to sector in the economy. These policies interact with each other over time to produce the behavior of the entire system. If this representation of the economy is correct, the National Model ought to produce the kinds of behavior observed in the real economic system. We find this is true.

A number of different behavior modes have been identified in the real economy. For example, there is the business cycle, with peaks of activity occurring some three to seven years apart and with a high degree of variation in the intensity and the intervals between peaks from one cycle to the next. There is also the Kuznets or construction cycle, with peaks 15 to 25 years apart. But much more important is the Kondratieff cycle or economic long wave, with peaks 45 to 60 years apart.

The Kondratieff Cycle

We believe that the present economic situation is dominated by the economic long wave, but thinking is confused because people try to attribute current unusual and extreme conditions to the business cycle. There is a great deal of controversy about the Kondratieff cycle: In American academic economics, the majority opinion asserts that there is no such thing. In Europe, however, theories on the economic long wave go back into the 1800s, well before Kondratieff.

My own belief in the Kondratieff cycle results from work with the System Dynamics National Model. We first saw the long-wave behavior in the model's output. After carefully examining the model for possible defects or mistakes, we realized that ordinary business and government policies can interact with one another to produce a cyclical economic behavior characterized by a large buildup and rapid collapse in the rate of capital construction.

The behavior seen in the model occurs in the real economy. Over the last 200 years of Western economic history, there have been four major economic peaks. The intervals between these peaks vary, but they fall generally in the range of 45 to 60 years apart.

Another Depression Ahead?

The economic long wave is the phenomenon responsible for the great depressions of the 1830s, the 1890s, and the 1930s and causes such episodes to occur approximately 50 years apart.

Present worldwide economic crosscurrents suggest that we are entering another such downturn of the long wave. Around 1931, as now, there was great concern about foreign debt and the possibility of default. Three to five years later, a number of major Latin American defaults did occur. In the past few years, we have again seen speculative bidding-up of prices of physical assets and land, and the collapse of those prices, as occurred during the 1920s and 1930s.

Throughout the economy, there have been replays of what went on before the 1930s. Defaults, unmanageable debt on agricultural land, and inflation turning into deflation are all part of working out the imbalances that have accumulated by the peak of long-wave expansion.

Looking at the National Model near an economic peak, we find that business cycles become progressively more severe. Likewise, in the actual economy, every business-cycle recession since 1965 has been more severe than the one before.

The peak period of the long wave is one of overexpansion of production capacity. Such overexpansion is worldwide today. For example, an executive of one of the large chemical companies told me recently that his company was closing down and dismantling two "modern world-class" polyethylene plants. He said that when these were taken out of service they would reduce excess capacity in the industry by 10%. This means that 20 such plants had been built beyond the number needed.

Another example is the worldwide excess capacity in the automobile industry. Some U.S. automakers blame competition from abroad, while others point to increasing consumer awareness and demands, causing companies out of tune with the market or less ef-

Failed bank in Haverhill, Iowa, during the Great Depression of the 1930s. The economic long wave is the phenomenon responsible for the depressions of the 1830s, the 1890s, and the 1930s, according to author Forrester. In the 1980s, more banks are failing than at any time since the Great Depression.

fective in their designs to suffer. Yet the fact remains that there would be no economic problems for the automobile industry if there were a shortage of cars rather than a surplus.

Fare cutting, which has led to the bankruptcy of a number of airlines, is an expression of overcapacity in air transportation. In steel and most other major U.S. industries the same situation exists, albeit with shortages in some of the newer and more innovative areas.

Productivity and the Long Wave

At the peak of an economic long wave, productivity no longer rises—a fact that I think has been misunderstood. To bolster productivity, the U.S. government has tried to offer incentives for investing in more capital equipment. But incentives do little when there is already excess capacity. In fact, productivity no longer rises because in many industries there is already as much capital plant as workers can use. However, within a decade the United States will begin a major shift in the nature of its capital plant after the present plant is worn out and depreciated.

Recently, a farm-machinery dealer in Omaha said that if no more farm machinery were sold in the United States for 10 years, the agricultural sector would not be inconvenienced. Go into a farmer's machine yard and look at the eight tractors there. The farmer may well tell you he hasn't the slightest idea why he bought that last $80,000 tractor. He uses it only three weeks a year. The other machines would have done almost as well. He bought it because it was stylish. He bought it because his neighbors were buying. He bought it because he thought it would pay for itself in increased profits. Now he's in trouble because his profits have failed to rise. Many industrial sectors have the same problems.

Return on investment has been declining since 1965. A downward trend means that expectations for paying back debt are in jeopardy

"The United States is now doing what South American countries have been doing for some time: borrowing money to pay the interest on what it has already borrowed. The result is a larger debt next year."

and profit margins are narrowing. Prices have been rising, partly as a result of the economic long wave and partly as a result of flooding the economic system with money from the monetization of government debt. Unemployment has been rising since 1965. During this same period, every peak of unemployment has been higher than the previous peak, while every low point has been higher than the previous low point.

These developments are not separate coincidental happenings. There is a driving force that links them together. They come together as an ensemble of symptoms, not as independent happenings that have coincided.

For example, the history of real interest rates is informative. Real interest rates peaked as high as 12% in 1930-1934, much higher than they have been recently. Today, we are moving toward another peak in real interest rates. The reason for this is deeply entrenched in the economy and is not a consequence of the Reagan administration or Paul Volcker or the Federal Reserve. It is part of the internal dynamic of the economic long wave and what happens to the balance of money, demand, prices, and inflation rates as one moves past the peak of the economic long wave.

Defaults on Debt?

Despite the present recovery, I think we will see more difficulty before we come out on the other side because major imbalances are yet to be corrected. The foreign debt has received the most attention. Foreign nations are likely to default on debts totaling more than the net worth of the entire American banking system. Even now, at the top of a business cycle, developing nations are barely able to pay the interest on their loans, let alone pay off the principal. The next downturn will cause them even greater difficulty.

To meet their payments, countries would be forced to demand greater economic austerity than their citizens will tolerate. The result will almost certainly be changes in governments. New governments will say, "We didn't take on the debt. We don't have responsibility for it. We are only partially to blame: After all, the people who lent us the money are supposed to be just as smart as we are. They lent money to someone who can't pay it back; it's their fault as much as ours. Therefore, we don't even have a moral obligation to pay it back because we were enticed into unmanageable debt."

These countries may well become quite at ease about defaulting.

Once countries have defaulted and their credit is ruined, there is no reason why they shouldn't expropriate the assets of the multinational companies in their countries, as was done in the late 1930s. This will produce repercussions in the developed countries.

Farmland and home mortgages present the same kind of problem. Several billion dollars' worth of balloon mortgages come due in California in each of the next several years. They were taken out with all interest and principal coming due in three years, on the expectation that prices would have risen enough that the owner could roll over those mortgages. If the mortgages can't be rolled over, the home-

Combines harvest corn near Coon Rapids, Iowa. Farmers who overbought equipment during the last economic downturn now are struggling with debt and low income. Other industrial sectors have the same problem, says author Forrester.

owners are in trouble.

We saw indications of this in the last recession: There were very weak housing markets in many parts of the country. We could run into a situation where home mortgages are in jeopardy, threatening a deflationary spiral. Once housing or farmland has to be put on the market on a distress basis and people realize that prices aren't rising anymore, there won't be buyers.

This is happening in agriculture now. Land is being put up for forced sale, and the expectation is that there will be more of the same in the future. Anyone who has the money to pay says, "Why should I buy now? It looks like the price is going to go down next year." So the buyer backs off and the seller is selling into a vacuum. The resulting deflationary spiral can go downward a long way once it gets started.

Another major issue to be resolved is the U.S. national debt. The United States is now doing what South American countries have been doing for some time: borrowing money to pay the interest on what it has already borrowed. The result is a larger debt next year on which interest must be paid.

Imagine for a moment that U.S. government revenues remained fixed where they are now and that expenditures for transfer payments and other expenditures, except for interest, remained fixed. Only interest is changing (at current rates). In this scenario, simply the compounding of interest into principal is sufficient to double the deficit in every four-year administration. On the average, the deficit has been doubling in each four-year administration for the last five administrations.

The United States is on the verge of a runaway compounding situation. If the deficit is not brought under control, it will rapidly get out of hand, with no solution available except for the United States to default on its debt. If we are to avoid future default, we must think (and act) rapidly. Given the major imbalances, we haven't yet escaped the consequences of the overexpansion of the 1960s and 1970s.

Inflation vs. Deflation

We now face an uncertain watershed between runaway inflation and deflation. Traditionally, the long-wave downturn has been a time of deflation, in which deflation feeds on itself. Debts are disposed of either by paying them back or by defaulting, either of which collapses the money supply and causes prices to fall. In a deflationary spiral, debt is paid back, but the remaining debt becomes progressively more burdensome due to the decline of prices and production. The burden of debt becomes greater because it is not being liquidated as fast as the ability to repay is declining.

If the government tries to buy its way out of social and economic difficulty by flooding the system with money, one can get a situation similar to Germany in the 1920s: hyperinflation. In hyperinflation, everybody's attention focuses on coping with inflation and not on producing things, so the economy declines.

"If one had to choose between deflation and hyperinflation, deflation is a better choice. It would end sooner and lay a more solid foundation for recovery than hyperinflation."

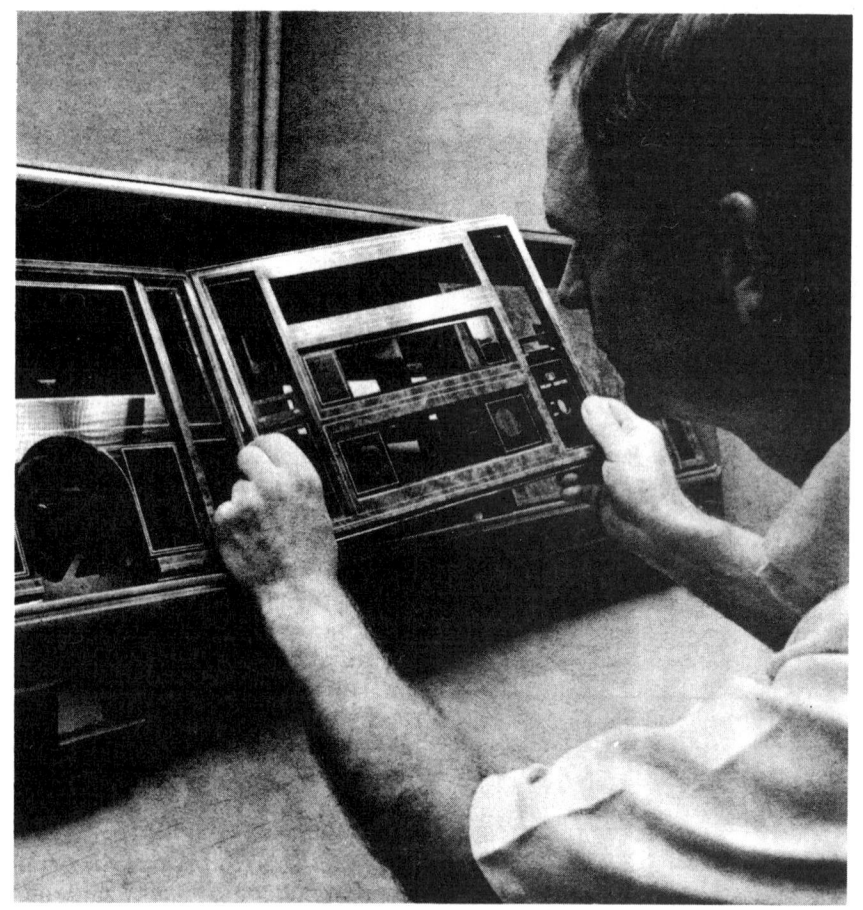

Worker adds parts to an automobile instrument panel. Overproduction of automobiles has led to a worldwide glut of autos, causing severe economic problems.

If one had to choose between deflation and hyperinflation, deflation would be the better choice. It would end sooner and lay a more solid foundation for recovery than hyperinflation. I am hopeful that there is a path between deflation and hyperinflation. It is urgent to find such a path.

Learning from the Long-Wave Theory

In the past, the Great Depression of the 1930s was not recognized as a downturn in the economic long wave. Rather, it was seen simply as a severe example of an ordinary business-cycle downturn, accentuated by mistakes made by the Federal Reserve. By failing to see the true cause, governments and economists have missed an opportunity to learn from the past.

Through use of the System Dynamics National Model, we have for the first time a cohesive, integrated theory of how the economic long wave can be generated. Now there is a chance for learning.

However, understanding might not remove the difficulties standing in the way of effective action. It is probable that, with an awareness of the economic long wave, we could have prevented some of the overshoot from which we must now recover. The excess expansion could have been restrained by engaging in severe restriction on liquidity and money since 1960. Tight money and high interest would have prevented the borrowing that fed decades of speculative excesses.

But which elements in our society would have backed tight money and high interest? I don't know of any group—Republicans, Democrats, labor, management, or universities—that would have supported such a move. But necessary moves might be supported the next time, if the nature of the economic long wave becomes well understood.

There is great merit in helping everyone understand the economic wave as the cause of present problems. Let them know that pointing fingers won't help, that the downturn won't last forever, and that we must try to alleviate personal hardships and move forward. If we do nothing else, I think this would be useful.

If there is a great technological military threat, we work on several different kinds of solutions, with ample resources, and we always get answers. It is equally possible, using a similar approach, to come up with answers to the problems posed by economic difficulties. But there is a lack of belief that economic behavior can be understood. One of our great national shortcomings is our failure to address social and economic problems with the same kind of aggressive research that has so successfully been applied to physical problems.

About the Author

Jay W. Forrester, Germeshausen Professor at the Massachusetts Institute of Technology, directs the System Dynamics Program in the Alfred P. Sloan School of Management. His address is Sloan School of Management, 50 Memorial Drive, Cambridge, Massachusetts 02139.

John M. Culbertson

Destructive Foreign Trade
Sowing the Seeds for Our Own Downfall

An economic heretic argues that unrestricted "free trade" will lead to falling living standards in developed countries. Eventually, it will bring global anarchy and degradation.

Destructive foreign trade patterns pose a great threat to the world in the remaining years of the twentieth century. One-sided, one-way-benefit foreign trade is undercutting the economies of the United States and other high-income nations. Unless it is corrected, this damaging kind of trade will cause a drop in the standards of living of high-income nations so great that it will raise the threat of political extremism and disorder. It will also, in effect, globalize mankind, undermine the capabilities of national governments, and thus destroy the political basis of human affairs.

In today's world, unregulated foreign trade—so-called "free trade"—throws peoples and nations with widely different wage levels and standards of living, population situations, economic laws, regulations, and policies into a destructive competition with one another. Massive, trade-caused shifts of industries and jobs from high-income to low-income nations—the most striking feature of recent foreign trade, causing real incomes in the United States to decline for the past decade—will continue on to a devastating outcome.

Attempts by the United States to force unregulated international trade upon the world, and the U.S. acquiescence to the massive and ongoing loss of its own desirable industries and jobs, have headed the world toward a crisis affecting foreign trade, international economic relations, and the political structure of human life. This free-trade crusade rests on nothing more substantial than the experience-refuted and anti-scientific doctrines of "laissez-faire" economics and its false interpretation of economic history.

The implied outcome of such a trade policy is the globalization of mankind: the creation of a one-world competition that leaves national governments helpless and

PHILIP WOLMUTH/UNFPA

Workers in an electronics factory in the Dominican Republic. Workers in developing nations often accept longer hours, poor working conditions, and drastically lower wages than U.S. workers.

THE FUTURIST, November-December 1986

"Actual foreign trade commonly benefits one of the trading nations at the expense of the other, and it may damage both nations."

inflicts a kind of one-world anarchy on mankind. In this situation, there is no power capable of preventing destructive competition, of protecting human values, or of preventing high birth rates and overpopulation in some parts of the world from dragging all of mankind down to poverty.

White Hats and Black Hats

The implications of destructive international trade patterns are little understood because discussion of the subject is dominated by a set of misleading stereotypes that conceal the real issues. For the so-fashionable proponents of laissez-faire economics—and for those who thoughtlessly accept what they were told in their economics courses—the issue is simply the choice between "free trade," which wears the white hat, automatically promotes economic efficiency, and makes everyone better off, and "protectionism," (one shudders at the very word) wearing the black hat.

Many liberals take substantially the same view of foreign trade on the basis of a different set of stereotypes. To them, "one-worldism," generosity, cooperation, and "helping behavior" wear the white hat, and "economic nationalism" wears the black hat. So, while Adam-Smithian individualists oppose limitations on U.S. imports and international trade as violation of laissez-faire economics, liberals oppose it as selfish nationalism. Thus, *The New York Times* and *The Wall Street Journal* both can luxuriate in righteous indignation over "protectionism," as they do *ad nauseum*.

Another stereotype that especially affect liberals is the 1960s notion of "economic growth" as a process that automatically will raise all nations to affluence, if only the so-called "rich nations" give enough "help" to the "poor nations." To those still governed by this stereotype, it may seem that the United States, as a "rich nation," should be oriented toward helping the "poor nations" to take off into sustained growth, rather than making its rich self richer.

How can all these people be wrong? Because they are all governed by stereotypes that basically misrepresent both the way international trade actually is working and the outcome that will follow free trade in today's world. These stereotypes offer simple solutions, panaceas that promise more than can actually be delivered.

Both laissez faire-economics and these "economic growth" stereotypes arise from ideological myth. Laissez-faire economics is predicated on the eighteenth-century myth that Nature preprogrammed the world so that things automatically work out for the best under self-seeking individualism. The "economic growth" stereotypes, in turn, are characterized by a belief in the efficacy of "helping" and good intentions (a result of misinterpreting Christian doctrine) and by the modern faith that "prog-

Metal worker in Wisconsin. Foreign competition has shifted many manufacturing jobs out of the United States to developing nations; ultimately, such competition could force the reduction of wage rates for U.S. workers.

REYNOLDS METALS CO.

Fewer Jobs for Blue-Collar Workers

The outlook is bleak for U.S. workers who don't have skills in demand or the right education. Millions of such workers lose their jobs each year because of irreversible changes in the U.S. economy. And the number of jobs available for such workers will continue to decline.

A continuing decline in the number of manufacturing jobs can be expected due to productivity gains, shifts of plants overseas, and stiff competition from abroad, according to a report by the Congressional Office of Technology Assessment (OTA). Over the five years from 1979 to 1984, 11.5 million American workers lost jobs because of plant shutdowns or relocations, rising productivity, or shrinking output.

Although manufacturing now accounts for less than 20% of U.S. employment, nearly half of all workers displaced during these years worked in manufacturing industries, especially those such as steel, automobiles, industrial equipment, and textiles, hit hard by international competition.

The situation for these workers is not expected to improve. In fact, according to OTA, it will be impossible for some industries even to maintain current levels of employment. And rapid changes in international trade and technology mean that displacement will continue in prosperous times as well as recession.

Many of these displaced workers face long-term unemployment. During the period of 1979 to 1984, nearly one-quarter of the displaced workers who had held their previous jobs for three or more years were unable to find new employment. Particularly hard hit were minorities; less than 42% of black displaced workers were reemployed.

"These workers are likely to face extended periods of unemployment, loss of health insurance and retirement benefits, and reemployment only at lower pay," says John H. Gibbons, director of OTA.

Within manufacturing, the most vulnerable jobs are those of unskilled and semiskilled blue-collar workers, according to OTA. These jobs are not only the easiest to automate but are also the easiest to move overseas to low-wage countries.

For individual workers, the exact cause of displacement is often unclear. Many firms, in response to stiffer international competition, automate production in order to cut costs and increase productivity. For people who lose their jobs as a result, the distinction between trade-related and technological displacement is blurred.

In all sectors of the economy, service as well as manufacturing, manual labor and routine mental tasks are vulnerable to computer-based technology. The fewer skills that workers have, the more vulnerable they are to displacement.

Another group of people with especially difficult problems finding adequate work is displaced homemakers. These are women whose main job has been home and family, but who must now support themselves because of divorce, widowhood, disability or long-term unemployment of their spouse, or loss of eligibility for public assistance.

Like workers displaced from factories and offices, these homemakers have lost their major source of income and face painful readjustment problems. The number of such displaced homemakers facing serious employment problems is estimated at 2 to 4 million and is growing.

Barriers to employment are often higher for homemakers than for mainstream displaced workers, because many have little experience in a paid job. Also, these women have no unemployment insurance or other income cushion to see them through training.

The methods for helping these workers, such as job training programs and education for adults, have not kept up. While the federal government has attempted to assist displaced adult workers, mainly through Title III of the Job Training Partnership Act of 1982, it has been estimated that no more than 5% of eligible workers are being served by this program.

According to OTA, "To meet the challenge of living with global competition while enhancing the quality of its citizens' lives, the United States will have to move on many fronts to upgrade the skills of its work force and to make the best use of the abilities of its people."

Among the recommendations made by OTA are:

- Giving all Americans a sound basic education.
- Giving adult workers the opportunity to retrain later in life, in classrooms or in the workplace.
- Designing jobs and organizing work to take best advantage of the skills people have or can acquire.
- Ensuring high-quality reemployment and retraining services to workers who find themselves in the wrong place at the wrong time and become displaced.

Source: *Technology and Structural Unemployment: Reemploying Displaced Adults*, Office of Technology Assessment. Available from the Superintendent of Documents, U.S. Government Printing Office, Washington, D.C. 20402. GPO stock number 052-003-01017-8.

"The most striking effect of unregulated foreign trade is to throw all the people of the world into a global wage competition."

ress" is to come to all humans as a gift of nature.

When the matter is approached in a realistic or scientific framework, it is clear that unregulated international trade, or free trade, is not automatically beneficial. Actual foreign trade commonly benefits one of the trading nations at the expense of the other, and it may damage both nations.

The very unbalanced trade between Japan and the United States, for example, has greatly benefited Japan and damaged the United States. Japan, through unbalanced trade between the two nations, took over many of the rewarding and promising industries and jobs of the United States and enjoyed a rapid rise in incomes, good jobs, and what economists vaguely call "productivity." The United States lost those rewarding and promising industries and jobs and suffered declines in incomes, good jobs, and "productivity."

The New World of Foreign Trade

Today's foreign trade operates in a new kind of world, one very different from nineteenth-century trade under colonialism. We now have a situation in which all nations are free to go after the rewarding industries of the times; in which transportation and communications are quick and cheap; and in which the latest in technology and management methods can be quickly copied and practiced anywhere in the world, with the aid of multinational corporations, if desired.

It is also a world bulging with 5 billion people, most of whom live in nations that are severely overpopulated, have great numbers of people who are unemployed or underemployed, and have rapid rates of population growth.

In this distinctive new situation, the most striking effect of unregulated foreign trade is to throw all the people of the world into a global wage competition and cause desirable industries and jobs to shift from high-wage nations to low-wage nations, and from nations that impose cost-incurring regulations for environmental protection and worker protection to nations with anything-goes production, child labor, or government-managed labor.

The current U.S. trade deficit of nearly $150 billion, the rapid rise of U.S. foreign debt, and the partial or complete loss by the United States of a very long list of industries reflect the perverse effects of today's international trade, a source not of economic efficiency but of global economic degeneration.

Economics textbooks say that, in international trade, low-wage foreign labor does not undercut high-wage domestic labor, according to the "principle of comparative advantage." But the facts of recent and earlier experience show that this is simply an error.

The textbooks present an example of foreign trade that is in bal-

The globalization of the world brought on by foreign trade would mean overpopulated nations would have no real incentive to limit population, since the burden would fall equally upon all, says author Culbertson.

ance and in which low foreign wages do not undercut high domestic wages, and they say that this shows foreign trade to be automatically beneficial. What this example actually shows is that low wages do not undercut high wages *in cases where the trade is required to be in balance.* That is, it shows that if the United States does not want its wage level and its standard of living undercut by low-wage foreign competition, what it has to do to prevent this is to limit its imports sufficiently to keep its trade in balance.

More broadly, a certain management of trade by the national governments generally is required to achieve efficiency-enhancing and beneficial foreign trade.

Since some industries and jobs are more rewarding and have brighter futures than others, to protect its nation's interests the national government must see that its pattern of trade does not drain away its desirable industries to other nations and leave it with unrewarding and dead-end industries. When a nation like Japan targets the desirable industries and gets them, the nation that leaves its future to be taken care of by mysterious natural forces winds up with the second-rate industries.

The Implications of a "Global Economy"

The effect of international trade in today's world is to undercut the wage level and standard of living of high-wage nations and to pull all nations down to a lowest-common-denominator standard of living that is determined by the world's overpopulated nations. This will be the case unless government policies curb destructive patterns of foreign trade.

Under competition, economics tells us, there can be only a single price. Thus, international wage competition will bring a single, worldwide wage rate. With existing—and worsening—overpopulation, this will be a very low wage rate.

The United States and other Western nations are accustomed to a high standard of living. Built into this standard of living are fixed costs for automobilized societies, expensive medical care, air-conditioning-dependent buildings, and the location of industries. These nations cannot compete on cost with nations accustomed to a simpler and cheaper pattern of life.

Moreover, the people of the United States and the West are not anticipating a future of increasing impoverishment, in which they give up the only way of life they and their ancestors have known for generations. Such a forced economic fall surely would threaten political extremism and disorder, which would not solve the problem but would instead introduce new dimensions of misery and degradation. Offhand, the idea of the "global economy" strikes many as trendy and exciting. When its implications are considered realistically, it presents a different picture.

There are some other points. Economic decline becomes a self-feeding process. As people become poorer, they no longer can afford products based on advanced technology and knowledge. As these become irrelevant, advanced technology and knowledge are lost.

Moreover, a low-income society cannot support the organizational structures and overhead requirements of advanced education and technology. So a declining society essentially moves back down the road up which it earlier had advanced, losing the knowledge and capabilities it had gained. This is what happened in the decline of the Roman Empire, when skills and capabilities were lost that were not again equaled for a thousand years.

Another implication of "international economic integration" or "the globalization of mankind" is the movement to a quasi-anarchic situation. Unregulated international trade and capital movements undermine the accustomed powers of national governments. Under worldwide wage and other competition, national governments would be put in the position (indeed, they now are in the position) of bidding against one another to try to gain industries and jobs so their citizens can make a living.

Such competition among national governments to gain the favor of businesses by offering them zero-regulation, minimum-subsistence wages, tax breaks, and subsidies precludes the government from performing those con-

AGENCY FOR INTERNATIONAL DEVELOPMENT

Japanese-manufactured computerized "chalkboard" electronically scans whatever is written or attached on it and makes photocopies of it. When a nation like Japan targets desirable industries and gets them, others like the United States are left with the second-rate industries, says Culbertson.

structive and civilizing functions that for centuries we have taken for granted. People with sufficient faith in the "free market" and the invisible hand of Nature may be cheered at the thought that meddlesome government in this new world would be decisively excluded from economic affairs. However, those who lack such faith and who lack a taste for living under anarchy would want to weigh carefully these implications of the globalization of mankind.

Workable International Economic Relations

The workable pattern for future international economic relations is one in which nations retain their independence and their ability to control their own destinies. From the diversity of experiments provided by independent nations, there will emerge, as always, some successes and some failures. As the top-level organizing unit of human affairs, nations are governed by the same evolutionary principles as other kinds of living systems.

We need a trade policy that promotes constructive, beneficial patterns of international trade, patterns like those depicted in economics textbooks. Such international trade benefits both of the trading nations rather than benefiting one nation at the expense of another. To benefit both nations, the trade must be a source of genuine economic efficiency—which, in large part, present-day trade is not.

For international trade to benefit the trading nations, it must to some degree be guided or managed by the national governments. Profit-seeking private trade across national boundaries presumably brings profit to the traders, but this in no way shows that it benefits the nations involved. Presumably, the slave trade was profitable to the traders, the shippers, and the slave buyers, but that does not show it to have been beneficial, in a broader sense, to the nations involved or to mankind. Some judgments as to what does or does not benefit the nation must be made by the government, acting on behalf of the whole nation.

For foreign trade to be beneficial to its people, the nation must ensure that it does not run a trade deficit without some special justification. A trade deficit drains away the nation's industries and jobs and runs up its foreign debt. The

> "Even with the very best policies—which in many respects would be the opposite of its recent policies—the United States probably faces a substantial economic come-down."

nation also must ensure that its pattern of trade does not cause it to lose its rewarding and promising industries. The United States recently is not coming anywhere near meeting these criteria.

Balancing Foreign Trade By Limiting Imports

In today's world, where low-wage nations increasingly can use the latest technology and production methods to produce goods for sales abroad, a high-wage, high-regulation economy like the United States must regularly impose limitations on its imports. Such limitations will keep its trade in balance and prevent the draining away of its industries and jobs and the undercutting of its wage level and standard of living. If imports are not limited, the country's workers will be thrown into wage competition with "developing" nations and will face a dismal future.

Many people misunderstand what is accomplished by changes in exchange rates. For the United States, whose goods are being undersold by low-wage foreign production, a reduction in the dollar exchange rate is not a way of bringing trade into balance while preserving the U.S. standard of living. Rather, it is a way of eventually bringing trade into balance by reducing the U.S. level of real wages and standard of living to the level of the low-wage foreign competition—not what the people of the United States are expecting.

Limitations on U.S. imports, rather than being termed "protectionism" and avoided like the plague, are precisely what is needed. Import limitations would move U.S. trade to a position of balance and replace one-sided, one-way-benefit trade with balanced and mutually beneficial trade. To accomplish this requires a coherent, consistent trade policy and system of import limitations that is designed to benefit the nation rather than any particular industry or group and that gives full consideration to finding trade patterns that also benefit our trading partners.

Even with the very best policies—which in many respects would be the opposite of its recent policies—the United States probably faces a substantial economic come-down. An effective trade policy is required to limit the decline in the nation's economic position and to prevent a disastrous economic crash. The nation is now living on borrowed time with its huge trade deficit, the continuing export of its industries and jobs, its skyrocketing foreign debt, its huge government deficit, its officially ignored insolvencies and declining guarantee funds for banks and financial institutions along with rising bank failures, the growing proportion of its people living on part-time or temporary jobs, and the continuing decline in real incomes.

In contrast to the popular image of preprogrammed and inexorable economic growth and progress, the United States and the world face in the rest of the twentieth century a time of trials and the shattering of unrealistic expectations.

The United States must shift from thinking about international trade and international economic relations in terms of ideological stereotypes to thinking realistically about what kind of trade policy is needed to replace destructive patterns of foreign trade with constructive and mutually beneficial trade between nations. This will not be accomplished under any of the popular stereotypes such as "free trade," "competition," "the free market," "one world," "the global economy," or "international cooperation." It will require new concepts, a new vocabulary, and nonideological analysis of the actual effects of different patterns of foreign trade.

Foreign trade threatens to undercut the only political structure modern man has known—the nation—and to globalize mankind into 5 billion undifferentiated creatures desperately competing against one another for a chance to earn a living in an increasingly crowded world. Foreign trade would have us give up something we once fought for—our national independence. In the brave new world, I suppose we would rededicate the Fourth of July, replacing the obsolete "independence day" with, say, "globalization day."

Foreign trade is working to make the whole world into a population commune in which world wage rates are equalized, in which no nation could gain by limiting its population, and a nation would not particularly suffer from having explosive population growth, since the burden of world overpopulation would fall equally upon all.

These great issues turn on policy toward international trade. The United States and several other Western nations seem committed to policies that can do untold harm, and Americans, with the best of intentions, cannot see beyond the stereotypes that will push their world into decline and degradation.

Editor's note: This article directly challenges much of the conventional economic wisdom of today, as well as many of the views expressed in previous FUTURIST articles. THE FUTURIST will publish selected responses from readers in a forthcoming issue.

About the Author

John M. Culbertson is professor of economics at the University of Wisconsin, 1180 Observatory Drive, 7438 Social Science Building, Madison, Wisconsin 53706. He has been an economist with the Board of Governors of the Federal Reserve System, has served as a consultant to the Subcommittee on International Finance of the House Banking and Currency Committee and to the U.S. Agency for International Development, and is author of *Macroeconomic Theory and Stabilization Policy*, among other books.

Lewis J. Perelman

LEARNING OUR LESSON
Why School Is Out

The same technologies that are displacing workers in the post-industrial age could be used to improve the efficiency of learning and adult retraining.

The age of schooling is over. A new, post-industrial "learning enterprise" is about to replace the outworn infrastructure of industrial-age education. The technology we call "school" will have as much place in the twenty-first century's learning system as the horse and buggy have in today's transportation system.

The economic, social, and technological trends pushing critical choices about learning to the top of the public-policy agenda include:

• The quality, value, and relevance of most educational services are declining, but the development of a post-industrial economy means that the population has growing, unmet needs for learning.

• The costs of education and training have become the biggest single item of spending in the U.S. economy and are rising several times faster than personal income.

• The demand for government subsidies to education is exploding, but the deficit crisis is going to require fiscal austerity.

• Modern information technology can be used to increase the productivity of learning, but an entrenched educational establishment obstructs its application.

The transition that these trends will force—away from a socialized educational bureaucracy and toward a competitive learning enterprise—will occur eventually worldwide. But delay will be costly. The nation that is first to adopt a high-technology, consumer-based learning system will enjoy a permanent competitive advantage in the global economy of the information age.

The Declining Value of Education

The quality, value, and relevance of most educational services have been declining for at least two decades. We no longer can assume that *more* education necessarily benefits either the individual or the nation.

More education has not led to stronger basic skills. For instance, the U.S. Defense Department has had to increase spending on training in basic skills by more than 40% in the past five years, despite the fact that the current crop of military recruits is the most educated in history.

Nor does *more* education guarantee economic improvement. In the 1950s, the cost of additional education was more than offset by greater earnings. Since the 1960s, real incomes of American workers have declined even as the average level of schooling has grown enormously.

Though the utility of much formal education is declining, the needs for learning are increasingly urgent. Learning is as strategically critical to a knowledge-based, post-industrial economy as steel was to a materials-based, industrial economy.

Despite the frenzied political attention given to childhood education in the past three years, the most crucial unmet learning needs are those of adults. More than three-fourths of America's workers in 2001 will be people who are already adults today. A fifth of the current adult population is functionally illiterate and another fifth is only marginally literate. On the other hand, 15% or more of today's workers are overeducated or overqualified in that their knowledge and skills no longer fit the requirements of a changing economy. The majority of workers at all levels need substantial retraining every five to eight years, regardless of whether they change careers or stay in existing jobs.

The Looming Cost Crisis

Total spending for education and training in the United States—more than $300 billion a year—is rivaled in size and growth only by health care. Just as in the health-care system, the immensity of the

> "The nation that is first to adopt a high-technology, consumer-based learning system will enjoy a permanent competitive advantage in the global economy of the information age."

THE FUTURIST, March-April 1986

"The U.S. Defense Department has had to increase spending on training in basic skills by more than 40% in the past five years, despite the fact that the current crop of military recruits is the most educated in history."

education and training market has led to a crisis of productivity and cost containment.

Per-pupil spending on public elementary and secondary schools grew by 22.5% during the past decade; at the same time, real income per capita increased only 6.5%. Experts estimate that the cost of bringing teaching staffs and schools up to the standards called for by numerous national commissions would add $100 billion a year to the $150 billion now spent annually on schools.

In the past 20 years, college costs for students grew 13-23% at various types of institutions. The cost of a bachelor's degree at a top Ivy League college is now about $100,000—and the cost in the next decade easily could be double that.

The investment by employers in employee training and education—some $80 billion a year—is now comparable in scope to all of formal higher education and is projected to grow 25-30% by 1990. Experts guess that a fifth or more of this expenditure is required simply to compensate for the failures of schooling.

The Government Crunch

The federal deficit crisis will finally become tangible to the American public in fiscal year 1987 as the provisions of the Gramm-Rudman-Hollings law begin to take effect. The impact of the fiscal crisis will affect state and local governments, too, and will endure through the end of this century. One consequence will be to halt and then reverse the long-term growth of the government role in providing, funding, and regulating education in the United States.

The main immediate effect of federal cutbacks will be on higher education. Nearly half of America's college students now receive financial aid from federal programs.

State governments will be the focus of the impending revolution in education policy. The states now pay half the costs of public primary and secondary schools. In the 1950s, half the higher education in America was provided by private colleges and universities; today, the great majority is provided by government-subsidized public (chiefly state) institutions.

Education expenditures now represent nearly one-third of state government budgets on average, and in some states account for more than half the budget. Without drastic changes in technologies and institutions, simply maintaining the current mediocre level of education for a growing population of children would require tax increases of 10-30%. Meeting the neglected learning needs of adults through conventional schooling would impose a comparable increase.

In the impending era of fiscal austerity, increased taxing and spending for education will be virtually impossible; reduced appropriations are more likely. Under these circumstances, cost containment and productivity are destined to become central concerns of public policies on education and training.

The Learning Technology Revolution

Out of sheer necessity, the demand for cost-effective instructional technology is about to explode. The same rapidly advancing computer and communication technology that is creating much of the need for lifelong training and education is also providing the technological means to meet these learning needs with vastly improved efficiency and effectiveness.

A study at MIT showed that traditional classroom instruction was the only one of nearly 20 communications media studied whose productivity actually declined during the past two decades—all others grew either steadily or explosively. A recent study by Education TURNKEY Systems Inc. found that the average cost of classroom instruction in elementary and secondary schools is $1.25/student/hour; equivalent computer-based instruction costs $1.10/student/hour. And the cost gap is steadily widening as schools grow more expensive while computer technology rapidly gets cheaper. Education delivered

Adult retraining program at the University of Maryland. Employers are now spending almost as much in employee training and education—some $80 billion a year—as is spent for all of formal higher education.

MADMUP Politics

Displaced, "overeducated" workers may be political time bomb

The next wave of unemployment and displacement of the U.S. work force will focus more on older, middle-class, white-collar and managerial/professional workers. Why? The aging baby-boom generation, the largest population group, is now past "entry-level" age. Also, the U.S. economy has shed so many production jobs that future employment problems will increasingly affect the predominant services sector.

Despite a higher level of education, most baby boomers already are worse off economically than their parents or even their counterparts of just 10 years earlier. Median income in constant dollars of men 25-34 years old declined 26% between 1973 and 1983. Average family income in this age group fell 14%, despite the increased number of two-career couples. The typical cost of home ownership for a couple in their early 30s has gone from about 20% of gross pay a decade ago to around 45% today.

The most educated baby boomers are becoming the most disillusioned by the growing gap between the rising cost of advanced education and its declining economic payoff. Only 53% of today's physicians in private practice are working at full capacity, and a surplus of 100,000 physicians is projected in the 1990s.

Many lawyers are now underemployed or unemployed; yet the number of law school graduates may double within a decade. Technology is expected to make most dentistry obsolete by the turn of the century. American corporations are steadily cutting out thousands of the staff and middle-management jobs that used to soak up MBAs.

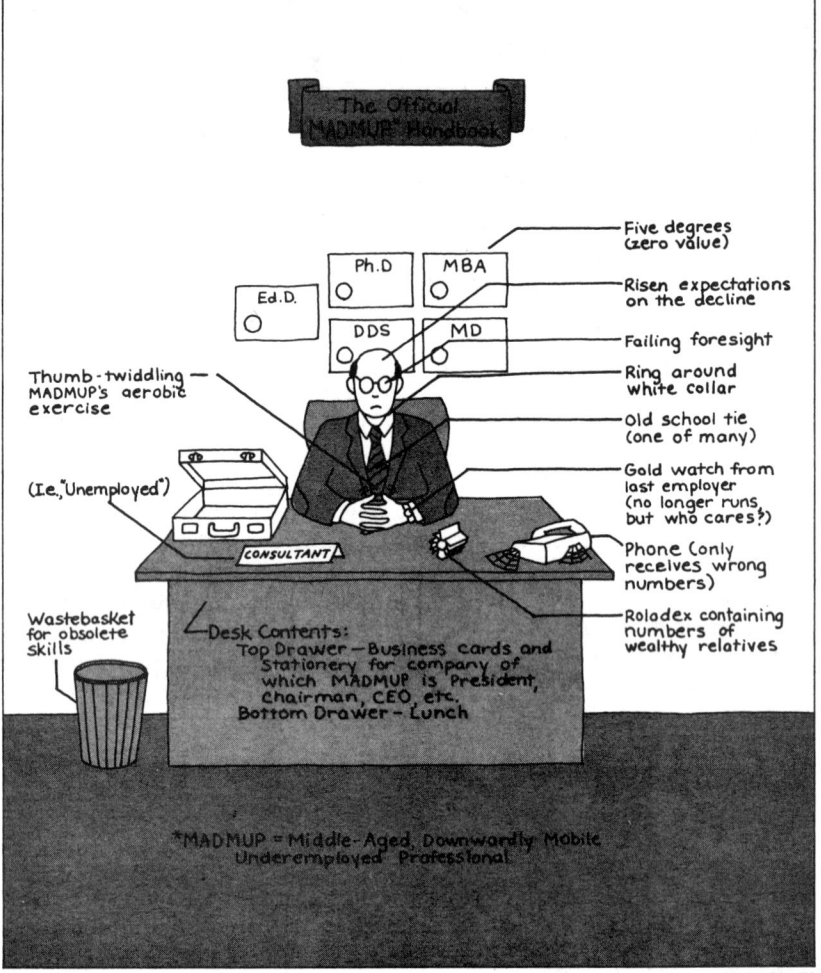

One consequence of this changing economic tide will be a political watershed. In the first half of this decade, political campaigners were infatuated with "Yuppies"—Young, Upwardly mobile Professionals. In the second half, politicians increasingly will be besieged by a growing, angry mass of MADMUPs—Middle-Aged, Downwardly Mobile, Underemployed Professionals.

MADMUP politics will be less concerned with simply the quantity of jobs generated by the economy and ever more concerned with social status and quality of work. The MADMUP phenomenon will be grossly understated or entirely missed by conventional econometric statistics because MADMUPs will go to heroic lengths to mask their true status—they will live off a spouse's or relative's income rather than accept "welfare"; they will call themselves "self-employed" or a "consultant" rather than "unemployed"; many will cling to unproductive jobs with apparent social status rather than shift to better-paying vocations of much lesser esteem.

The disappointment and frustration of this group of overeducated, overqualified, and underemployed workers will affect other strata of society besides their own. Their failure at upward mobility threatens faith in an "American dream" subscribed to by their parents, by their children, and by a host of other working people with less-esteemed vocations and credentials.

—**Lewis J. Perelman**

> "Had the productivity of education increased during the last 40 years as rapidly as the productivity of computation, a bachelor's degree from Harvard could be attained in 10 minutes at a cost of about 10¢."

via telecommunications can be even more efficient. For instance, *Sesame Street* (one of the most expensive but also most successful educational TV programs) costs 1¢/viewer/hour.

Computers also can help cut costs and improve effectiveness in education and training by being applied to the management of instruction. Much of the cost overhead in schools is bureaucratic paperwork that can be vastly reduced by automation.

The combination of computers and optical-storage devices—videodiscs—has already been applied successfully to industrial and military training. The new compact-disc data-storage systems promise to vastly expand the market for computer-based instructional technology. One disk holds as much information as 20 encyclopedias or a full set of textbooks required for four years of college.

Had the productivity of education increased during the last 40 years as rapidly as the productivity of computation, a bachelor's degree from Harvard could be attained in 10 minutes at a cost of about 10¢. Perhaps the comparison is too extreme, but even agriculture, a pretty conservative business, has managed to increase its productivity by an order of magnitude in the past hundred years, while schools have been technologically stuck or going backwards.

Policy Impact

The technology exists to greatly increase the productivity of the learning process. But institutions are technologies, too, and fundamental technological innovations inevitably require social and political transformation that established institutions instinctively resist.

Where learning consumers are accountable for costs and where competition offers choice, the application of innovative systems to improve the cost-effectiveness of learning can be readily observed: in the military, in corporations, in proprietary schools, etc. Where government shields academic institutions from competition and dilutes or prevents consumer accountability for costs—notably in elementary and secondary schools and also to a growing extent in formal higher education—educational productivity is poor and declining.

America's hopes for future economic and political leadership will depend on when public policy catches up with economic reality: In the information age, learning is in, school is out.

Computer Tutor

BRITISH INFORMATION SERVICES

A computerized training system designed in Britain helps teach workers how to run an automated machine shop. Companies can thus avoid using expensive production equipment for instruction.

The Denford Flexible Machining System (FMS), said to be the first package designed exclusively for training purposes, includes two small industrial robots, a computer-controlled lathe, a milling machine, a conveyor, and software. In the photo, an instructor shows how to program one of the robots.

According to author Lewis Perelman, the technologies that are displacing many workers can also be used to improve training programs, so that displaced workers can quickly learn new skills.

Source: Denford Machine Tools Ltd., Birds Boyd, Brighouse, West Yorkshire, HD6 1NB, England.

About the Author

Lewis J. Perelman is president of Strategic Performance Services, P.O. Box 5500, McLean, Virginia 22103. He is author of *The Learning Enterprise: Adult Learning, Human Capital, and Economic Development* (Council of State Planning Agencies, 1984).

Rowan A. Wakefield

Home Computers & Families

The Empowerment Revolution

Home computers will give the American family vast new powers over information and services. This new power will make families increasingly self-reliant, says author Rowan Wakefield.

The really big home computer revolution is about to explode. Studies comparing society's assimilation of the home computer with other home-related technologies (television, radio, the automobile, etc.) each show the latter half of this decade as the beginning of major penetration of the American home by computers, with market forces turning the 1990s into a golden era of home computer use.

Such growth is not surprising. Indeed, it is inevitable, for the family and the home computer form a potentially unique and ideal marriage. Their relationship is potentially a powerful one in our emerging information society, where information has become America's principal product and access to it offers power.

The family, society's truly multipurpose institution, is unique in its potential to take full advantage of the vast capabilities of the computer, civilization's first complete multipurpose technology. With a computer, the family can create, manipulate, transmit, store, and retrieve information, and gain access to economic, political, educational, social, and cultural information. The computer-empowered family thus has a greater degree of self-reliance as it becomes increasingly less dependent on many outside information-based services, public and private.

"People have become more selective about buying software. They want quality, not just color, bells, and whistles," according to Nancy Dillon, owner of Phoenix, Arizona-based Strictly Software, which publishes software directories. She sees the home computer market, stimulated by increasing availability of quality software, growing in many areas, including

Computerized compact-disc system contains the entire text of the Encyclopaedia Britannica on one disk. Such developments in computerized educational material will shift the balance of power from the education establishment to the home, says author Wakefield.

home education for children in cooperation with schools, home education for adults, and senior citizen involvement in communications, security, etc.

The home computer revolution is so new that we are only beginning to get results of meaningful studies of its impact on families. But such studies already show several benefits from home computer use. Families using home computers, for example, tend to spend much less time watching television; parents and children tend to spend more time together when the family uses home education programs. In general, home computer use is showing that it can be a positive, enhancing influence on family life, outweighing most potential disadvantages.

Family Empowerment By Home Computer

"Family empowerment" is a great social revolution in the making. The question is not, "Will it happen?" but rather, "How soon?" Its coming is inevitable, a direct result of the marriage of the home computer with the family in our emerging information society. It is the natural evolution of the democratization of information use begun more than 500 years ago by Gutenberg.

Family empowerment means not only putting the family in the forefront of the information society but also using home computers to bring back into the home many functions that were there before the industrial revolution—before education went to school, work went to factories and offices, and health care went to hospitals and clinics. This means reversing a long-term trend that has left many homes little more than places to eat, sleep, and watch television.

Now, thanks to the home computer, expert systems, and self-help programs, these functions can come back home without loss of literacy, job security, or life expectancy. In fact, these functions can be enhanced when done at home, as families regain control of their lives, become more cohesive and stronger, and restore a large measure of their fundamental reason for being: mutual self-help and caring.

The following sections describe areas of potential family empowerment by home computer.

Power Over Entertainment

Computer games have changed radically since PAC Man™. Today's "interactive fiction" programs, for example, are like book or short story writing; in them, you are the main character, playing the part of a detective, a wizard, a ship's captain, or whatever. Far from eliminating the written word—as many critics feared—these new computer games take the written word a step beyond the one-dimensional world of the novel and give us a preview of a different form of literature in the future.

Role-playing games, in which the computer is an integral part, tend to blur the line between entertainment and education as they offer new and often revolutionary ways of learning and solving problems. The value of such entertainment, according to Bob Albrecht, president of DragonQuest of Menlo Park, California, and editor of *Adventures in Learning*, is that youthful players use a variety of computer programs in playing: word processing, spread sheets, data base management, etc., all of which stand them in good stead when they enter the world of work later.

Home computers—aided by such video developments as the VCR—are helping to speed the trend of giving families greater control over their leisure time, including entertainment that they can select to fit their values or create themselves. Thus, families will become less dependent on major TV networks, movie companies, the mass media, and the major purveyors of games.

Power Over Education

Families are spending (depending on whose statistics you use) from two to ten times the amount of money spent by schools on computer education programs. Future Computing, Inc., estimates that, well before the decade's end, home purchases will account for 70% of a billion-dollar computer education software market. That represents a significant shift in the balance of educational power from the education establishment to the home.

But such family empowerment should be measured not only quantitatively but qualitatively as well. Families can select home computer education programs to suit individual values, intellectual interests, learning speeds, or other preferences. And they can adapt or create their own programs infinitely faster than it takes a new textbook to reach the market, continually enriching these teaching and learning materials from child to child, generation to generation.

Power Over the Health Professions Field

The 1979 U.S. Surgeon General's annual report pointed out that increasing our life expectancy is largely a matter of how we use information. Seventy percent of the increase is information-use-based

---

"'Family empowerment' is a great social revolution in the making."

(50% lifestyle information and 20% environment information). Of the remaining factors, 20% is genetic and only 10% involves intervention by the formal health-care establishment.

Since the computer has become our information manager *par excellence*, home computer programs dealing with physical and mental health promotion, diagnosis, and treatment may become a multi-billion-dollar market.

In the area of treatment, we will see more programs like the federally operated Physicians Data Query, or PDQ, an authoritative cancer textbook updated monthly, including a list of experimental treatments and a directory of 10,000 U.S. physicians who specialize in cancer care. The physicians on the PDQ staff, who estimate that 40,000 more people annually could be cured of cancer with uniform available application of the best therapy, welcome patients using the program to pressure their own doctor into using the data base. Those familiar with PDQ see no reason why the concept can't be extended to any disease.

For prevention, the family can now use simple computer programs in diet, exercise, drug and alcohol abuse, stress control, health-risk appraisals, and other related areas. Exciting new programs involving life-cycle histories may well become the omnibus family health program vehicle. A psychologist I know has already started one for his newborn son. This could tie in ideally with Blue Cross's "Life Card" or with the forthcoming personal laser cards, which can store two megabytes of information.

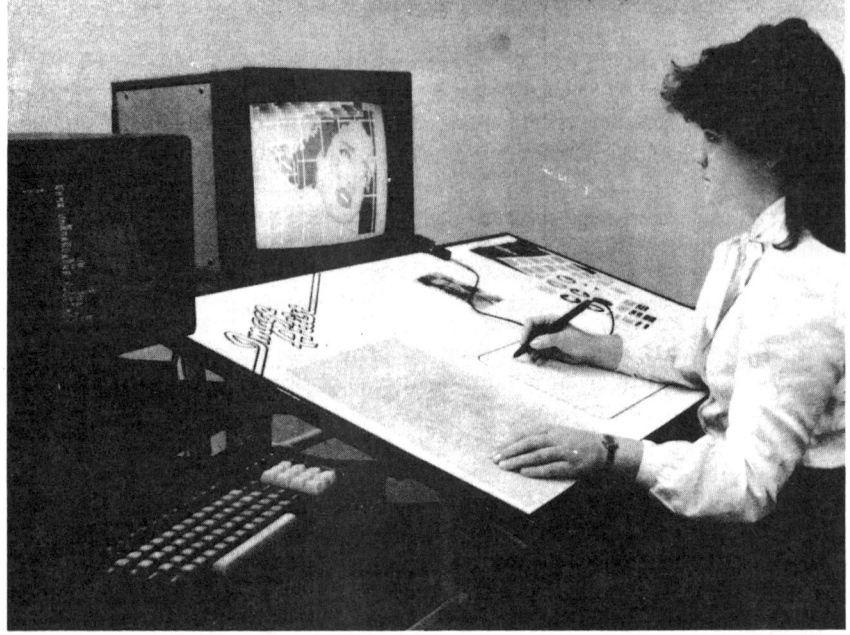

Power Over Government

Family empowerment here takes two thrusts. First, home computers linked to telecommunications systems can give families more power over elected representatives and government bureaucrats by more effectively monitoring their activities. This is becoming easier as congressmen are increasingly getting personal computers to link them to their home constituencies.

Second, families tapping into the world's many data bases can gain direct access to and use of information affecting complex government policy decisions. This may become one of the most significant forms of citizen/family empowerment. It is made possible by taking advantage of the growing number of on-line data bases (currently more than 1,500 worldwide) linked to home use of econometric modeling and more sophisticated expert systems and decision-simulating programs as they become increasingly available to home computer use.

The latter, drawing on data base and networking information, enables family members to be just as knowledgeable as any government expert. For example, families could examine the impact of tax reform on the whole range of family activities, including family businesses; the impact on student loans of decreasing government subsidies; or even the impact of an Iraqi victory over Iran on the future of Israel or world oil prices. They could manipulate the data in numerous ways, looking at various options in the public domain and others they could create themselves.

Power Over Other Professional Service Fields

There will be no shortage of program material for families in virtually all professional service fields. Much will be created specifically for family use. But there is a gold mine in programs on which professionals, including physicians, lawyers, accountants, stock brokers, travel agents, etc., have spent hundreds of millions of dollars developing for professional use—never intending their use independently by clients, patients, or families.

Bright entrepreneurs are constantly digging into this gold mine, stealing, adapting, or otherwise creating *de novo* programs to meet more and more types of consumer needs. The Educational Testing Service has spent years and a great deal of money developing SIGI, a college and career counseling computer program. They have gone to great lengths to restrict its use exclusively to institutions. Similar programs, however—practically clones—are constantly coming on the market for consumers at affordable costs.

The American Library Association surveyed use of on-line computer services available in libraries. They expected to find business market research coming in first, with library use second. To their great surprise, lay use was first to tap into MEDLINE, the National Library of Medicine's data base. It was being used to supplement or check information beyond what these lay people believed their doctors had given them.

HDG Software, Inc., a Sherborn, Massachusetts, company, offers LegalEase, a do-it-yourself computer disk with 150 contracts, agreements, leases, a simple will, power of attorney, a real estate brokerage agreement, and other binding business forms—all for less than $100. "Take the law into your own hands," its promotion urges. A California company offers computer programs for filing for uncontested divorces, or drawing up living-together contracts, etc.

In accounting, home tax preparation programs have been on the market for several years. Already, home investment service programs, linked with discount brokers, give family members quick, easy, low-cost home service. In England, family members can bypass travel agents and make on-line travel arrangements from home terminals directly with British Railways.

"Image Artist" system provides a low-cost, computerized drafting and illustration system for designers. Such tools will help expand the working-from-home movement.

In the field of religion, the *Church Computer Users Network Newsletter* recently listed over 200 program resources, predominantly for church management, but many also for religious education and Bible study that could be used by families.

Power Over Work

The growing trend toward self-employment and working at home gives family members increasingly greater power over their work environment and working conditions. Self-employment in the United States has risen steadily since the early 1970s, with the computer helping turn work at home—especially for women and the disabled—into a viable, recognized business activity. Some predictions call for 25% to 35% of all paid work to be done out of the home by the turn of the century.

Marion Behr, vice president of the National Alliance for Home-Based Business Women, estimates that as many as 15 million homemakers, widows, retirees, etc., are potential home-based businesswomen. For these women, working at home, assisted by a computer, is about the only way to get into business with virtually no capital investment.

Power Over the Marketplace

The use of the home or office computer to get information more effectively on goods and services is already increasing consumer and family power over the production and distribution of goods and services. Computers give family members immediate, direct access to extensive public and private consumer information bases.

The business community itself is moving in this direction. For example, the Ford Motor Company has begun replacing salesmen with interactive computer programs that potential buyers can use directly. The computer has much more factual information, is consistent, is quick, and doesn't forget. The company says this program is aimed at buyers who are becoming "more sophisticated." I read this as "more empowered."

Families, as they change their traditional economic role from exclusively consumers to producers as well, become "prosumers," as Alvin Toffler calls them in *The Third Wave*.

Power in the Creative Arts

Families using computers can now produce music without instruments or musicians, graphic arts without models, video dramas without leaving home—all using fast-moving electrons and their own creativity. Of course, word processing programs are already demonstrating many ways of stimulating or improving writing ability.

The use of the home computer for these purposes, as a powerful new aid to creativity, may well become one of the greatest growth areas in home use. It could, for the first time in history, enable vast numbers of people to attain close to their full creative potential. Relatively inexpensive programs capable of doing these things are coming on the market almost weekly.

Power Over Home Management

This includes the many areas already penetrated by home computers: home security, home energy control, home banking, home shopping, and indeed virtually all recognized forms of household and family management. The increasing use of computerized personal and household robots will also play an important role in this area of family empowerment.

Power Over Communications And the Mass Media

Use of the personal computer linked—usually via a modem—to the world's telecommunications systems is one of the biggest and most significant changes since the initial burst of home computer purchases in the early 1980s. Communications is now a major use of the computer. More than 75% of U.S. businesses will have modems by 1990. In homes with computers, 30% now have modems; more than 60% are projected to have them by 1990, and by then most computers will come with modems built in. The French government has begun giving computer terminals to telephone subscribers in lieu of phone books because they are cheaper in the long run and can be kept constantly updated.

The growing use of computers for communications has led to the emergence of information utilities that combine the functions of an electronic encyclopedia with a central switching station, enabling users not only to gain access to all kinds of data bases but also to communicate with other users. For example, CompuServe, an information utility with over 250,000 subscribers, has an index of services available covering more than 1,000 entries, from news/weather/sports services to medical, travel, legal, educational, and reference library services.

Computer bulletin boards give home computer users access to vast information resources, which are exchanged, given away, or sold for nominal fees. There are currently 1,500 bulletin boards in existence, covering just about every interest imaginable, and there will be many times this number by the 1990s.

Using the home computer as an alternative or supplemental form of communication gives the family its own communications medium. Families can thus communicate more easily with other family members, friends, businesses, congressmen, etc., and have easy access from home to libraries, schools, original information sources, and the world's rapidly growing number of data bases. All this tends to make families less dependent on the mass media and large information-related institutions.

"Some predictions call for 25% to 35% of all paid work to be done out of the home by the turn of the century."

> "Today's youth will bring computer skills to their own families and households in the 1990s, finally giving families the in-house computer competence they have lacked."

How Can All This Happen?

Family empowerment will inevitably continue and grow. There will be a steadily growing need by families for all kinds of professional services—from marriage and family therapy and counseling to legal, financial, educational, and religious services.

At the same time, while there is an enormous reservoir of professional services available to meet these growing family needs, there are serious barriers, such as high costs, restricted delivery of services due to high insurance costs, inaccessibility, inconvenience, insensitivity to widely varying family values, and a computer technology that is often difficult for the layman to use and that lacks adequate programs.

These barriers are rapidly being overcome or bypassed, as home computers become faster, more powerful, smaller, more versatile, cheaper, and easier to use; as better, more varied, more sophisticated, and more practical consumer programs become available at affordable costs; and as home computers linked to telecommunications systems become more widely accepted, with less costly linking operations. Especially significant is the growing trend of adapting complex expert-system programs from large to small computers.

The key ingredient that will make all of this happen is the estimated 96.8 million households that will be in the United States in 1990. That's eight times the number of U.S. businesses, and 840 times the number of schools, two of today's largest markets for personal computers. The Census Bureau projects that more than half of these households—52 million—could be earning more than $20,000 by 1990.

Today's youth will bring computer skills to their own families and households in the 1990s, finally giving families the in-house computer competence they have lacked. Only then will we see the family/computer marriage fully consummated.

Computer-competent families and households will form an enormous market for U.S. and foreign technical and business entrepreneurs. But to reach this mass market they must create and sell machines that are cheap, versatile, powerful, and easy to communicate with. And software must be created and marketed to meet the needs of these households. All of this is technologically possible.

Assessing Families' Computer Needs

Sales of home computers have slacked off after the phenomenal growth of the early 1980s. From 1979 to 1984, computers in American homes jumped incredibly from virtually zero to almost 10 million. Recently, however, not only has growth slowed precipitously, but surveys show that many home computers are gathering dust as families cannot find uses for them.

What we are now experiencing is a healthy shakedown period in both the industry and the user community prior to another period of major growth. This is the time to pause to assimilate, to evaluate, and to find out how to take full advantage of what has been learned so far about this powerful new phenomenon.

Now is also the time for high-tech industry and small entrepreneurs to reassess and upgrade the quality of programs and to increase program diversity. It is the time for industry to step up the power and expand the utility of the computers, to make them far easier for the masses to use.

It is the time for the research community to begin providing more results of studies of the impact of home computers on families and society. Now is the time for families of computer users to seek out and create a demand for a greater diversity of quality computer programs that can be used to help strengthen virtually all types of home and family activities. And it is time for everyone to think seriously about what regulations, if any, may be required to control or liberate this technology for consumers.

Almost all of these things appear to be happening, in various stages, as society prepares for the real home computer revolution soon to come.

We must accept this home computer revolution as inevitable. It is too late for the Luddites. So we must try harder to understand what is happening as this technology permeates our society and act on this information intelligently and rationally.

What about a society filled with computer-empowered families? Will empowered families turn their new power inward, seeking ever-greater self-sufficiency? This could lead to the fulfillment of de Tocqueville's worst fears. The great French historian foresaw clearly that America's great sense of freedom, its rugged individualism, were the sources of its strength but could lead to its demise if freedom and independence were to run rampant and become anarchy.

Or will families use their new power for the common good and thus vastly strengthen not only themselves but society as a whole? It is too soon to know the answers to these questions, but the greatest tragedy would be to let our ignorance or fears of this awesome technology stop us from taking advantage of its vast potential for family empowerment and for improving society.

About the Author

Rowan A. Wakefield is senior editor of *American Family*, a national newsletter on family policy and programs. His address is Deer Island, Maine 04627.

This article draws on material from an article by Wakefield that appeared in a recent issue of *The Journal of Family and Culture*.

New Challenges for the Information Age

TERRY GRAVES

The last 30 years have seen rapid growth and evolution of entire industries to support the information needs of the organization and the individual. These industries have now become the engine that drives the economy, and they provide the key to future prosperity.

Despite the rapid progress of the information technology revolution, we are still in the early years of the information age. Over the next several decades, information technology will be a principal contributor to profound changes in how we do business, how we work, and how we play.

Surveys project a tenfold growth in the next decade both in numbers of personal computers and in central processing capacity. They show office automation budgets growing at an equal rate. By 1995, the terminal or workstation will be nearly as common as the telephone is today, and in many cases the phone and terminal will be the same device, using the same networks and linking the same people together.

So much human time will be tied up using computers that people will demand 100% availability and instantaneous response time, and both will be cheaply available. Basic information utilities will be as economical and taken for granted as light, power, and phone. And we will be comfortable using them.

During the 1990s, we can expect a crisis—one so subtle we would be wise to begin guarding against it even now. The cheapening of information brings with it the potential devaluation of quality and creativity. We will have spent enormous amounts of energy for systems to store, process, and dispense incalculable varieties and quantities of data, documents, and messages.

We will have made the cutting and pasting together of all ideas into new formats easy beyond belief, and we will have opened the libraries of the world to infinite replications. It is not too soon to start thinking about what we will do with it all. How will we be able to sort out the useful from gibberish? How will we recognize and reward creativity and new insights when we have access to so much we haven't begun to explore?

The availability of limitless information also provides great opportunities to remain competitive. Large organizations in Japan manage their information resources very effectively. They study worldwide trends such as resource allocations, production standards, marketing statistics, and trade policies. They then disseminate information to all departments; each division in turn uses whatever is pertinent to its specific operation.

In the not-too-distant future, you will be able to tap "expert systems" to get whatever information you want. It will be like having the leading scientist in England, the most renowned heart surgeon in Africa, the newest computer specialist in Silicon Valley, or even the best cook in France as a first-hand adviser. How we make use of information and communications available to us—locally as well as globally—by merely pushing a button is a wonderful opportunity and challenge.

The challenges in the 1990s will require enormous efforts beyond those already begun. We must use our computer resources to assure greater quality in service than we now accept. For example, artificial-intelligence products will run our computers and networks, and they will apply other tools to indexing and abstracting, to error analysis and detection.

Certainly we will not have reached the limits to growth of information and information technology in the mid-1990s—and perhaps we never will, as the technology continues to develop and evolve.

—John Diebold

John Diebold is chairman and founder of The Diebold Group, Inc. (475 Park Avenue South, New York, New York 10016), an international management consulting firm. He is author of the 1952 management classic *Automation*.

Philip Kotler

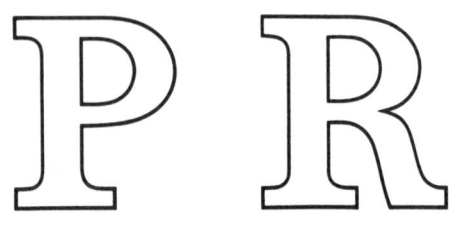

PROSU

Prosumers—consumers who produce goods and services for their own consumption—will bring changes to the way business is transacted in the future.

Alvin Toffler, in his book *The Third Wave*, prophesied the emergence of a new class of consumers in the post-industrial world: "prosumers." Prosumers are people who choose to produce some of the goods and services they consume. They can be found making their own clothes, repairing their own cars, and hanging their own wallpaper.

All of these goods and services could be purchased in the marketplace, and, in fact, most people today purchase them from others. This is the essence of being a consumer. The essence of being a prosumer, on the other hand, is to produce goods and services for one's own consumption.

Mature consumerism is, for many, increasingly unfulfilling. So few of us make anything that we consume that we lose all sense of ourselves as producers, or at least as producing consumers—that is, prosumers. Yet many prosumers can be found, and more are emerging.

Toffler distinguishes between "production for use" and "production for exchange." When people produce for use, production and consumption are fused in the same person. When they produce for exchange, production and consumption are separated; people put all their time into producing one thing and use their earnings to acquire needed goods and services that they don't have the time or skill to produce.

Moving Toward Prosumerism

Toffler argues that production and consumption activity became separated during the Industrial Age. In the pre-industrial age (or First Wave, as Toffler terms it), agriculture was the dominant institution. The vast majority of people were prosumers. They hunted or grew their own food, made their own clothing, and created their own amusements. They made up Sector A, the largest sector of society.

A few members of the community specialized in some mode of production, such as candlemaking or blacksmithing. They traded their surplus output for things that others produced. They were consumers in their nonwork life and made up a much smaller Sector B. The dominant process of First Wave societies was self-production, the norm was survival, and the social nexus was kinship, friendship, tribe.

The Second Wave appeared with the Industrial Revolution in England. The factory became a dominant institution, and an increasing number of people spent their productive hours there. Most people worked in factories 8 to 12 hours a day and used their income to buy what they needed in the marketplace.

Most people produced for exchange, not for use. Sector A (prosumers) grew small, while Sector B (consumers) grew large. The major group of remaining prosumers were housewives, in that they cooked, cleaned, sewed, knit, and shopped for their own use, not for pay. Prosumption activity is so undervalued in Second Wave societies that these societies don't even record the value of homemaker activities in estimating their gross national product.

THE FUTURIST, September-October 1986

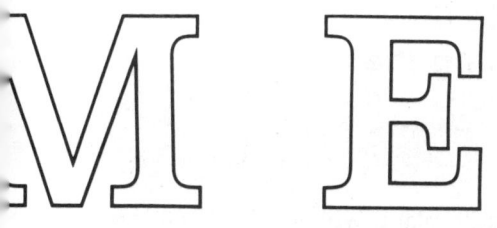

MERS: A New Type of Consumer

Toffler says that the dominant processes in Second Wave societies are industrialization and marketization. Second Wave societies are marked by the establishment and elongation of exchange networks through which people obtain needed goods and services. Goods are produced under the norm of efficiency and are consumed under the norm of indulgence. The social nexus holding people together is contracts and transactions instead of kinship and social relations. With industrialization and marketization, people increasingly become specialized producers and are increasingly unable to produce almost anything else—even cooking.

Toffler sees the post-industrial age as moving toward a synthesis of First and Second Wave societies: the Third Wave. The dominant institution in Third Wave societies is the home, or electronic cottage, where most people carry on their production and consumption. More people shift more of their time to prosumption activity, and Sector A starts increasing in size relative to Sector B.

Because people now produce more of their own goods and services, markets become less important, since they exist to meet exchange needs in those societies where most production is for exchange. Toffler sees the dominant process in Third Wave societies to be "demarketization," including demassification as well. The norm of Third Wave societies is individual (rather than mass) consumption. The social nexus is the family and, secondarily, the neighborhood.

The Rise of the Prosumer

Why will people move toward more prosumption activity? Toffler presents several arguments. First, the workweek will continue its long decline, from 80-90 hours during the early days of the Industrial Revolution to 40 hours today to even fewer hours in the future. The scarcity of jobs will lead some companies to adopt work-sharing schemes. Furthermore, some people will volunteer to work less than 40 hours, preferring to work part time.

Second, people will be more highly educated. They will not accept boring work as readily. Advancing technology, especially in computers and telecommunications, will tempt them to use their time in other ways.

Third, the rising cost of skilled labor—plumbers, carpenters, etc.—will drive more people to do their own work. And if they are unemployed or underemployed, they will have time to take care of these tasks. Thus, rising service costs will lead to more prosumption.

Fourth, people want more physical activity as their work becomes increasingly mental in a technologically advancing society. Those sitting at desks all day will seek physical activities, including some involving self-production.

Fifth, some people will feel that they can produce better goods and services than are available in the market, especially if manufactured goods and services decline in quality. People who have developed a high sensitivity to quality and a strong instinct for workmanship will undertake projects at home that normally would be contracted for in the marketplace.

Sixth, more people will turn away from mass-produced goods and seek more self-expression by producing their own goods and services. They will increasingly attend

CORBETTE/ANKELE

Woman tends garden and fruit trees. Gardening is an ideal prosumption activity, producing at least part of a family's food needs.

> **Modern computers will permit people to participate more actively in designing the products they want.**

courses on cooking, gardening, knitting, weaving, painting, and so on.

In advancing these points, Toffler presents scattered rather than comprehensive evidence. He notes, for example, that self-care items—do-it-yourself pregnancy-testing kits, throat cultures, etc.—have grown into a multi-billion-dollar industry. He cites the high number of electric power tools bought by "do-it-yourselfers." He notes that more people are attending more colleges and continuing-education centers to learn more crafts and skills than ever before.

Selling to the Prosumer

If Toffler is right about a swelling wave of prosumption activity, then marketers face a challenging—if not frustrating—future. They will find fewer customers for mass-produced goods and services and less consumer interest in brands. On the other hand, alert marketers will discover new opportunities in a number of areas.

Marketers will find it increasingly hard to sell those goods and services that people can produce themselves. Therefore, marketers need to research which goods and services people are most likely to start producing themselves.

For example, if more people learn how to repair their own automobiles, garages will have less work to do. If more people hang their own wallpaper, professional wallpaper hangers will find less work. If more people bake their own bread, automated bakeries will find fewer customers for their output.

Prosumption activities that are likely to attract consumers will have four characteristics. They will promise high cost saving, require little skill, require little time and effort, and yield high personal satisfaction.

One activity, for example, that satisfies many of these criteria is home improvements and decorating. The homeowner who paints his own walls saves the high cost of hiring a painter, finds it easy to paint well with modern paint rollers, and feels some satisfaction both while painting and when finished painting. We can therefore predict that house painting would move toward the prosumption camp.

People will want to play a larger role in designing or producing certain goods and services. One is reminded of the classic marketing situation in which consumers rejected a brand of cake mix that included egg powder because they wanted to add fresh eggs themselves. They wanted more participation in "giving birth" to the cake. Instead of moving toward task simplification, some consumers are moving toward task elaboration in the interest of achieving better quality, such as grinding coffee beans and brewing their own coffee instead of just adding boiling water to instant powdered coffee.

In Japan, many scroll painters make their own brushes, mix their own paints, and even make their own paper. These painters are thoroughgoing prosumers. Most Western painters, on the other hand, buy their paints, brushes, and canvases. Manufacturers will need to study which stages in the production process people might want to perform themselves.

The Prosumer and Modern Technology

Modern computers will permit people to participate more actively in designing the products they want. General Motors' Saturn project visualizes car buyers entering a showroom, sitting down at a computer terminal, and responding to questions about what they want in the way of the car's color, engine, seat material, radio, and so on. Their order is transmitted to the auto plant, which proceeds to produce the desired car.

Similarly, future home buyers could enter an architect's office, sit down at a computer terminal, and specify room sizes and layout, examine the results, and modify them until satisfaction is achieved. Or a person will enter a clothing store, stand before an electronic mirror, and press appropriate buttons that will superimpose various suits on him or her in different colors, styles, and materials. After finding the most pleasing look, he or she will press another button, and laser beams will cut and prepare the clothing.

The fact that people enjoy participating in production is demonstrated by a number of situations. Salad bars are increasingly popular in restaurants because many people prefer to "compose" their own salads. Certain ice cream parlors allow people to make their own sundaes. The success of the "Bradley GT kit"—with which a person can turn a Volkswagen into a sleek sports car—shows the interest of some people in producing complicated (and less expensive than ready-made) goods. A direct mail order company sells a set of step-by-step blueprints for making one's own helicopter.

Marketers, instead of fighting prosumers, should look for opportunities to facilitate prosumption activities. One way to facilitate prosumption is to create better tools for prosumers to use, including better electric power tools for carpentry work, better tools for farming small plots of land, and so on. Another way is to simplify the production process. Adhesive wallpaper, for example, allows more people to hang their own wallpaper.

One of the major growth markets spurred by prosumption will be the instruction market. More people will want to acquire skills for producing their own goods and ser-

Thirties-style car can be assembled from a kit. Prosumers enjoy participating in the production of the products they use.

vices. They will attend day and evening classes in cooking, gardening, auto repair, and dozens of other subjects. "How-to" books, magazines, audio and video tapes, and computer-aided instruction will flourish. Some marketers will develop "cool lines" (as opposed to crisis-oriented "hot lines") where they will sell information over the phone on how to make or fix things.

Different Goals, Different Needs

Whereas producers in Second Wave societies continued to add new consumer benefits to an elementary offer (called "product augmentation"), the tenor of Third Wave societies will be to pare down the number of "built-ins." The price of goods and services will therefore fall because their content has been reduced. The only marketers who will command premiums are those who add benefits most valued by consumers that consumers cannot add themselves.

Stores will have to revise their **strategies**. They will carry lower inventories of those goods that people will want to produce themselves, and they will carry higher inventories of those goods that prosumers will need, such as tools, gloves, etc. With people spending more time in their electronic homes, they will want goods and services to be located reasonably nearby. We can predict a dispersion and deconcentration of retailing and a renewal of neighborhood life.

Prosumers will show preferences for certain forms of retailing. They will rent more goods to clean their rugs, repair their cars, and maintain their gardens. Car washing establishments, where people drive their cars into bays and wash their own cars, will boom. People will also drive their cars into do-it-yourself garages and rent the testing equipment and tools to fix their cars. They will enter picture-framing workshops and rent tools and buy materials to make their own frames.

Marketers will have to direct their promotion appeals to themes stressing skill-building and productiveness. They will find it hard to combine mass consumption goods with self-fulfillment values.

Specialized (as opposed to mass) media will continue to grow in popularity. People will want to follow their own interests, not mass-produced programs. They will search for others with kindred interests, finding them and communicating with them through electronic media, such as computer networks and citizens band radio. Marketers will have to develop more specialized messages and media designed to reach highly segmented target markets. One sign of this segmentation is the phenomenal growth in special-interest magazines concurrent with the circulation decline of mass-audience magazines.

How Far Will Prosumption Go?

Any movement or change is always the result of opposing forces. Several forces could lead to more prosumption activity. Among them are the growth of structural unemployment, the rising cost of labor, the desire for higher-quality goods and services, the development of new technologies that enable people to participate in the design of customized goods, and a general increase in education and therefore desire for self-actualization.

At the same time, we should not underestimate the forces that will inhibit prosumption. First, threatened interest groups will use the law to prevent people from producing certain goods and services themselves. Thus, construction trade, unions will support the enforcement of building codes to prevent people from building their own garages, doing their own electrical work and plumbing, and so on. Physicians could discourage people from buying self-care and self-medication products. Teachers' unions will oppose families who want to take over their own children's education. Professionals of all kinds will sell people on the idea of buying services from professionals rather than performing those services for themselves.

> **Prosumerism will not suddenly burst on the scene but will emerge gradually from trends already in existence.**

Second, corporate America will increase its efforts to sell people on the life of ease and high consumption. Advertising will appeal to people's interest in convenience and comfort.

The effect of rising incomes on prosumption activity is ambiguous. Consumers with higher incomes can buy more of the services they need. On the other hand, they may also have more leisure time and want to spend it more productively.

We should recognize that few people will opt for 100% prosumption, even if prosumption activity increases. The 100% prosumer would be a hermit living in the woods like Thoreau, who produced his own food, clothing, and shelter. Other examples of complete prosumers would be Robinson Crusoe and the Swiss Family Robinson.

We can, in fact, distinguish two major types of prosumers who will be found in society.

1. The Avid Hobbyists. These are people who spend most of their time producing for exchange but who fill their leisure time with one or a few dominant hobbies. The avid gardener, the versatile home repairer, and the skilled cook are producers in two domains: their main occupation and their major hobby or hobbies.

2. The Archprosumers. These are people who want to practice a lifestyle that is closer to nature, where they produce more things themselves. They want to grow and can their own fruits and vegetables, knit and sew their own clothing, and be more independent of the mass production, mass consumption society. Their themes are "small is beautiful" and "less is more."

If Toffler is right, prosumerism will not suddenly burst on the scene but will emerge gradually from trends already in existence. Already, we see people who are spending more time producing goods and services for their own use than buying those goods and services in the marketplace. These people would rather walk to work than "taxi" to work. They would rather cook at home than eat in restaurants. They would prefer fixing their own plumbing to calling in a plumber.

In order to learn more about prosumerism, we should study certain groups more intently. Do young archetypal prosumers continue their lifestyle as they get older? Do older retired people with time on their hands move toward more self-production? Do poor people perform more prosumer activities?

The prosumer phenomenon represents a search for more creative and fulfilling lifestyles in an increasingly mechanistic world. People want to see themselves as cause, not effect; as players, not spectators, in producing their life results.

Customers shop in hardware department. Marketers will need to research which goods people are likely to produce themselves and what tools they will need to produce them.
SEARS, ROEBUCK AND CO.

About the Author

Philip Kotler holds the Harold T. Martin Chair of Marketing at Northwestern University and is author of *Marketing Management*. His article "'Dream' Vacations: The Booming Market for Designed Experiences," appeared in the October 1984 FUTURIST. His address is J.L. Kellogg Graduate School of Management, Northwestern University, Nathaniel Leverone Hall, 2001 Sheridan Road, Evanston, Illinois 60201.

Bernard I. Forman

Reconsidering Retirement

Understanding Emerging Trends

Dealing with the social and financial problems of older people entails much more than just piecemeal modifications of retirement policies in the United States. There is a need to change popular attitudes toward work and toward the concept of retirement itself. Yet, sensitivity to emerging social trends and understanding of forces underlying these trends are often conspicuous by their absence.

While the effects of the changing demography on political and socioeconomic realities are widely discussed, practical measures to moderate their impact are mainly temporizing evasions and circumventions. It is seldom disputed, for example, that wholesale reform of the American pension system is sorely needed to make it more equitable and comprehensive. Yet, very little actual improvement has emerged so far from the efforts of several congressional committees and presidential commissions specifically assigned to address the problem.

It is generally acknowledged by most students of American government that the necessary changes will not take place without some form of government intervention. It should be equally evident that no combination of makeshift, patchwork reforms can succeed in resolving the intricate, interlocking problems that arise from retirement. The economic advisability of continuing to encourage early retirement is especially doubtful. However, there is little agreement among advocates for the aging and

> Workers are opting for early retirement in increasing numbers. But this trend could have several serious long-term consequences—including an acute labor shortage in the not-too-distant future.

United Nations interpreter works in a booth overlooking a meeting room at U.N. headquarters. Mandatory retirement often forces highly skilled, experienced workers off the market. A recent congressional report suggests that the wasted know-how of older workers could be the key to increasing American productivity.

THE FUTURIST, June 1984

"The American public no longer accepts without question the thesis that retirement is an unadulterated blessing that provides a cure-all for our social and economic ills."

pension-fund experts as to the best way to treat retirement.

Balancing Benefits and Consequences

One valid concern is the balancing of short-term benefits of certain common employment practices—like that of mandatory retirement—against their long-term consequences. How wise is it, for example, to focus our current efforts on assuring full employment for young workers when dropping birthrates may bring an acute labor shortage in the not-so-distant future? Who will fill the vacant slots if qualified, experienced older workers are prevented from doing so or are encouraged to withdraw from the labor market? Social considerations aside, can commerce and industry afford to ignore the obvious need to retain the older worker who is willing and able to continue working? Can older workers continue their jobs without jeopardizing the opportunities for younger replacements?

During the Carter administration, Congress tried to find answers to such thorny questions, with mixed results. One report suggested that the know-how of older workers, now being wasted, was the key to increased American productivity. Other studies supported these assertions.

The American public no longer accepts without question the thesis that retirement is an unadulterated blessing that provides a cure-all for our social and economic ills. Nevertheless, Labor Department figures show that American workers continue to opt for early retirement in increasing numbers. The paradox is hard to explain, except in terms of the customary time lag between the availability of information and its digestion by the general public.

International Retirement Policies

In Europe, this trend has been even more pronounced. Max Horlick of the U.S. Social Security Administration describes the anomaly as follows: "Long-range planners discuss the need to extend the working career in order to defer payment of benefits and gain a longer period of contributions. The trend, however, tends to be toward earlier and earlier retirement."

Despite warnings that lowering the retirement age would create additional problems as the aging community grew, social and political pressures caused the warnings to be ignored. European planners seem to be fully aware of the contradictions, but are even more wary of the growing political influence of the elderly.

A substantial number of European countries, including both capitalist and Communist-bloc nations, have experimented with a variety of financial inducements designed to reduce or control unemployment by fostering the retirement of older workers. West Germany lowered the retirement age from 65 to 63 in 1968, with allowances for part-time employment under certain conditions. Denmark has permitted early retirements for reason of failing health since 1965, as has Norway for "premature aging." Both Norway and Sweden lowered the permissible age for retirement from 70 to 67 in 1974, and then to 65 in 1976.

In these countries, social planners have responded to the perceived needs of their older citizens in a manner that they consider the most humane and equitable. They have reacted to popular criticism of the policy of forced retirement with carefully crafted programs allowing for partial retirement, partial pensions, and other innovative options. They have, in short, tried to provide flexible choices. Yet some form of withdrawal from employment seems to be regarded as an absolute prerequisite for eligibility for government benefits.

Social and economic problems related to aging have become even more troublesome in Great Britain than they are in the United States. The long-held postulate that help for the old and underprivileged is a basic responsibility of government has come under serious challenge. For the first time in decades, it is being argued that even such a previously sacrosanct assumption has practical limitations. The result is that in Britain, as in the United States, the poor, the elderly, and the disadvantaged are the ones most profoundly affected by the reduction of public benefits and subsidies.

It is incontestable that maintaining even minimal standards of living among the world's vast numbers of unemployed is becoming an overwhelming problem. Even in Sweden, a country long associated with progressive social-welfare policies, the electorate seems to be having second thoughts about the feasibility of unlimited public support of social programs. To more and more people it is becoming manifest that if increasing masses of pensioners must be supported by decreasing numbers of the still-employed, the burden will eventually become unbearable.

The major political and economic systems of the Western world have responded to the current labor glut with what amounts to the same old failed remedies. They have tended to revert back to the solutions of the Great Depression, when it was believed that promoting earlier retirement of older workers would magically solve all problems of mass unemployment. They seem to have forgotten that the relief was only temporary and purchased at great cost.

France, under President Francois Mitterand's socialist government, has once again taken to trying to encourage earlier retirement in an attempt to "distribute" the country's jobs and stem the rising tide of unemployment. Much the same policy is being followed in Great Britain, Belgium, West Germany,

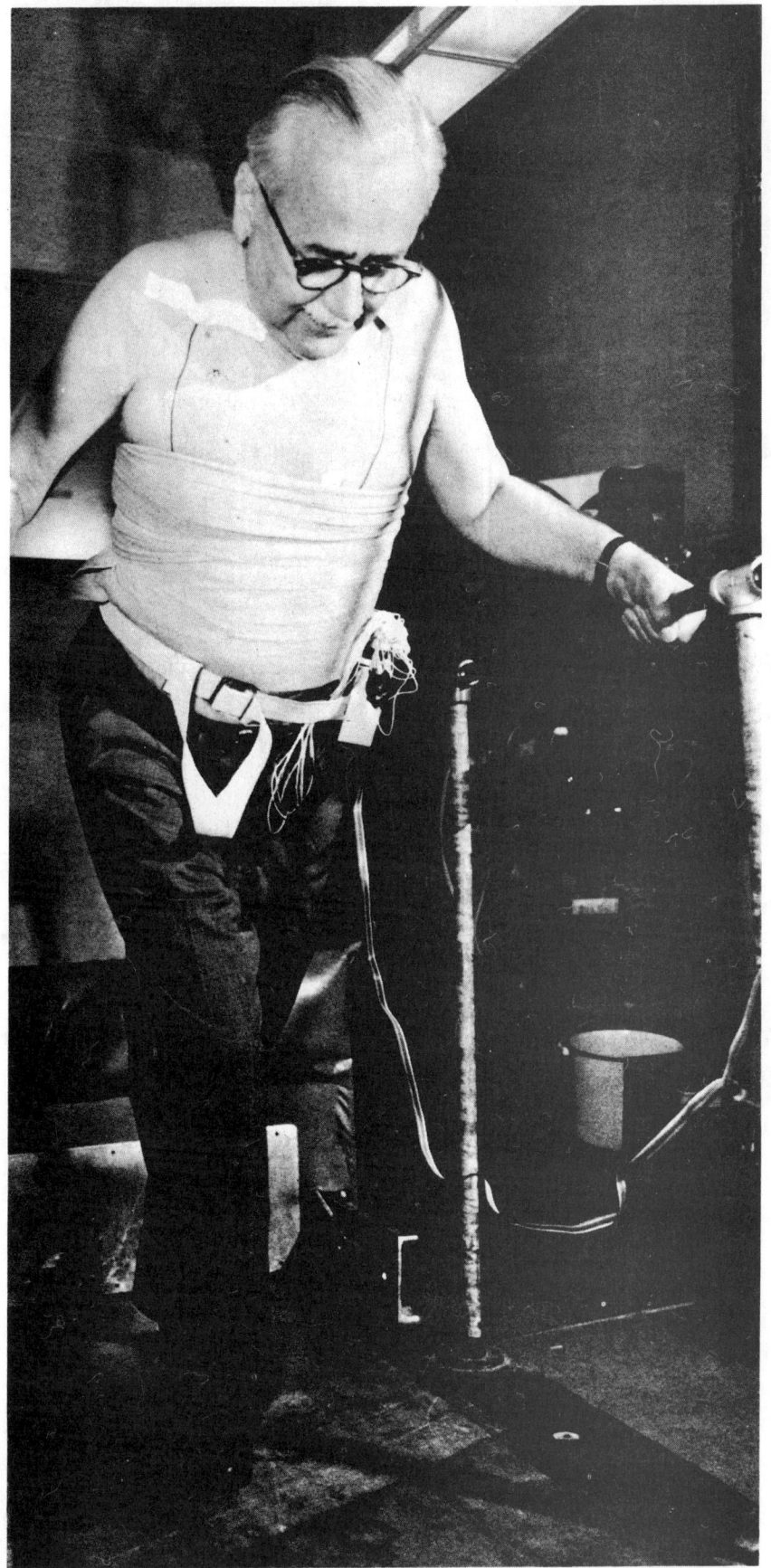

Elderly man undergoes an exercise test at the National Institutes of Health. Surveys have shown that declining health is no longer a major factor in early-retirement decisions; in fact, a majority of retirees would like to return to work.

the Netherlands, and Italy. Even among Communist-bloc nations—in Yugoslavia, Bulgaria, Czechoslovakia, Hungary, and the Soviet Union—the same tendency is manifesting itself.

In the Orient, we have a somewhat different picture, colored largely by massive overpopulation. Japan, for all its industrial and technological wizardry, is deeply troubled by the clash between the old tradition of reverence for the aged and the new demands of a modern technocracy. Lines have become sharply drawn between the mass of younger workers and a deeply entrenched gerontocracy. Still other cultural factors affect conditions in China, India, and other Asiatic societies. Even with cheap and abundant labor, none of them has completely escaped the socio-economic consequences of a worldwide increase in the number of older survivors.

Future Implications

The inclination to ignore the implications for the future of an aging work force is not necessarily shared by all government agencies. Serious efforts have been made by several governments to encourage later retirement in order to ease the strain on pension and retirement systems. In the Soviet Union, for example, some key officials have argued against removing experienced older workers from the labor force prematurely on the grounds that such actions are wasteful, uneconomic, and ultimately counterproductive.

The United States seems to be trapped between two equally important concerns. On the one hand, the public is becoming increasingly conscious of the aging of the population and the illogic and injustice of current retirement policies. On the other hand, there are worries about the possible effects that changing present retirement policies may have on the employment prospects of younger

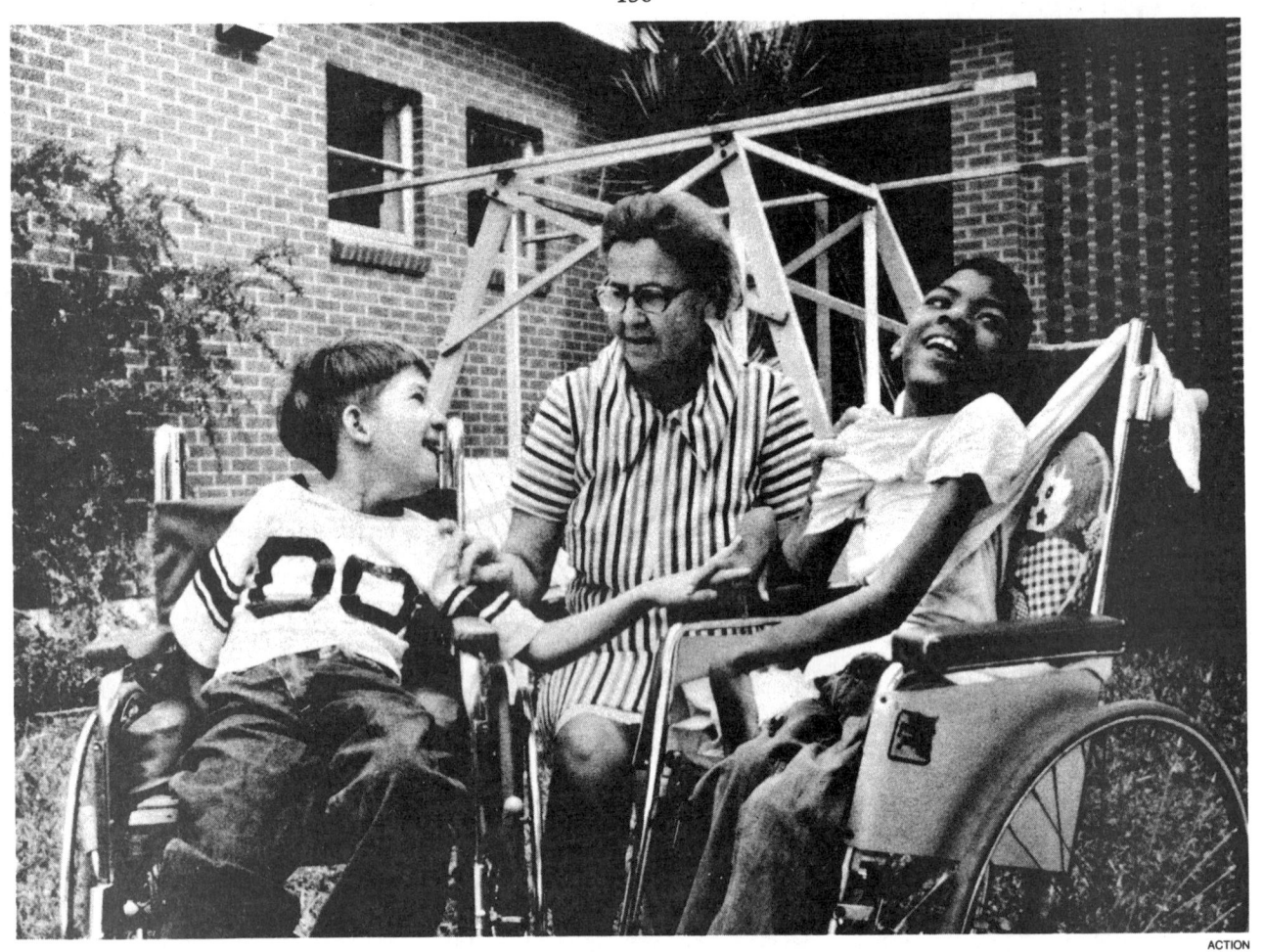

Retired woman cares for two handicapped children as part of a "foster grandparent" program in Mississippi. Increasingly, it is seen as good social and economic sense to better utilize the skills and abilities of older Americans, says author Bernard Forman.

workers. The concerns may be equally important, but they cannot be treated with a single "generic" remedy, appropriate for all economic ailments.

A 1979 Department of Labor-sponsored study contended that most early-retirement decisions were motivated by declining health rather than by an actual desire to withdraw from work. It saw those decisions as only minimally affected by the mandatory-retirement policies of employers. A Harris survey of the same year, however, disputed that conclusion. It showed that a majority of retirees regretted being induced to leave their jobs and would like to return to work, if that were possible. Harold Sheppard, President Carter's counselor on aging, stated that there were signs the trend toward early retirement was undergoing a definite reversal.

Several recent studies by Jerome Rosow and others at the Work in America Institute make detailed recommendations for alternatives to current retirement policies. One outlines some of the available new options for an "extended working life." Another describes some of the model retirement programs already in operation.

The Changing Public Opinion Of Retirement

There are signs of awakening public awareness of the wastefulness of premature retirement, along with a willingness to rethink and redefine the concept of retirement itself. Innovative pilot programs sponsored by both public and private agencies, aimed at providing meaningful employment for workers at or near retirement age, have emerged. Among notable examples are:

● The personnel policy of Baltimore's WMAR-TV, which deliberately attempts to match older employees with appropriate new jobs.

● The Travelers Insurance Company's ambitious retraining program for older employees, and its allied "Corporation for Older Americans."

● The "Retirement Planning for the 80s" project of the National Council on Aging.

A wide variety of alternatives to total retirement are already available. Among current variations of flexible or partial retirement are combinations of delayed or postponed retirement, in-company part-time work, or temporary assignments. There are also opportunities presented for phased-in or "tapered" withdrawal from full employment and a variety of novel shared-job arrangements.

Some firms offer continued accrual of pension benefits and others are pro-rated, proportionately reduced, offset, or postponed until full retirement occurs. In a few exceptional cases, in-service retraining programs that make pos-

> "The real question is not whether but how to assure all retirees of a comfortable old age without compelling them to retire either too early or too late."

sible the "redeployment" of older workers are available. Some companies have even tried copying the Danish experiment of voluntary demotion, which they have found preferable to involuntary retirement. However, it remains inescapable that the continuation of benefits in any situation is still contingent upon the good will and generosity of the employer, in the absence of federal mandates or regulation.

Even if this promising new trend develops into a full-scale readjustment of American employment patterns, some crucial questions remain to be answered. Among them are the feasibility (from the actuarial point of view) of continuing accrual of pension benefits after "retirement" and the political risks of raising the age of eligibility for Social Security.

Dissatisfaction with current retirement policies was seen in Congress with the passage of the Age Discrimination in Employment Amendments of 1978. The drive to eliminate mandatory retirement altogether has most recently been reactivated by Congressman Claude Pepper and others. President Reagan's own personal opposition to mandatory retirement has reinforced the movement, which is strongly supported by public opinion. Still, most labor unions continue to be ambivalent, mainly because their leadership views the issue as a useful weapon in labor-management negotiations. Academe remains, for its own special reasons, equally resistant to change, while other special-interest groups also persist in favoring traditional retirement policies.

In the business community, the picture continues to be mixed. However, there is evidence of a rising tide of opposition to present retirement practices, along with a belated recognition of their adverse social and economic consequences. More and more businessmen are beginning to see that the mushrooming army of unemployed and unproductive retirees is placing an intolerable strain on younger workers, on Social Security, on the American pension system, and on the economy as a whole. Changing demography, occupational shifts, labor-force composition, pension systems, and the whole gamut of employment issues play an interactive role in affecting the health or sickness of the national economy.

Changes Needed in Retirement Policies

Few Americans seriously question the right of every employee to some kind of livable income (whatever it may be called) after many years of service to an employer. Whether it is received in the form of an earned pension or as a Social Security payment, it is the deserved reward for services rendered. The real question is not whether but how to assure all retirees of a comfortable old age without compelling them to retire either too early or too late.

Should the income derived from a public or private pension be adequate to enable the retired worker to retain his or her pre-retirement style of living? Since no one has yet come up with a satisfactory estimate of what an adequate or decent standard of retirement living is (or should be), that must remain a moot question.

Nevertheless, there can be little doubt that some combination of private and public income maintenance is necessary to shield the average retired employee from inflation and impoverishment. For that reason, substantial improvements in the administration and distribution of both public and private pension funds are desirable. Yet it is equally important to be sure that the required reforms are not used merely as a pretext by the employer to spur accelerated retirement and circumvent the desire of capable older employees for continued employment on a full- or part-time basis. Some authorities, in fact, maintain that making pension plans more generous for a larger number of workers is tantamount to offering irresistible financial incentives for early retirement.

From a broader perspective, it seems to make good social and economic sense to do whatever we possibly can to utilize the wasted know-how of older workers much more effectively than is being done now. Creating a new, unproductive leisure class of parasitic elders is hardly an acceptable cure for intractable societal ills anywhere in the world. Nor is there any law that decrees we must follow blindly in the footsteps of other nations that have been mistaken in the past and may be repeating the same mistakes today. We are not obliged to use foreign social security programs as absolute models, especially if we are convinced that they are wrong.

American policy-makers are now recognizing that retirement has many faces, not all of them attractive. Some have even begun to reconsider the very idea of retirement. The realization may finally have begun to sink in that a great number of older people are going to have a lot of time ahead of them to weigh the advantages and disadvantages of having nothing really meaningful to do.

About the Author

Bernard I. Forman is a part-time Mandatory Retirement representative of the National Senior Citizens' Law Center in Washington, D.C. He has a doctorate in education from Rutgers University and is professor emeritus of art at Mankato State University, Mankato, Minnesota. His address is 14329 Astrodome Drive, Silver Spring, Maryland 20906.

Mary K. Kouri

From Retirement to Re-Engagement
Young Elders Forge New Futures

There is a restless element among today's young elders, the 55- to 75-year-olds. They have refused to go quietly to retirement villages, golf courses, or senior-citizen centers—places where the elderly are supposed to collect their reward of rest and leisure after a career of full-time employment. For them, retirement is banishment from important sources of meaning and satisfaction in their lives.

"You've gotta get used to not being invited out to lunch or not being called. Then you have to create your own world," states 71-year-old Arnold McDermott, who retired as director of personnel for the city and county of Denver at the age of 64. He saw it as an

Rejecting the traditional retirement lifestyle of full-time leisure, restless "young elders" today are showing the way to "re-engagement."

opportunity to "get into more creative work": writing, teaching, and consulting. Not once did he consider a life of full-time leisure such as golfing, traveling, card playing, or fishing.

Once retired, though, McDermott faced exclusion from the professional mainstream with which he wanted to maintain his connection. "One of the problems of retirement is that you go from activity to non-activity. They don't call you and ask you for your advice. You have to be aggressive in a way not necessary before. You have to find your own device to get into the circles, meetings, and other things without being socially offensive about the whole thing. It's not easy."

The Young Elder: A New Kind Of Person

"A lucky minority of people now over sixty-five have had the good fortune to enjoy the education, comforts, choices, and encouraging environment that were a birthright for almost everybody born after World War II," Carolyn Bird

Arnold McDermott, a former municipal administrator, advises Irene Scott, a community association board director. Since his retirement seven years ago, McDermott has actively carved out a meaningful life for himself, consulting for management and employee organizations, writing articles for professional journals, and teaching seminars on management, among many other activities. Young elders are increasingly discovering the potentials of late adulthood and, through the life-design process, finding ways to help meet the needs of their communities.

Arnold McDermott (center) consults with directors of the Colorado Association of Public Employees. Accustomed to problem-solving and other "knowledge work" as a municipal administrator, McDermott, 71, wished to continue meeting such challenges in retirement. The information age will produce increasing numbers of knowledge workers who will find it difficult to retire, says author Mary K. Kouri.

observes in *The Good Years: Your Life in the Twenty-First Century*. While representative of a restless minority of today's older generation, young elders may well characterize the aged population that will emerge from the post-World War II "baby boom" in the years 2010 through 2030.

- **Education.** Today's young elders have a higher level of education than any group of 55- to 75-year-olds who preceded them. In 1950, Americans aged 65 and over had completed a median of 8.1 years of schooling. By 1970, the median had risen to 8.7 years. The median level will rise to 11.9 years by 1990, or just short of a high-school education, according to gerontologist Robert Havighurst. One in every three of the 4,128,000 Americans born in 1955 has been to college. This unprecedented level of education will mark their thinking, their openness to change, and their expectations throughout their lives.

- **Work.** A significant number of the young elders today are "knowledge workers." The move from a society engaged mainly in the production of goods to one increasingly occupied with information and provision of services has drastically changed the nature of work.

Knowledge workers are those who work in technical, professional, managerial, and administrative capacities. Such individuals are accustomed to meeting challenges and solving problems. In retirement they want activities that yield similar kinds of satisfaction.

Economist and educator Peter Drucker wrote in *The Age of Discontinuity: Guidelines to Our Changing Society* (1968), "The knowledge worker ... cannot easily retire. If he does, he is likely to disintegrate fast."

America is rapidly moving into the information age; S. Norman Feingold points out in THE FUTURIST (February 1984) that as much as 80% of the work force will be information workers by the year 2000. As the baby-boom generation retires from knowledge work, they will have to "plan for something to do," as one young elder advised. "You cannot sit and watch the boob tube or you will lose your mind. You've got to keep your mind active."

- **Health.** Young elders today enjoy better health and a longer life expectancy. While 75 used to be considered a ripe old age, a healthy 75-year-old can now reasonably expect to live another 10 years. This health and extra time come from two sources. First, scientific research has encouraged health maintenance and longer life through proper diet, adequate exercise, abstinence from smoking, and moderation in drinking.

Second, knowledge work is not as debilitating to the body as were the earlier forms of work. Having been given access to health maintenance knowledge, and having

"Retirement itself has become a problem.... Many older Americans find that retirement separates them from the kinds of lives they are capable of living."

been spared the drain of backbreaking physical labor and dangerous workplaces most of their lives, the baby-boom generation can expect another decade of life beyond that enjoyed by the young elders of today.

- **Planned retirement.** The work careers of today's young elders were structured by the new social invention of planned retirement ushered in by Social Security in 1935. Before then, most workers retired only when they were ill. For many of them, economic support was uncertain. It was most often provided by their families, sometimes by the scarce welfare programs of the time. The years after retirement were few, and the choices of lifestyle were limited by poor health.

Social Security legislation passed in 1935 made it possible for workers to retire at 65 regardless of their ability to continue working. Pensions, which came to prominence after World War II, have supplemented Social Security and contributed enormously to financial well-being in late adulthood.

The irony facing the baby-boom generation is that they have never known a world in which workers did not retire. They have never received a paycheck without a Social Security deduction. Yet they are justifiably pessimistic about getting their share before the system collapses.

Solutions-Turned-Problems

Some of the well-intentioned solutions to the problems of the elderly have themselves become problems: they no longer serve many young elders of the late twentieth century. (Today's solutions would have been more appropriate for the parents, aunts, and uncles of today's young elders.) As the baby-boom generation enters young elderhood, most will resemble their forebears of the late twentieth century, and the problems will escalate.

Retirement itself has become a problem. It was intended to serve as a respite and reward for many years of labor. Now with better health and longer life expectancy, many older Americans find that retirement separates them from the kinds of lives they are capable of living.

Social Security, which started in 1935 with 150 workers paying in for each beneficiary, had only three workers paying for each beneficiary in 1980. After the turn of the century, when the baby boomers enter their 50s, 60s, and 70s, the ratio could drop to two workers for each retiree. Medicare, too, is in trouble, with expenditures having doubled in the past 10 years.

It is time to question whether American society can sustain the marginal involvement of a growing proportion of its members. The demographic realities of the baby boom—and the subsequent "baby bust" resulting from baby boomers' lower rate of reproduction compared with that of their parents—

JOAN KELLEY/ACTION

Foster Grandparent Addie Hayes feeds her young charge at the Portland (Oregon) Child Care Center. Many young elders find that retirement separates them from the lives they are capable of living; society, too, may ultimately suffer from the marginal involvement of so many vital citizens, says author Kouri.

Volunteer in ACTION's Foster Grandparent Program teaches shop at Alabama Rehabilitation Center. Many young elders look ahead to their 60s and 70s as a time when they can be of service to the community rather than only to themselves.

"I think retired people should have some part-time work to do so they could continue to help society in some manner," says retired civil engineer Otis Deetin. "There ought to be an overlap between the generations. . . . When people are approaching retirement there should be younger people who have worked with them preparing to take over their responsibilities so there will be continuity in the work."

When asked what he thinks a man such as himself should be doing in modern America, Arnold McDermott replied, "Contributing. I think he has an obligation to contribute and an obligation to find out how he can contribute."

Young elders of the future could continue to be involved in the mainstream of society in an individually rewarding, as well as socially and economically productive, fashion. This continued involvement or "re-engagement" would be an alternative to retirement.

"Re-engagement" is a new form of involvement in life—perhaps different from that in earlier years and suited to the energies, interests, and capacities of one's present age. The forms of re-engagement discussed below are just a few of the many possibilities of new involvements in young elderhood.

From Retirement to "Re-Engagement"

Retirement as currently practiced will clearly become economically untenable as the proportion of older persons increases and the number of younger workers available to replace and support them diminishes. We must rethink the suitability of complete withdrawal from employment in late adulthood—or the timing of it, at the very least.

In *The Good Years*, Bird predicts, "The most compelling reason that people will continue to work past sixty-five is that older people will be needed. The work that machines create and leave behind is the human work that requires understanding acquired slowly over years of living."

The young elders of today who refuse to be banished into complete rest and leisure while still capable of leading vigorous lives have much to say about alternatives to full retirement.

are forcing society to reconsider Social Security, Medicare, and other institutions designed as humanitarian solutions.

Re-Engagement I: Phased Retirement

In several western European countries, the practice of gradual or phased retirement is well established. This gradual retirement is accomplished in different ways. The worker may have extended periods away from work for one to five years before full retirement—or gradually work fewer hours a day or fewer days a week. Most European employers report satisfaction with phased retirement, both at the organizational and individual levels, and will continue to offer it as an alternative to abrupt withdrawal from the work force.

"Young elders can help the young learn how to adapt to change. Skills at adapting that have been acquired and finely tuned through experience can be a gift to the young."

Phased retirement could serve as the transition into re-engagement for young elders. For example, if the individual plans to go into another area of work on a part-time or full-time basis, the change could be started during phased retirement from his former work career.

Re-Engagement II: Mentoring

Mentoring traditionally has consisted of an older adult teaching a younger person the ropes of the working world. While this will continue to be a valuable bridge between the generations, there are needs for two other kinds of mentoring.

First, young people need to learn to adapt in a society marked by rapid and unceasing change. In *The Aquarian Conspiracy*, Marilyn Ferguson describes adaptation as knowing how to learn, ask good questions, pay attention to the right things, be open to and critical of new concepts, and gain access to information. Young elders can help the young learn how to adapt to change. Skills at adapting that have been acquired and finely tuned through experience can be a gift to the young.

The second kind of mentoring addresses adolescents' need for strong adult ties. As family structures change, more teenagers find themselves without satisfactory adult relationships. They need new kinds of connections with adults wherein they can find encouragement, positive examples, and support with the difficulties of growing up.

Top: Grace Monroe, 96, of ACTION's Retired Senior Volunteer Program (RSVP) trains teenager to shop for the elderly. **Bottom:** RSVP volunteer Frank Wilkins, 76, helps woodworking students at the Colorado Boys Ranch for less-fortunate youngsters. The need of young people for strong adult ties and the need of young elders for continued involvement can both be satisfied by mentoring, a form of "re-engagement."

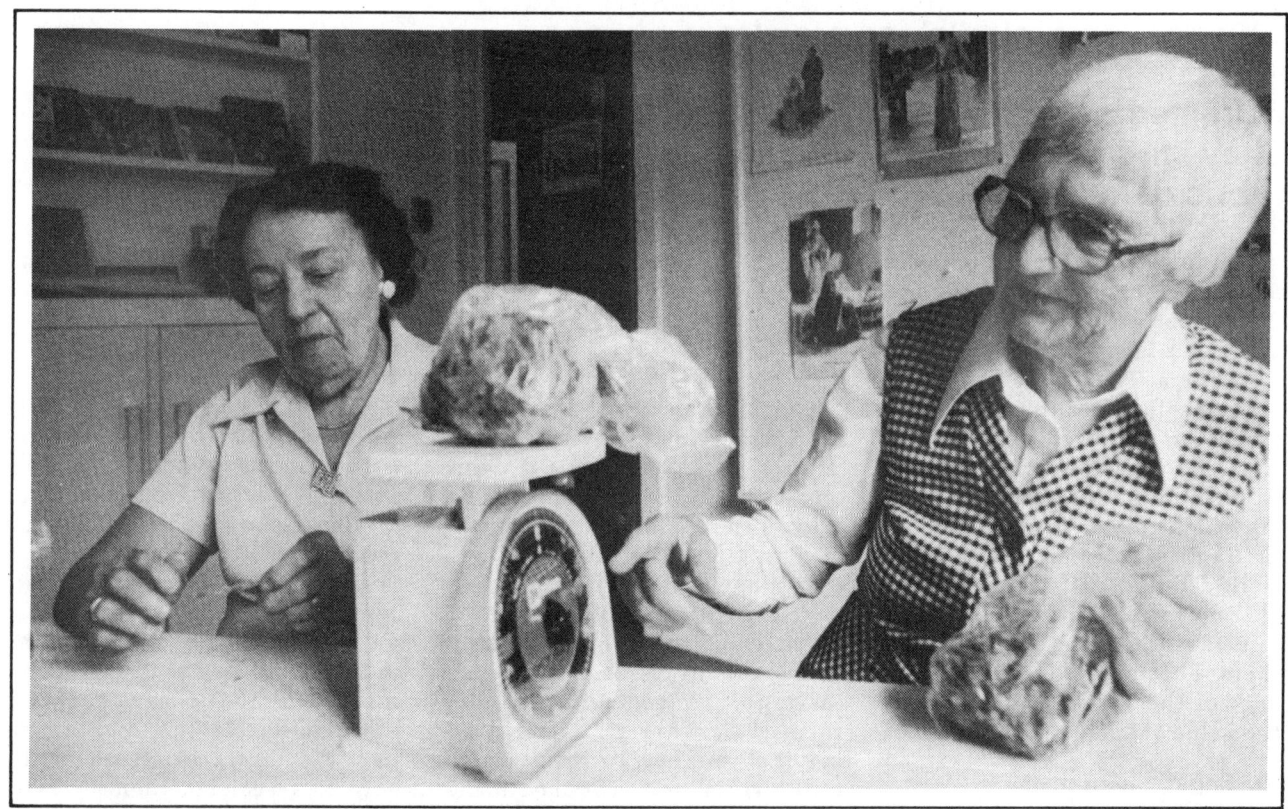

Volunteers in Babylon, New York, weigh dates for RSVP food co-op. Most young elders consider community service crucial to their life satisfaction, and their participation in the volunteer work force may help make up for the mass movement of young married women into the paid work force, says author Kouri.

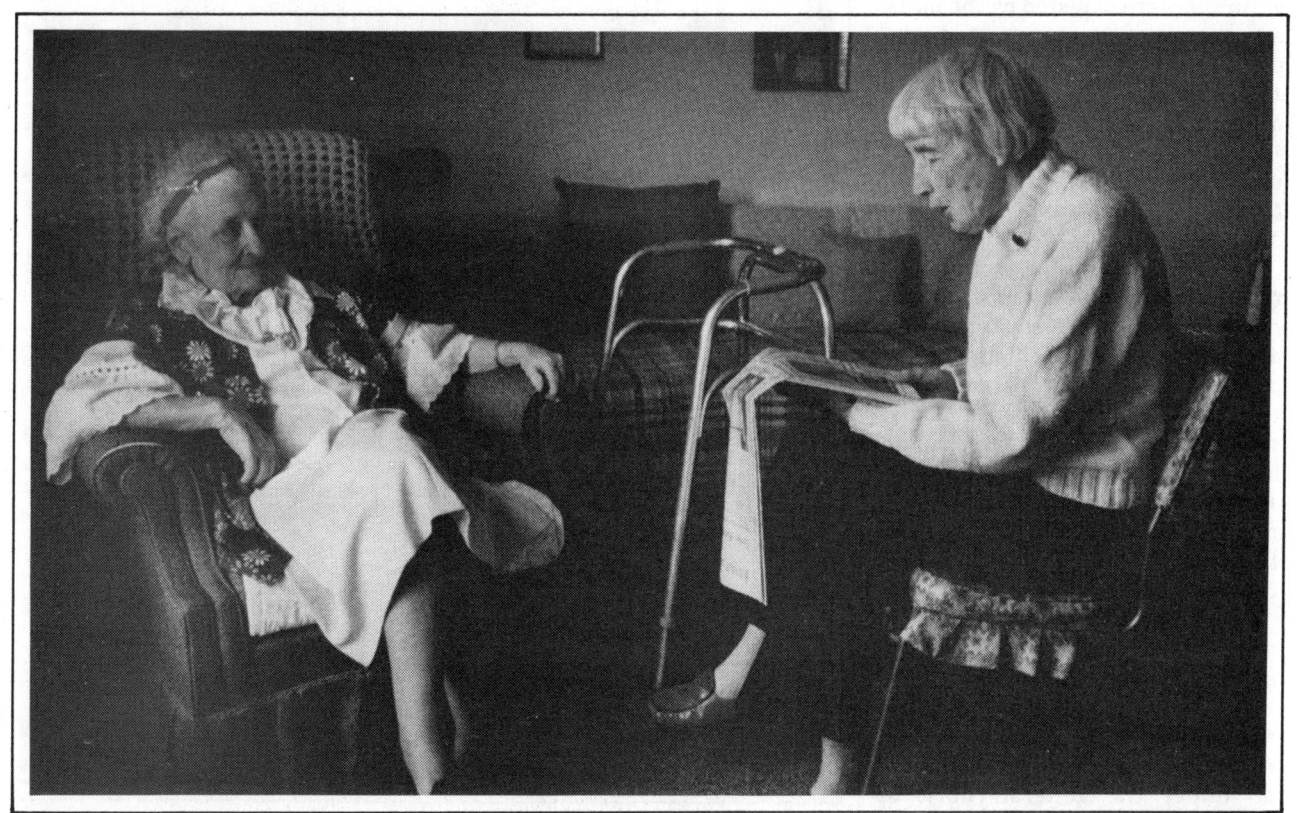

Senior Companion Program volunteer reads newspaper to housebound woman in Ellsworth, Maine. The years after retirement can be used in service to the community. This form of re-engagement consists of the unnamed work that "keeps the system running" and allows young elders to again become community leaders.

" 'People past middle age are already bearing more than their share of the extracurricular, unnamed work that keeps the system running. They shrug off what they do under the general rubric of helping. . . .' " —Carolyn Bird, *The Good Years*

Young elders can often provide these connections. They have the savvy that can only come from having made mistakes and learned from them. They can bring to the relationship a healthy objectivity that is often difficult for parents and school personnel to achieve. An example of this type of mentoring is portrayed in the film *On Golden Pond*. Norman, a veteran of eight decades of life, and 13-year-old Billy form a bond of respect and affection that enriches both of them. The positive effects on both ends of the age spectrum suggest the value of such mentoring.

Re-Engagement III: Community Service

Young elders represent a gold mine of badly needed assistance as the ranks of community service volunteers are depleted by the mass movement of young married women into the labor force. From 1947 to 1975, the percentage of married women—the traditional source of community service volunteers—who worked outside their homes escalated from 20% to over 44%.

A recent study of a group of 20 retired men found that some form of community service was counted as crucial to life satisfaction. One of the participants, retired industrial negotiator Lawrence Aidle, said that in earlier years, as he looked ahead to his 60s and 70s, service was his main interest. "To me, the time of life has come when I can be of service to others rather than to myself."

In *The Good Years*, Bird observes that "people past middle age are already bearing more than their share of the extracurricular, unnamed work that keeps the system running. They shrug off what they do under the general rubric of helping. . . . People over sixty-five are the leaders in services that we are going to label Experience Sharing, Conserving, Systems Patching, Matchmaking, and Whistleblowing."

Prospects for Re-Engaging

Today's America "hails old age as an achievement and treats it as a failure," as *Newsweek* put it. How can we bridge that chasm so young elders can be fully involved in the mainstream—an economic as well as humane necessity?

Young elders today are showing us the way. Resisting banishment to the fringes of society, they are carving out meaningful lives for themselves. They are demonstrating that the key to involvement in the social and economic mainstream lies as much within the individual as it does in public programs and policies.

When the individual believes that late adulthood can be a productive and rewarding period of life, he or she will arrange to make it so. We must revise our image of the older years so that more individuals will take the initiative to design rewarding, socially and economically productive lives as young elders.

We train our adolescents and young adults for their work careers. We are beginning to recognize the need for parenthood training. We are even awakening to the benefits of teaching people to cope with the upheavals of life in the middle years, the "mid-life crisis." We must also teach adults how to re-engage themselves in life as young elders to make the fullest use of longer life and better health.

ACTION

Foster Grandparent Alex Archuleta reads to Headstart student in Colorado. Young elders today are demonstrating that late adulthood can be a productive and rewarding time of life. But society must change its image of older people and encourage them to re-engage, says author Kouri.

"The life design process for re-engagement in young elderhood should include raising the awareness and appreciation of the possibilities of these years."

The Life Design Process

The life design process for re-engagement in young elderhood should include raising the awareness and appreciation of the possibilities of these years. The SAGE (Seniors Actualization and Growth Explorations) Program is a unique series of growth and self-discovery experiences developed by Gay Luce and described by her in *Your Second Life*. Such a program can heighten appreciation of these years.

The first step, and cornerstone of the life design process, is the identification of what the individual wants at the present stage of life. As Richard Bolles points out in *The Three Boxes of Life and How to Get Out of Them*, all stages of life must include a mix of work, learning, and leisure.

The second step of the life design process for young elderhood includes taking stock of one's skills and competencies in much the same way that job seekers and career changers do. This shows the individual the array of choices that can be made based on personal preferences, energy levels, and other criteria.

The third step is selecting those skills and competencies one wants to use at this phase of life. For some young elders, this means using highly developed skills from the past in different ways. A skilled secretary, for example, might use his or her skills in a voluntary capacity in a community service organization.

For other young elders, renewed vitality is better found in the use of skills that were perhaps never fully developed in the past. For example, retired school principal Ray Rebrovick developed a skill in woodworking and now has a small business building custom-designed picture frames.

The fourth step is determining how and where these skills and competencies can be applied. Here, bartering can be used creatively. For instance, a family of four—mother, father, and two teenage sons—all pitch in with year-round outdoor maintenance of their 72-year-old neighbor's property. The neighbor, a retired baker, keeps them supplied with homemade baked goods plus two completely prepared dinners each week.

The fifth and final step in designing a rewarding and productive life is connecting with people. Networking is invaluable—telling friends and acquaintances about the skills, services, and ideas one has to offer, and learning of persons with similar interests or possible needs.

Enlarging one's network is useful at this stage of life design. New awareness of the potentials of late adulthood can aid in venturing into new contacts with people and organizations. With this final step, the process begins to gel into a synthesis of the young elder's goals and skills and the needs of individuals or groups in the community.

Eight Ways To Live Longer

The U.N. World Assembly on Aging in 1982 listed the following ways people can live longer:

1. **Exercise your mind.** Like your muscles, your brain atrophies with disuse. Senility is six times greater in elderly who withdraw from people and from life.
2. **Live well.** The surest way to live longer is to be born in a rich country. (Life expectancy in Sweden is nearly twice what it is in Ethiopia.) A clean, warm home, safe water, and a full stomach all reduce vulnerability to infectious diseases.
3. **Eat properly.** Malnutrition causes half a billion deaths annually. But obesity helps kill 50% of people in industrial countries by putting pressure on heart and joints, causing heart disease, strokes, and arthritis. There are very few fat 80-year-olds.
4. **Keep moving.** Too much rest can kill you by making your circulation sluggish and your muscles weak. Just one year of exercise can make a 70-year-old as fit as a person of 40.
5. **Stop smoking.** Every cigarette you smoke shortens your life by five and one-half minutes.
6. **Watch your eyes.** Old age usually affects eyesight and hearing. The answer is a health system offering effective diagnosis and referral.
7. **Stay happy.** Stress increases blood pressure. Depression makes you apathetic. Both contribute to heart disease. The death rate is 50% higher among lonely old people than among married couples.
8. **Get involved.** If your needs are not respected or taken seriously, complain. The best person to fight for better housing, employment, and health care is you.

For more information, write to United Nations, Department of Public Information, New York, New York 10017.

About the Author

Mary K. Kouri is a career development counselor and gerontologist with Human Growth and Development Associates, 1675 Fillmore Street, Denver, Colorado 80206. She works with the Health Support Council for Capital Hill Seniors, Inc., a group of young elders in Denver who are engaged in self-help programs.

WORLD FUTURE SOCIETY
THE FUTURIST LIBRARY

World Future Society books help people to look ahead by describing important developments that could occur in the future. They explore many of the greatest issues of our time in clear, concise language directed to the general reader. These eight anthologies of articles from THE FUTURIST explore topics ranging from computers, communications, and work to education, the environment, and space.

Global Solutions: Innovative Approaches to World Problems. Ways exist to solve such problems as overpopulation, energy shortages, environmental pollution, and international tensions. Practical solutions presented include macroengineering projects, preventive health care, new foods, even do-it-yourself housing.

Habitats Tomorrow: Homes and Communities in an Exciting New Era. Exciting descriptions of many possible developments for the homes and communities of tomorrow. From Arcosanti to space colonies to Auroville and the home of the future, this book explores many new ways of living.

Careers Tomorrow: The Outlook for Work in a Changing World. New careers are emerging, and new developments in the working environment such as the paperless office or telecommuting will change the working routine. This book explores the many changes in the way people will work in the future.

The Great Transformation: Alternative Futures for Global Society. A dramatic transformation in human life will lead to a more creative, humane world based on treating humanity and the world as a whole system. A look at tomorrow's consciousness and community.

Communications Tomorrow: The Coming of the Information Society. A well-illustrated, comprehensive overview of the future of communications—from satellites and computers to the future of the English language and the search for self-knowledge.

1999: The World of Tomorrow. A breathtaking glimpse of what may happen in the years ahead, including the future of architecture, aviation, offices, space colonies, medicine, energy, and technology.

The Computerized Society: Living and Working in an Electronic Age. Specific suggestions about how people can use computers to be more successful in their careers, education, businesses, even their sex lives—and how computers can help solve the great problems the world faces.

Mail to: The Futurist Bookstore, World Future Society, 4916 St. Elmo Avenue, Bethesda, MD 20814, U.S.A.

Name _____

Address _____

City _____ State _____ ZIP _____
80F5

☐ Check or money order enclosed.

☐ Charge my ☐ MasterCard ☐ Visa ☐ American Express

Acct. No. _____ Exp. Date _____

Signature _____

Please send me the following volumes:

	Regular Price	Member Price
☐ Global Solutions	$6.95	**$6.25**
☐ Habitats Tomorrow	$6.95	**$6.25**
☐ Careers Tomorrow	$7.95	**$7.15**
☐ The Great Transformation	$6.95	**$6.25**
☐ Communications Tomorrow	$6.95	**$6.25**
☐ 1999: The World of Tomorrow	$6.95	**$6.25**
☐ The Computerized Society	$6.95	**$6.25**
☐ WFS Membership ☐ New ☐ Renewal		**$25.00**

Use member prices if you join with this order.
Postage and handling $ __2.50__

Total Order $ _____

THE FUTURIST

A journal of forecasts, trends, and ideas about the future.

Membership Application

☐ Yes! I accept your invitation to join the World Future Society. Enclosed is payment of $25 (in U.S. currency or the equivalent in another currency) for a one-year membership, which includes six issues of THE FUTURIST and a 10% discount on books and other products available through the WFS Bookstore.

☐ Check or money order enclosed. *Please address envelope as shown on reverse.*
☐ Please bill me.
☐ Charge my credit card: ☐ MasterCard   ☐ VISA

    Card No. _____
    Expiration Date _____
    Signature_____

Name _____

Address _____

City _____ State or Province _____ ZIP or Country _____

4001

THE FUTURIST

A journal of forecasts, trends, and ideas about the future.

Membership Application

☐ Yes! I accept your invitation to join the World Future Society. Enclosed is payment of $25 (in U.S. currency or the equivalent in another currency) for a one-year membership, which includes six issues of THE FUTURIST and a 10% discount on books and other products available through the WFS Bookstore.

☐ Check or money order enclosed. *Please address envelope as shown on reverse.*
☐ Please bill me.
☐ Charge my credit card: ☐ MasterCard   ☐ VISA

    Card No. _____
    Expiration Date _____
    Signature_____

Name _____

Address _____

City _____ State or Province _____ ZIP or Country _____

4001

THE FUTURIST

A journal of forecasts, trends, and ideas about the future.

Membership Application

☐ Yes! I accept your invitation to join the World Future Society. Enclosed is payment of $25 (in U.S. currency or the equivalent in another currency) for a one-year membership, which includes six issues of THE FUTURIST and a 10% discount on books and other products available through the WFS Bookstore.

☐ Check or money order enclosed. *Please address envelope as shown on reverse.*
☐ Please bill me.
☐ Charge my credit card: ☐ MasterCard   ☐ VISA

    Card No. _____
    Expiration Date _____
    Signature_____

Name _____

Address _____

City _____ State or Province _____ ZIP or Country _____

4001

BUSINESS REPLY CARD
FIRST CLASS   PERMIT NO. 10485   BETHESDA, MD

POSTAGE WILL BE PAID BY ADDRESSEE

WORLD FUTURE SOCIETY
4916 St. Elmo Avenue
Bethesda, MD 20814-9968
U.S.A.

NO POSTAGE
NECESSARY
IF MAILED
IN THE
UNITED STATES

BUSINESS REPLY CARD
FIRST CLASS   PERMIT NO. 10485   BETHESDA, MD

POSTAGE WILL BE PAID BY ADDRESSEE

WORLD FUTURE SOCIETY
4916 St. Elmo Avenue
Bethesda, MD 20814-9968
U.S.A.

NO POSTAGE
NECESSARY
IF MAILED
IN THE
UNITED STATES

BUSINESS REPLY CARD
FIRST CLASS   PERMIT NO. 10485   BETHESDA, MD

POSTAGE WILL BE PAID BY ADDRESSEE

WORLD FUTURE SOCIETY
4916 St. Elmo Avenue
Bethesda, MD 20814-9968
U.S.A.

NO POSTAGE
NECESSARY
IF MAILED
IN THE
UNITED STATES